MARK MY WORDS

Mark Nicholson

Contents

As Tears Go By

It is the evening of the day
I sit and watch the children play
Smiling faces I can see
But not for me
I sit and watch
As tears go by

My riches can't buy everything
I want to hear the children sing
All I hear is the sound
Of rain falling on the ground
I sit and watch
As tears go by

It is the evening of the day
I sit and watch the children play
Doing things I used to do
They think are new
I sit and watch
As tears go by

Marianne Faithful, 1966

Introduction

This book is a memoire with a difference. It's about an average (or regular if you prefer) sort of person: an average size male person, English, white, heterosexual, average ability (above average in some things, lower in others), experiencing ups and downs throughout life. What makes the book different is that it details the thoughts I recorded at the time, showing my frustrations, feelings and joys, particularly regarding the fairer sex. Whether these thoughts are typical is up to the reader to decide. The book is a record of a life through the 1950s, 60s and 70s and onwards to his 70th birthday in 2020, capturing the sounds, scenes and smells that help us recall past times.

All our lives are affected by how we felt and what we did as a child. As a teenager we are at our most impressionable; more gullible to peer pressure, sensitive to feelings and receptive to suggestions. As a child I experienced warm, loving feelings towards a girl in his dreams. Is that girl the woman I now love and will happily share the rest of my life with?

Some of the things I did and ways I felt in my earlier years may make you cringe, but that's how it was. Most of the time I was just an ordinary sort of bloke. I wrote when in a particular frame of mind, often bitter-sweet, sometimes melancholic, when feeling lonely, fed up, bored or sentimental, but always with an urge to record memorable moments of my life. It was not a diary, more of a Thought Book. That was the name his wife later gave to it. It records the way I felt at that time so that in the future I could look back and see my lows at their lowest and highs at their highest. At the time, I didn't intend anyone else to read it, but it felt like I was writing to someone.

We all make mistakes and behave badly at times but if we could live our lives again would we act any differently? Maybe. More than likely we'd make the same blunders again. It's easy to look back with the benefit of hindsight and wisdom.

In my early forties I learnt to apply the following principle:

Anything you can conceive and believe you can achieve.

This gave me a new outlook on life and with the lessons from the past experiences and by observing those who already achieved success, I become a better person and my life turned out for the better.

The book is not just about girls. It's about the sights, sounds and smells of the places I lived, especially Bradford in Yorkshire, the joys of canoeing, photography, my pet dogs and many more things, and love of my three daughters. The book tells of my work and the challenges I both faced there and at home.

What was life like for a lad who grew up in England during the second half of the 20th century? It was quite different from the 21st century: worse in many ways, better in some. Things we take for granted these days, such as mobile phones, computers, the internet, motorways and cheap air travel, either didn't exist or were unavailable to the average person. It was a time of great social change: traditional conventions were challenged and old attitudes faded as the century drew nearer its end. The 'swinging sixties' introduced new-fangled music, fashion, psychedelia, flower power, more television, different interiors and better cars. It was the time of Mods, Rockers and Hippies, a decade of great music - the Beatles, the Rolling Stones, Dusty Springfield, The Who, The Monkees, Procol Harum - the list could go on and on. Music has a great way of reminding us of the past, so passages from the author's favourite songs are included.

Are people any different now? Teenage boys are still overcharged with testosterone and presumably still spend much more time thinking about sex than actually doing it. But social attitudes have changed over the years, particularly towards sex. What was considered deplorable at one time can become acceptable at another. Normal behaviour for one generation might be seen as bad taste for the next. The 1960s were a particularly exciting time for changes in social behaviour. The contraceptive pill became available and sex outside marriage became acceptable for a lot of society, although it was still frowned upon by many.

Whilst copying words written 50 years ago I recaptured the same feelings and emotions I had at that time. It was like being there, saying and doing what I described, feeling the same emotions, but with the benefit of wisdom lacking in youth. It was as if a time machine had taken me back all those years.

Enjoy the story, whatever your age and compare or contrast it with your own feelings and experiences.

Mark Nicholson
2020

Baby me with my parents and sister

Chapter 1: Pre-teen years

My name is Mark. If you look it up you will find that it means 'consecrated to the god Mars', 'god of war or 'to be warlike'. None of those apply to me. I was given that name because I have a birth mark on my bottom. The brown stain looks like I haven't wiped my bottom properly. It's been a source of embarrassment for me every time I'm seen naked such as in school showers or swimming pool changing rooms. Now I've told you a secret about myself that I've never told before. That's just the beginning. When I was in my teens and twenties I recorded a lot of secrets in what I called my 'Thought Book'. But let's start at the beginning.

I was born in May 1950 at Northampton General Hospital. Mum and dad were both in their 29th year and my sister Dorothy was 4 years and 9 days old. My dad Edward was a teacher and mum, Catherine a nurse. When I was born they lived in Steeple Bumpstead, near Haverhill, in Essex so why was I born 80 miles away? I think it was because whilst waiting for me to be born mum was staying with her parents who lived 12 miles from Northampton and dad was at Cambridge University. The hospital where I was born is still there off Cheyne Walk. In later years we lived in the town for four or five years but I have lived in other parts of England much longer. When people ask me where I come from, I tell them Northampton. If I meet someone who has spent say the last 20 years of their life living in Northampton but was born elsewhere, I feel that I am the true Northamptonian, not them.

I don't remember living at Steeple Bumpstead because when I was a year old we moved to Weston Coyney near Stoke-on-Trent in Staffordshire. Dad had a teaching career and every few years he would move to a better position in a different town. My sister Mary was born in Stoke when I was 4 and a half.

In 1956 we moved from Staffordshire to Northampton. Dad had got a job as a teacher at Delapre Secondary Modern School. Our house was in Towcester Road. As you went out of town, it was up the hill on the left, just past a field and half way between stops for the red number 7 bus. The fare for the two-mile ride into town was tuppence ha'penny and I would often travel by bus alone, perhaps to cubs, to the swimming baths or to the Gaumont cinema. When it was cold, the best place to sit on the bus was downstairs at the front. Behind the window of the driver's cab, in between the aisles, there was a shiny round metal hump that was always warm. If you were in a hurry, it was best to be at the back so you could jump off the platform before the bus had stopped properly. Upstairs was my favourite spot because you could see more outside. However, you couldn't always see clearly inside the bus if there were a lot of people smoking.

Our blue Jowett Bradford van, registration LLG 742 had a distinctive smell. Dad told us it was previously owned by a chemical company. There were no proper seats in the back. I sat on a makeshift seat made from old cushions and blankets next to my 8-year old sister, Dorothy and our Skye Terrier dog called Ash. I was 4. We were going on holiday to Anglesey. It took a long time to drive from Staffordshire to the Menai Bridge and we were bored. After such a long journey it was exciting to cross the Menai Bridge and peer down at the wreck of the old wooden sailing ship HMS Conway, a training ship that ran aground and became wrecked in 1953. It meant that we were nearly there.

Dad with Bradford Jowett at Weston Coyney

We stayed in a cottage at Dinas which is at the eastern side of Traeth Bychan, a couple of miles north of Benllech. I enjoyed stepping over the rocks above the beach and looking in the pools for starfish and crabs. I was doing just that when one morning my legs suddenly stopped working. I couldn't move. I called Dorothy and she fetched mum and dad. I was taken to Bangor hospital where I was placed in a cot with high sides in a ward by myself. Nobody spoke English so I didn't know what was happening. Later, I learned that I had a mild dose of polio so I had to be kept in isolation. Dad had to sign several forms to release me after those four or five days of imprisonment. The only nice thing about the hospital is that I was given a lovely Dinky toy – a car transporter; but when I was discharged they took it away from me. I was very upset to lose it. Having to stay in that hospital was a nightmare but it was the loss of that toy that upset me for many years after. The only lasting physical difference was that, according to mum, my left leg was a little bit shorter than my right, but I've never noticed.

We continued to enjoy future summer holidays in Anglesey. The wreck of the Conway remained until 1956, when during work to remove it, the ship caught fire and was burnt down to water level. Dad changed the Jowett for a more modern van, a cream Austin A35, registration PUC 334. We stayed in a rented holiday cottage at Ty Mawr at Dinas. That means 'big house' in Welsh, but the cottage was tiny. You had to climb a ladder to reach the upstairs bedroom. Hefin, who lived at the farm, was about my age and we often played together. It was fun to dare who could stay the longer on a rock before a large wave broke over it.

Ty Mawr and A35 van

On some Sundays we went to the Memorial Free Church in Oakamoor, Staffordshire. I think dad used to take services there whilst the usual minister was away. We children didn't have to sit through the whole boring service because we were allowed out of the church after the first 20 minutes or so. When the service finished we had a tasty Sunday lunch at the Lord Nelson. Then we would go to Lightoaks, home of the Bolton family. They had a massive garden with a Wendy house for the girls and trollies for me to pull them on around the lawns.

Mary and Mark in 1956

Saturday Club at the Gaumont cinema was brilliant. They showed cartoons, road safety films and had sing-alongs. They always started with this song:

'We come along on Saturday mornings, greeting everybody with a smile.
We come along on Saturday mornings knowing that it's all worthwhile.
As members of the GB club we all intend to be.
Good citizens when we grow up and champions of the free.
We come along on Saturday mornings greeting everybody with a smile, smile, smile.
Greeting everybody with a smile'.

The best bit of Saturday Club was the serial. Gene Autry played in "The Phantom Empire". He's in the Junior Thunder Riders club of cowboys who come from the underground city of Murania. Their futuristic secret headquarters has lots of electrical gadgets including giant levers and pistons, spheres making huge sparks, flickering gauges, giant ray guns and welding torches that emit huge flames. The city has lots of uranium that nasty scientists want to pinch. At the end of every episode Gene Autry is about to get blown up but at the start of the next episode he miraculously escapes.

My best friend was called Snowy. His last name was White, but he was called Snowy because he had white hair. He had a sister, a brother, a mum and a dad and although they were all Whites he was the only Snowy. He was a small lad.

Snowy cooking garden picnic

The Whites lived together in a small house called a prefab. I didn't know then why they called it a prefab, but later I found out it was short for 'prefabricated bungalow'. Thousands of them were built just after the war; I guessed the reason was to replace all the houses that had been bombed, but it might also have been because of the 'baby boom'. I didn't know it then, but apparently at around the time I was born people kept making babies. I wondered what people did with their time before the baby boom years as an alternative to making babies. Anyway, after the war they needed a lot of houses quickly so they built these prefabs. The word 'prefabricated' indicates that the houses must have been made already before they were actually built. How could that be? If they were made before they were built then they were being built as they were being fabricated. Like bricks are made before being used to build a brick-built house, like trees are grown, sawn and seasoned before they are used to make a wooden house. I live in a brick house but it's not called a prefab even though the bricks are prefabricated. Anyway, we all knew what a prefab was. It was a single storey house in an estate containing hundreds of identical ones, connected by concrete roads and concrete paths which went all round the prefab. The building sat on wall that was about a foot high, so you had to go up a couple of steps to get inside. The prefabs were all made of smooth light grey sheets with strips of wood over the joints and they all had corrugated roofs. I suppose the sheets were made of asbestos, which was good because it stopped them from burning down. They were intended to last only 10 years but they were still being used 15 years after the war ended. It was always warm and cosy inside Snowy's house. His mum often used to cook chips on their gas cooker in a big pan full of hot oil. I don't think it ever caught fire. They had a big telly and it was always turned on. When I went there after school we would watch Popeye. Our telly was a small one. There were just two channels, BBC and ITV. I liked Dixon of Dock Green. Blue Peter started in 1958 and I remember them showing the building of the SS Canberra ocean liner in 1959. I was very impressed. She was fitted with the most powerful steam turbo-electric units ever installed in a passenger ship and had a top speed of about 27 knots. She also had a bow propeller for manoeuvring in port.

My other friends were Andrew, who lived just three doors up the road from us and Nigel who lived further up on the other side of Towcester Road. Nigel called his mum mother and his dad, dad.

Usually we would play in our garden or in the field next to it. There were some apple trees and an almond tree in the garden. The trees were good to climb. On one of the apple trees there was a swing made of rope and a piece of wood. Someone had lifted a bed frame into the branches of the almond tree. It was a metal frame with a mesh of wire in diamond shapes held to the frame with coiled springs. The springs were missing in one corner so you had to be careful not to go near that part. The springs made it difficult to walk on in any case so it wasn't a very good tree house because it didn't even have a proper floor, let alone walls or a roof. You had to jump up to reach the lowest branches on the almond tree and climb up by wrapping your legs around its smooth trunk, which gave me a nice feeling. In the autumn we picked the spiky green fruit and if you were lucky there would be two or more white nuts inside.

Sometimes we lit a bonfire. I invented a game of heating up the end of a metal pipe in the bonfire. When the pipe got really hot I would pour some water down the pipe. A moment later there would be a satisfying pop and a jet of steam would fire back out of the pipe, a bit like a cannon. I never understood why it did that but I knew the hotter the pipe the better it worked.

Once I lit a bonfire in the field next door and it got a bit out of control and started to burn the gorse bushes. We had to rush back and forth to the house with buckets of water to put it out. I thought the fire brigade would have to be called out but we managed to put it out. I got told off.

It might have been Snowy who introduced me to smoking. You could buy cigarettes from a corner shop one or two at a time for about a penny each. We knew you weren't supposed to smoke until you were 16 and that made it a bit special. Dad caught me once so I got into trouble for that too. It wasn't like being told off. I knew dad was cross with me though. He marched me home, told mum what I had been doing then made me smoke another one in front of them both. It made me choke after the first puff. I never liked the taste anyway. After that I never smoked as a habit.

At the back of our garden there was a tumbled down low building. It had very thick walls because it used to be an air raid shelter. It was dark and damp inside. I found an old projector and some glass slides buried under the rubble in there. By shining a torch through it you could show pictures on the white cement walls. I once arranged a show and people gave me a penny ha'penny to enter. The show wasn't very good because there was only three or four pictures and the torch battery went flat so you couldn't see them anyway. I didn't give the money back but I didn't spend it either. The fourpence ha'penny just stayed in a jar on a ledge in the den. Alison came to the show. She was my girlfriend; she had fair hair and wore a yellow and white dress. I liked her. Not in the same way as I liked Snowy. Snowy and I played games, had fun and got into trouble. Alison played games too but it felt different being with her. My favourite dream must have been about her. The dream was more about colours and feelings than about Alison and what we did, but it always felt like it was her. The colours were white and yellow like her dress and green like a caterpillar. You had to be careful when you picked up a caterpillar or it would squash in your hand and make a gooey mess. Caterpillars are green and squelchy but if they don't get squashed they turn into beautifully coloured butterflies. In my dream I cared for the caterpillar and the caterpillar was pleased to become a beautiful butterfly. The yellow, white and green were bright and gave me a warm feeling, which was how I felt when I was with Alison.

I liked bumble bees too. I would catch them in my cupped hands and move them from one flower to a better one. They don't sting: at least that's what I believed and I never got stung.

I slept on the top bed of a bunk. Bedtime was announced by the radio theme tune of the Archers at 6.45. If we were good, we could stay up until seven, following the 'bedtime music' at the end of the programme.

I liked making things. I once found a stick shaped as a walking stick. I sandpapered it smooth and treated it with the linseed oil that dad used on his cricket bat. It had a nice smell. Boys often built trollies from soap boxes and other pieces of wood that were always easy to find. Wheels were more difficult to acquire. Typically, they would come from old prams. I used Mary's dolls' pram and I enjoyed towing it with my trike. Towcester Road was quite steep outside our house so you could build up a good speed going down the pavement. I crashed my trike into the bed of nettles outside the wood next door. My arms and legs were covered in itchy rashes.

Mark and Mary with pram and trike

I took Mary for rides in her pram. You didn't need to go with your parents. I could push the pram around the field or down to the 'rec' (recreation ground) where we would play on the swings, roundabout, slide and climbing frame. These were big, heavy pieces of equipment and the ground was either bare earth or compacted ash. We learnt to watch out for ourselves and endure minor injuries: most of the time we had scabs on our knees and elbows.

Nearly everyone had a bonfire and fireworks on November 5th. One year I went by bus with Dorothy and mum to a bonfire party outside the Quaker meeting house. Mum carried our fireworks in a basket and we were all looking forward to lighting them. At the party a spark must have dropped into the basket and the whole lot went off together. I was really sad that all our fireworks were lost. Mum carried the soot-blackened basket back home in the bus. In the morning after bonfire night it was fun to collect spent shells of rockets that had landed in the streets. I took Mary out in her pram, which made a useful container for my collection. She must have thought that the cardboard tubes were sweets because they looked just like the tubes of sherbet that we loved. It wasn't until we got home that I noticed the black coating around her mouth and face. Then she was sick. I got told off.

We had a couple of goldfish in a pond dad built in the corner of the garden. He couldn't have done a very good job because the water kept leaking away. A cat stole one of the goldfish. When dad next saw the pussy sitting by the pond he caught it and ducked its head in the water. He said it would teach the cat a lesson. I wonder if that's the sort of way he taught children at school. Anyway, it can't have convinced the cat because next time I looked in the pond there weren't any goldfish in it.

Football didn't interest me. Boys at school kept talking about the great Nobby Clark, but apart from seeing his name on the back page of the Chronicle & Echo nearly every week, I can't say I paid much attention. From the road Northampton Town Football ground looked like a huge pink hoarding pierced with very narrow turnstiles at intervals with signs such as Boys 1/6, Adults 3/- or 'Season Tickets'. The first of my only two visits to a football stadium was when grandad took me to watch the Cobblers play. They were third in division 4, got promoted in 1961 and won 3rd div title in 1963, scoring 109 goals. I witnessed none of the goals because at the game I attended either I was too small to see over people's shoulders or I wasn't looking in the right place or they just didn't score at all in that game. It was very crowded and noisy so I just shouted when everybody else did. At about that time another footballer, named George Best, appeared on the scene, but it wasn't until 1964, by which time we were living in to Swindon, that I noticed. More about that later.

The town football ground was quite close to the church we had to attend. On Sundays, most of the day was wasted by having to go to Abington Avenue Congregational Church. First of all, the service started at 11 so there wasn't time to do anything in the morning, especially as I had to dress up in posh clothes. These included sissy short trousers so I hoped none of my school friends would see me. During the quiet parts of the service I had to keep swallowing. I don't know why I did this but it worried me. I'm sure everybody in the church could hear me swallowing and if they looked they would see my Adam's apple move and know I was guilty of disturbing the silence. The best part of the service was the end, when the minister said benediction and the organist played the "going out" music, the louder the better, something like Handel's "Arrival of the Queen of Sheba". Then you filed out of church and shook hands with the minister. Sometimes, we children (Dorothy, Mary and I) had to wait in the car before mum and dad left church. Job's dairy was not far from the church and there always seemed to be milk floats going in and out of their yard. When we got home from church we would have a big Sunday lunch. Mum would have put a beef joint in the oven before we left home so it was ready when we got back. The accompanying vegetable always seemed to be marrow, which I hated. It was a horrible slimy yellow-green mess with a nasty taste and unpleasant smell. I was made to eat it.

"You'll eat it AND you'll like it," insisted mum.

Finally, I was able to get changed and play out, but by then the day was nearly gone and the thought of having to go to school the next day made me miserable. Sundays were not good.

Sundays were a bit better when after church we went to mum's parents. Grandma and grandad lived in a little house in Lavendon, about 12 miles away on the other side of Northampton. You went in through the kitchen. Fresh food was stored in the 'cool cupboard' which had marble shelves and a wire mesh door. There was no fridge so you had to buy fresh food nearly every day. Meat came from Mr & Mrs Lay's butcher's shop at the corner of the lane on Northampton Road. On top of the cupboard there was a mangle for squeezing water out of the washing. Hot water came from a gas fired boiler that had to be lit if you were having a bath, which was not very often. The gas cooker had to be ignited with matches or using a lighter at the side. When you used the lighter it clicked loudly and if it worked, which it usually didn't, a jet of flame would shoot out of the nozzle. There was often a smell of gas around the cooker.

When we entered the cottage there would be a lovely smell of roast beef. There would always be crackling with it and grandma made brilliant Yorkshire Pudding. The living room on the right smelt nice too. It had a sweet smell of snuff. Grandad kept it in the cupboard next to his chair. There was a pendulum clock that was always ticking and chimed every half hour. At twelve o'clock the chiming seemed to go on for ages, especially if it needed winding up. Grandma's chair was by the window. On the built-in cupboard next to it was a big radio. When you turned the radio on you had to wait a minute for it to warm up before any sound came out. Then you had to turn a knob to find the right programme, such as the Home Service if you wanted the news, weather, shipping forecast or the Archers. On the display was a list of cities that I'd never heard of, such as Hilversum. On the back wall there was a door with a latch that made a metallic clack sound. The door led upstairs. To its right was the table. When we stayed to eat, the table had to be opened out and pulled away from the wall. It took up nearly all the space in the room.

Beyond the table was the door to the front room. We really only went in there on Sunday afternoons so mum and dad could watch television. The Brains Trust was really boring. On Gardeners Question Time, Ted Moult's reply to most things seemed to be, "The answer lies in the soil." Grandad grew chrysanthemums in the garden and tomatoes in the greenhouse. You could get to the greenhouse from the kitchen by going through the bathroom and then the toilet. There was no flushing toilet: they had had an Elsan which was okay to use if it had been emptied recently and just contained the blue Jeyes fluid. If it was full I worried about being splashed by the foul contents.

At the top of the narrow dark stairway were two bedrooms. Grandma and grandad's room was on the right. They had a big wooden blanket chest near the door. The other bedroom overlooked the front garden. It had a big bed that was high to climb up to. On the wall was a brown and white picture of a field being ploughed. When we stayed at grandma's we slept here with a long narrow pillow called a bolster separating me from my sister. The chiming of the church clock could be heard clearly when we were in bed.

After lunch we might go for a walk up the lane to Mr Thomas' pig farm. If we went into the yard goosey gander would squawk and hiss at us and we would run away.

Grandma's neighbour was Miss Cooke. She was a district nurse and went out on her moped. Mr and Mrs Freeman lived in the bigger house beyond Miss Cooke's. They gave us a tin of chocolates every Christmas.

Dorothy said that she always felt more a part of our maternal grandparents than I did from our more professional relations. She got the warmth and affection from them that she didn't feel at home at that time. Could this have been because she was so difficult herself? Perhaps by this time I was a much better son than my naughty big sister!

I liked grandma and grandad better than mum and dad and better than dad's parents who we called grandmother and grandfather. In 1958 they had a house built for them at Overstone, which was 7 miles from our Northampton house. After they moved in we helped move countless wheelbarrow loads of soil up to the back of the garden. He had a petrol lawnmower and my priority during our visits was to mow the lawns with it. The largest upstairs room was the study. It had a big desk and a typewriter for grandfather to write his sermons. He was a church minister. I used to write stories with the typewriter. The key for the letter P had lost part of its enamel coating. There was only one bedroom, so when we stayed I slept in a bed on the large landing. The upstairs toilet was separate from the bathroom. It was always smelly. They had two sorts of paper: Jeyes medicated, which was hard and kept in a box inside a dispenser on the wall; and a roll of soft tissue. Most people preferred the hard paper because it stopped poo going through to your hand. You could use the Jeyes as tracing paper too if you didn't mind the "Wash your hands now please" that was printed on each sheet. If you just had a wee you didn't wash your hands because mum, who was a nurse, said it was perfectly sterile.

Downstairs, by the front door there was another toilet and that was smelly too. In the lounge there was a piano, on top of which was the sweet tin, that always contained delicious soft centred fruit lozenges. There was a coal fired Aga cooker in the kitchen with big heavy lids over the two hobs. The dining room usually smelt of mint sauce. I liked the coconut pyramids that grandmother cooked.

Grandfather's chair was on the left of the fireplace and grandmother's on the right, next to her knitting cupboard. Grandfather had an 8mm cine camera that he used mainly for pictures of his garden, particularly the roses, and of the guests leaving by car. Later, I assembled all the clips of us driving away and added dance music to accompany it.

The worst thing about Sundays was the thought of Monday - back to school day.

Far Cotton junior school was a collection of dirty red brick buildings, black tarmac playgrounds and iron railings. My classroom had big iron radiators below tall windows which were too high to reach. On the corridor side was a wooden partition with windows you couldn't see through. The worst lesson was maths. The best lesson was when we went outside for country dancing, such as to the Barn Dance or waltz to the Valeta.

There were railway sidings next to the school. My teacher told mum that I spent more time watching the trains than learning. You could hear the trains from our garden when they were shunting at night. I knew that from when I slept out there in the tent. Sometimes we went train spotting. We would sit on the embankment between the road bridge and the tunnel. When we got bored of waiting for a train we sometimes walked down to the track and looked inside the tunnel, but never went inside it – you might get squashed by a train. We put pennies on the railway lines and retrieved them after a train had passed: they were squashed to nearly twice the size.

The Northampton arm of the Grand Union Canal was nearby. The overflow from the lock made an excellent water slide. It was near here that I played with friends on Saturdays. To get there you passed the Euclid factory, where they built huge earth moving trucks, so large that they were scary to pass. We stayed out all day. Providing we got home in time for tea it didn't matter how long we were away from home.

I learnt to swim at a pool on the other side of town: I still have a certificate for swimming 60 yards and it's dated 14/11/59. I would cycle to the pool after school and afterwards buy 4 penn'th of chips with bits. In summer we sometimes swam at Midsummer Meadow outdoor pool. The bottom of the pool was sandy and the warm water came from the power station cooling towers on the other side of the River Nene.

On some Saturdays I played with a friend who lived at Rothersthorpe Farm. He had a tree house that was better than ours. One of our favourite pastimes was to build tunnels from bales of hay. The barn used to store animal feed smelt delicious, and the feed pellets tasted pretty good too. The farm was somewhere near what is now the motorway services next to junction 15A of the M1. The motorway wasn't there then: its construction began a bit later. A few weeks before the motorway opened I cycled along a short section of it so I can claim to be one of few children who has ridden his bike on the M1!

Dad was the English teacher at Delapre Secondary Modern School. At his school they called him Eddy so the pupils from there called me 'Eddy's son'. I didn't like that. Being the son of the hated species of teacher was bad enough; being named after one was even worse. Fortunately, I didn't go to Delapre school – I was still a junior – but some of my school friends had a brother or sister at Delapre so I was 'Eddy's son' to them.

I went with dad on some of his school youth hostelling trips and in Easter 1960 we went to the Lake District. I have a photo of me squatting beside a waterfall in Far Easedale. More than 50 years later I have since walked through this lovely valley several times and on each occasion have tried to recapture that scene. The water level is always changing and it's difficult to identify the right angle and position, but the rock is still there and of course the mountains behind must be identical.

The photo below shows the group on the corner of Howe Head Lane, just up the lane from Wordsworth's Dove Cottage in Grasmere. We were feeding ducks then but now the pond is mostly overgrown, so you couldn't reproduce this scene today. There was none of the modern hi-tech outdoor gear in 1960. I wore heavy shoes with metal studs and got blisters, as most of us did. To keep off the rain we wore cycling capes. These were better than the latest breathable jackets. They were 100% waterproof, kept your rucksack dry and made a cosy tent when you stopped for a break. Air circulated underneath so you didn't get sweaty. You needed to be careful when it was windy though. We also wore metal badges that we bought from each youth hostel we stayed in, to commemorate our visits there, like trophies to prove our great achievements.

Easter 1960: Walking group near Grasmere

Frequently, the group would sing together as we walked. A favourite was 'My Old Man's a Dustman' by Lonnie Donnegan:

My old mans a dustman
He wears a dustman's hat
He wears cor-blimey trousers
And he lives in a council flat
He looks a propa 'nana in his great big hobnail boots
He's got such a job to pull 'em up that he calls 'em daisy roots

If we had to walk through mud, dad would start off with the Hippopotamus song:

Mud, mud, glorious mud.
Nothing quite like it for cooling the blood.
So follow me follow,
Down to the hollow,
There we can wallow in glorious mud.

Dad would then remind us that during the war, he served in the Friends Ambulance Service and was friends with Donald Flanders, who recorded that song.

The boys were always up to mischief and the 'ring leader' was usually Terry. One of the places we stayed at was Patterdale Youth Hostel. It's not far from the cricket field. One evening, some of the boys, led by Terry, picked up a bench seat from outside the pavilion and hurled it in the beck. I don't know why they thought that was funny. It was much more fun for us to roll boulders down the steep fell slopes.

Some years later, we were sad to learn that Terry was tragically killed whilst riding his bike round the M1 roundabout. You don't have to be old to die.

We set off from Patterdale to climb Helvellyn. It was a cold, wet and windy day and the climb was too hard for my 9-year old legs. I was not the only one to complain so dad agreed that I could go back down with two of the older lads. Part way down we got lost. Fortunately, we met a group carrying huge rucksacks and maps in waterproof cases. They told us which way we needed to go. I didn't hear everything but I did catch one of them saying, "Duke of Edinburgh." Back at the youth hostel I told mum about our adventure and that we had been rescued by the Duke of Edinburgh! It's a story mum often repeated.

Naturally, I believed everything I was told. Our head teacher, Mr Adams once came into our classroom and announced that it was his birthday. Someone asked how old he was and he replied that he was 100. When I told this to mum she said that he wasn't a hundred. I insisted that he was because that's what he told us. Mr Adams was clearly older than dad and dad was approaching 40, which was really ancient. I didn't like the idea of getting old. One night in bed the thought upset me badly and when mum came to comfort me she asked why I was crying I told her, "I don't want to die."

I was pretty near the bottom of class at Far Cotton junior and dreaded the thought that I was bound to fail the eleven plus and end up going to Delapre Secondary Modern School as Eddy's son.

The method of teaching was learning by rote. It was not necessary to understand. You just had to able to repeat what you were told. For example, when testing my knowledge of multiplication dad would say,
"Seven eights."
I hesitated.
"Quick quick – seven eights"
Further hesitation as my mind went into panic mode.
"Silly boy."
I hated school. I hated learning.

At the end of the 1960 summer term we moved to Pinxton, Derbyshire. Dad had got his first appointment as a headmaster at Adelaide Coke Secondary Modern School on Kirkstead Road. The school opened in 1860 and was maintained by Messrs Coke and Co until 1876 when it was taken over by Pinxton School Board as Kirkstead Board School. In 1903 it became a council school and in 1937 the boys and girls departments merged to form a senior mixed school.

Pinxton was a great contrast to Northampton. It was a mining village and many of the miners lived in an estate of terraced houses called Kirkstead Row which was just above the school. The miners could often be seen squatting by the side of the road or outside the Miners Arms which was on Church Street at the top of Kirkstead Road. I guess they preferred squatting to standing because they were so accustomed to that posture 'down pit'.

Adelaide Coke Secondary Modern School

We lived in the school house that was joined on to the school. Living in the school house meant that I could use the school playground as a private recreation area. I could ride my bike, chase cats and look inside the girls' outdoor toilets. They were the same as the boys' except they didn't have an outside wall coated in black bitumen with a drain gulley at its base and they didn't smell as bad.

Cycling on school playground

At the bottom of our garden there was a stream that ran beside the hedge. I built a dam. The stream came down from Kirkstead Row and often smelt of paint or oil or goodness knows what. The best part of the garden was the dirt track I made for my bike. There was no such thing as a BMX bike then. I built a shed and a tree house with walls and a roof. To get to the treehouse you climbed up an inclined plank. I'd nailed some slats across the plank to make it easier to climb. There was an old sofa in the treehouse and I'd slept in it for at least one night. The shed started as a hole in the ground that I had dug, but I can't remember why. It was about four feet square and two feet deep. On top of the hole I built a platform with a trap door. Using some old floorboards (they must have refloored the school hall) I built five feet high walls and a put a roof on top. It looked like a box. You got into the shed by climbing into the hole and up through the trap door. Once inside there wasn't really anything to do because it was just a dark empty space. One day a strong wind blew the whole thing sideways because it wasn't secured to the ground.

The main room in the school house was the living room where we ate meals and watched television.

Our favourite television programme was Supercar. In the puppet programme, the baddies Masterspy and Zarin fly the Mastercar.

"Mastercar has its port engine running successfully and stabilised at 15,000 revs. Masterspy calls out from the cockpit "Charging starboard". The rev counter on Mastercar climbs slowly. Masterspy calls out "five thousand, eight, ten, twelve, ... fifteen thousand!". Zarin flicks a switch on his remote console and shouts out "Interlock on". Masterspy exclaims "Fire two" and the engines blast into life."

A clever electromagnet is used it to pick up the car and deposit it on the top of a tv transmitter mast, where the villains are left to cool off. Thus, precariously balanced, Masterspy and Zarin are left having to lean backwards and forwards to try and keep the car from toppling. "Lean forward Masterspy!" thus became one of our favourite catch phrases.

There was a cellar in the school house. It had an electric light and a small window and it was always damp. We kept pet hamsters there so it always stank. I was given a chemistry set and this was where I experimented. My concoctions produced a pleasing range of colours and smells so I wrote them down and submitted my work for publication in the school magazine. Unfortunately, my submission was rejected as being too dangerous.

In the garden, we kept tortoises and guinea pigs. Dad made a run for them out of old floorboards. His joinery was not good. In the end, the pets either escaped or were captured by a cat.

I went to the adjacent junior school, which was at the top end of the playground. Miss Gibbs was my teacher. For the first time in my life, school was OK. As I didn't have a northern dialect I was asked regularly to read aloud in class. I was also able to sing and was proud of my rendition of "Oh for the wings of a dove".

Oh for the wings, for the wings of a dove
Far away, far away would I rove
Oh for the wings, for the wings of a dove
Far away, Far away, Far away, Far away would I rove

In the wilderness build me a nest
And remain there forever at rest
In the wilderness build me, build me a nest
And remain there forever at rest

In the wilderness build me a nest
And remain there forever at rest
Forever at rest
Forever at rest

And remain there forever at rest
And remain there forever at rest

Miss Gibbs taught by reward whereas others taught by punishment. Whether it was Miss Gibbs, the confidence given to me by my lack of northern dialect or because the people in Derbyshire were not as clever as those in Northampton I will never know. The result was I went from bottom of class in Northampton to top in Pinxton. I passed the eleven plus. I wasn't going to dad's school. Hooray!

Whilst I enjoyed riding my bike, other children preferred football. I was never taught how to play the game. It was assumed that every boy knew all the rules and had the necessary skills. Most boys did, but not me. Consequently, when teams were chosen, I was picked last and usually given the position of goalie. This meant standing around most of the time becoming cold and miserable, then being blamed for failing to save a goal. Playing ball games in the school playground often resulted in broken windows. Anyone breaking a window was expected to repair it from a stack of spare panes kept under the building. Some boys must have become expert glaziers by the time they left school.

On some evenings, dad and I played chess in his school office. It was the upstairs room in the gable end of the building below. The game lasted hours, with each of us sometimes taking half an hour to complete a move. In the office there was a Gestetner stencil copier, so a sweet smell of meths often pervaded the room. Perhaps it was the alcohol in the atmosphere that caused us to take so long in moving the chess pieces.

School office building

The building on the right was the cookery room and below that the woodwork room. The school's claim to fame was that it featured in the TV programme 'Whicker's World' because we were one of the few (perhaps even the only) school at that time which had a cookery class for boys. I must have Alan Whicker's autograph somewhere.

Teachers who had cars parked them on a sloping part of the playground between the school and Kirkstead Road. One of them was a three-wheeler with registration letters WEE. It must have had a faulty handbrake because one day Mary ran into the house and announced,
        "Daddy, I've just seen WEE running down the playground!"
The school hall also served as a gym. One day I challenged dad to a race up to the ceiling on the climbing ropes and he beat me. I was disappointed that someone as old as 38 could do that. At Christmas, they built a stage supported by old desks and performed a scene featuring words from the Bible in the Book

of John. Every time I now hear these last five words I am reminded of that performance because of the way they were spoken - loudly and with emphasis on each word:

"FULL. OF. GRACE. AND. TRUTH."

The school woodwork teacher, Mr Bolton supported the building of canoes of the kayak type. They already had a heavy wooden double called Pioneer and a 10-foot canvas single called Kingfisher. Three more doubles followed. These were much lighter than Pioneer, being made of wooden laths and covered with canvas, which was coated with gloss paint to make them waterproof. The type was PBK14, the letters referring to the designer Percy Blandford and the number to the length in feet. One was painted red and called Mallard, the blue one Dipper and ours, which was green, Bittern. They would be transported on the car roof rack or on a trailer (also made at school). We practiced on Thursday evenings in a pond at the nearby Brookhill Hall and sometimes in Cromford feeder reservoir. Brookhill Hall was once a coach house for families descended from Sir Edward Coke, the Attorney General for Elizabeth I. It was currently owned by pianist and composer Roger Sacheverell Coke, who gave us permission to use the pond.

Mr Bolton and canoes

On Tuesday evenings we went dinghy sailing at Ogston Reservoir, which is on the other side of Alfreton. Derbyshire Schools had several GP14 dinghies there. Our boatbuilding skills led to the construction of an 11-foot Heron sailing dinghy, which was also painted green. Dad named it Ardea, which he said is the Latin word for heron. We sailed the dinghy at Sutton in Ashfield Sailing Club. I soon developed a commendable skill in sailing and helped to train other children.

Loaded for canoeing and sailing

I bought my first camera from the chemist shop in Pinxton. It was a Brownie 127. The first pictures I took with it were at my cousin Anna's wedding in Wales. They were good pictures. My life-long interest in photography had begun.

My best friend was Robert. He and his family lived at the Miners Welfare, which was up across the field at the back of the schoolhouse. His father, who ran the Miners Welfare, had puffy hands. I thought that was because of the beer he handled.

Children of my age could wander freely. We would go down Wharf Road, past the 'fleapit' cinema, over the railway crossing and along the old canal. It was filthy and had an oily smell. Around the bushes on the waste ground near here some of the older boys would be delighted to announce they had spotted a 'jonnie' but I had no idea what they were talking about. In the opposite direction there was the remains of a disused coke works that we could explore. That had an even stronger smell.

My secondary education started at Swanwick Hall Grammar School. It was a seven-mile bus ride from the village going through Alfreton, and took about half an hour. Sometimes in the morning it was foggy when I walked to the bus stop. The fog had a distinctive smell and taste and was often coloured yellow. Boys sat upstairs on the bus. On the first day I wore my new school cap. I don't think I used it after that. Someone cut the strap of my brand-new satchel so I had to fasten it short thereafter. One afternoon a boy smeared me with a piece of greaseproof paper which he had found on the floor. It was covered in honey. The smell of honey reminded me of that unpleasant incident for years afterwards. It was important to avoid the bullies. They seemed to be predominantly those who didn't join the rest of school in morning assembly because they were Catholic. It didn't seem right for a religious person to treat his fellow human beings with such abuse. I never enjoyed grammar school. I might have liked art had it not been for the mockery a teacher gave me. I had painted a colourful illustrated drawing of my name and was so engrossed in the art work that I mis-spelt my own name. The teacher held up my masterpiece to the whole class and said.

"Look what MANK drew!"

Everyone laughed at me. I felt ridiculed. The only school sport I enjoyed was cross-country running.

In July 1961 I spent two weeks at the Derbyshire Schools Camp at Sutton on Sea in Lincolnshire. I hated the first week. We slept in tents on sacks filled with straw. I never had a bath or shower but that didn't matter because I didn't get dirty. The second week was OK. The Caramac chocolate bar had just been invented.

Postcard to Mark, Tent 23, Schools Camp at Sutton on Sea, Lincs.:

Dear Mark,
I hope you are having a very good time. We went to Pinxton in the coach and brought Ash back. She has settled down very well. Shall you be living here for a few days after you get back?
Grandmother and Grandfather

I got another card from dad saying he was getting ready to go to France and one from grandma and grandad who were on holiday in Eastbourne, their favourite resort..

A popular game was called "Snakey Snakey On Your Back". You covered your eyes and one of your group drew a snake like figure across your back, then stepped away. You then turned around and announced a forfeit and picked out who you thought had drawn the snake on your back. If you were correct they had to complete the forfeit; if not you had to carry it out yourself. If you were sure who drew the snake, you would choose a difficult forfeit such as to run around the garages and back; if unsure, an easy one that you wouldn't mind doing yourself, such as turn around three times. Good tactical training.

At one time, the back of my left hand became covered with warts. To have them removed I had to attend a series of treatments at the hospital in Nottingham, to which I travelled alone by bus. The treatment involved 'burning' them off with dry ice. I almost fainted from the pain.

Derbyshire Education Committee ran (and still do) an Outdoor Adventure Centre called White Hall in the Peak District. I stayed there and enjoyed their courses on canoeing and rock climbing. One of their trainers was the renowned climber Joe Brown. He demonstrated his amazing skills by scaling the outside stone walls of White Hall. His indoor trick was to climb under a dining table and chair without touching the floor. One of our days was a canoe trip down the Derbyshire River Wye. Joe's kayak capsized and the image I remember is of him standing in shallows in the middle of the river whilst smoking a cigarette.

In 1962 I went with White House to the Isle of Arran. Joe was one of the leaders there too. Another of the leaders was called AB (rhyming with maybe). I never discovered why he was called AB, whether it was his initials or short for something like Abraham: I guess I never will know. AB was my favourite leader and everyone else's too, a really nice man.

Postcard from Arran:
Dear Mary,
Is the weather good at Pinxton? We have had only one rainy day so far. This picture [of Glen Sannox] is one of where I have been swimming twice. At this time of year, the river is much higher but I only swam to the other side and back on the first time in. The second time I was looking for a pan someone had dropped under a waterfall (this was just an hour ago). The current there was very strong and I kept losing my grip and went speeding downstream. Today it was so hot that AB, a few other boys and I went swimming in the sea and did very little walking. Arran is an island with the most different kinds of rocks in the world (I think) and I have some to show you when I get back. Having a good time.   *Love from MARK.*

Joe Brown at Arran

On some Saturdays I would catch the bus to Alfreton and spend some of my pocket money in Woolworths buying things such as sweets and model aeroplanes. The goods were laid out on counters arranged as islands with the assistant standing in the centre. I attended the Saturday cinema at the Alfreton Empire, although it wasn't as good as the Gaumont in Northampton. Occasionally, I earned extra pocket money by potato picking. We had to follow the plough, collect the potatoes in one hundredweight sacks and load them onto a trailer. In those days, it was expected of men and boys to lift loads of 50 kilograms or more.

In 1962 the first James Bond film 'Dr No' was made. When it was on at the Alfreton Empire I invited one of the girls from school to go with me one evening,. We were to meet outside the cinema. I was excitedly looking forward to the date as I rode the bus from Pinxton to Alfreton. I stood waiting for twenty minutes beyond the agreed time but she didn't turn up. I caught the next bus back home and cried all the way.

Chapter 2: A teenager in the sixties

In May 1963 I became a teenager. I don't think that birthday was particularly different from the one before. Mary thinks by then I had stopped being obnoxious to her, but I don't remember being that way previously. At least I didn't have any big disagreements with my sisters. Mary remembers being a dutiful sister and ironing my new, colourful, polyester shirt, which ended up as a sticky mess attached to the iron. Poor mum had to go into full de-escalation mode.

Like any other boy of this age I was changing physically and mentally. Peer pressure was having a greater influence. As parental influence became less important, what everybody else of my age was doing became more so. Anyway, parents are so old, how can they possibly understand a thirteen-year old? Mum and dad had already passed forty, which seemed a really old age. An advert that said, "Phyllosan fortifies the over-forties" confirmed that everyone passes their best at that age.

During the summer of 1963 we moved away from Pinxton to Swindon, Wiltshire. The Pinxton school closed in 1964 to be replaced with an Evening Continuation School. Dad had got the job as headmaster at the brand-new Merton Fields Secondary Modern School, which was on the northside of Swindon. Dad was pleased to be able to select all the staff himself because there were some members of staff at Pinxton that he found difficult. When the school was being built dad showed me the school layout plans. He was pleased to point out that his office was right next door to the room labelled sec's office (pronounced 'sex office'). While we were waiting to be allocated a council house we stayed in our small caravan that was parked in front of the school. We used the school toilets and showers as our bathroom. Soon afterwards we moved temporarily into a council house in Downton Road, Penhill.

One morning in November 1963 I awoke to find part of my anatomy already awake, upstanding and demanding satisfaction. I did what boys do to fulfil that need. And I had just finished when mum suddenly appeared at my bedroom door. I thought she knew what I was doing and had come to chastise me! But no, she had come to tell me that President John F Kennedy had been shot dead. It wasn't so much the news that shocked me but the fact that I almost got caught.

I went to Headlands Grammar school, which was not far from Merton Fields. It was a fairly typical grammar school of that era, one of two such selective schools in the town. A third was built as the new estates stretched eastwards and the numbers grew. Commonweal was the more established. It was the middle-class school in old Swindon, the part of town that pre-dated the coming of the Great Western Railway works and the first big industrial expansion in the 19th century. Justin Hayward, the Moody Blues singer/songwriter born in 1946 was brought up in Swindon and went to Commonweal school. At the age of nineteen he wrote and composed 'Nights in White Satin'. The song was a tale of a yearning love from afar and was titled after a girlfriend gave him a gift of satin bedsheets. Its mournful tune often matched my mood.

Nights in white satin
Never reaching the end
Letters I've written
Never meaning to send

Beauty I'd always missed
With these eyes before
Just what the truth is
I can't say any more

'Cause I love you
Yes I love you
Oh how I love you

Headlands was the amalgamation of two older schools in the town centre but acquired its distinct identity as a grammar school with the opening of the new building on Cricklade Road, Stratton St. Margaret to the north of the town in 1952. The 20% of students who passed the 11 plus exam were offered places at grammar schools and went on to take GCE 'O' level exams at the age of 16. Over half would then leave for the world of work and craft apprenticeships. The rest would stay on for a further two years of the sixth form and take 'A' level exams. About half of that number then would head for university and the rest to colleges or work.

I joined Headlands Grammar School in the third year. The top class was 3U (university), the second was 3A (advanced level), the third was 3O for ordinary level and then there was 3E and nobody seemed to know what that stood for. It probably meant 'education only' and was the class for those with no hope of achieving any qualifications. My class was 3E.

Our headmaster was Mr Magson – always known as "the Boss" and head of the school from 1949 until he retired in 1974. A few years before his death at the age of 90, Tom Magson was still describing Headlands as 'the best school of its kind in the area'. Many of the pupils agreed. The Boss was a stickler for discipline and once suspended a 15-year-old girl who was seen outside the school talking to a friend who was smoking. He liked to use florid language, preferring to say 'iced confectionary' for ice cream, fried chipped potatoes for crisps and pantechnicon for lorry. According to the Boss, it never rained or snowed, but we occasionally had 'inclement weather'. We would hear these expressions at morning assembly where we were arrayed by age and class. The Boss would sweep into the hall, glasses flashing and gown flowing. We would rise to our feet as the expected mark of respect while he and the teachers sat up on the stage. Two hymns, a prayer, the Lord's Prayer, a reading from the Bible and then the announcements, ending with a 'naughty boys' list of pupils who had to wait for punishment outside his office. Twenty minutes to start the day.

Headlands school song was written by our history and English teacher, Mervin Comrie. It had a rousing tune written by Mr Gilbert.

Home of our youth, our future's mould,
Our guide when young, our love when old.
Give us the strength to face the fight,
To shun the wrong, uphold the right.
Floreat Semper Schola!

Teach us the joy of effort made,
Of work well done, of games well played.
Of friendship which can stand the test
Of time and trial, and so prove best.
Floreat Semper Schola!

Hand us the torch, whose steady glow
We will maintain and later show
Undimmed for all who follow here,
That they, like us, may keep it clear.
Floreat Semper Schola!

Arm us with truth and courage sure,
That we may all attacks endure,
And show in later life that we

Were worthy to belong to thee.
Floreat Semper Schola!

The Latin words mean may the school always flourish. Well, it did in my mind.

Morning assembly was held in the school hall. Normally we sat on tubular steel chairs with canvas seats and backrests. The chairs were often faulty: sometimes the screws that supported the canvas frames were missing (possibly by intent) or the canvas split (perhaps aided by a penknife). A typical boy's prank was to push his feet up under the seat of the chair in front, especially if the seat was occupied by a girl. This was a perfectly acceptable way for boys to harass girls.

Sometimes, the chairs were not set out so we had to stand up during assembly. On one such occasion, after a while of standing still I suddenly felt hot and dizzy. I needed to sit down. I bent my knees but there was no room to sit and anyway how could I sit whilst everyone around me was standing? The next thing I knew I was being lowered onto a chair outside the back of the hall. I don't know why I fainted. Perhaps I had skipped breakfast. Maybe it was the cold cycle ride to school. Perhaps I was ill. Totally embarrassed by the event, I don't think I even told mum and dad about it. The fear of having to stand still in a crowd haunted me for years afterwards. Whenever there were no seats out for assembly I would panic and position myself in a space, such as by the windows, where I could sit on the floor without being noticed by anyone that was bothered. Often my legs would wobble and it would take all my concentration to stay conscious until at last we filed out of the hall.

I wasn't keen on the main lunchtime activity which seemed to be kicking a tennis ball aimlessly around the playground. Instead, I would often visit the school library. One of the delights there was the sight of Veronica or Vanj, as she was called. She always wore high black leather boots and her legs really turned me on.

Girls were addressed by their first name, boys by their surname. Wasps were called jaspers; plimsolls were daps. To keep the daps white, they needed to be regularly coated with Blanco White Cleaner. When we arrived at school we had to change into daps in the cloakroom.

If a boy's hair touched the collar Mr Magson would tap the boy's head and tell him to get a haircut. Boys could get a detention if we were seen without the school cap. Miss Jacobs, the senior mistress, would stand outside the doors of the hall and pull the girls aside if their skirts were above the knee. One girl got a detention for eating an ice cream on the way home from school; she was told it lowered the standard of the uniform. The punishment for a minor offence, such as talking in class, would be an imposition, which might be to write 'I must not talk in class' fifty times. The 'impo paper' had two red lines between the main lines to help improve your writing skills. The best technique was to repeat each of the words in turn down the page instead of writing the whole sentence. Chewing gum, which one teacher called 'transatlantic sticky residue', was also prohibited whilst wearing school uniform. Our favourite sweets were Fruit Salad & Black Jacks because you got four of these a penny. Boys' comics were Dandy and Beezer whilst the girls read the Star and Twinkle.

In April that year, the school invited a famous football player to meet the boys in the small hall. I thought the young man was George Best but if it was I cannot understand why he would have been in Swindon, so it can't have been him. Not being a football fan, it made no difference to me. All I remember is that we were invited to ask him questions. We all just gazed at him and nobody said anything. Very embarrassing.

Four weeks before the School Fête, which was at the end May, a Talent Scheme was started. All those willing to take part were given a half-crown (two shillings and sixpence) and challenged to increase this as much as they could by the day of the Fête. 235 half-crowns were handed out and when the money was collected a profit of over £70 was made. The most successful pupil gained three pounds fourteen shillings. Staff and pupils were constantly waylaid and tempted with cakes, biscuits, fudge, and many other (sometimes indefinable) tasties. Coconut ice was my favourite. It was either pink or white.

The Fête started officially at 2.30, but several hundred people were already wandering around by 2.15 – a form of punctuality rarely seen during school hours. Admission was free, but not much else. Visitors could have their car washed for 2/6. The Broken China Stall was the first attraction. Some of the cups and saucers donated were so good that they could have gone to the Fancy Goods Stall. There were stalls for flowers, cakes, groceries: the lot. One lady even presented her weekly grocery list and asked the pupils to assemble it for her. There were stalls for model railways, cars, radio, chemistry: there was no end to it. Paul's Pop Shop was full of swinging children gyrating to the blast of umpteen-watt amplifiers in an enclosed space. Patient ponies plodded up and down the playing field and there was a never-ending queue for rides. 'Guess the number of Smarties in the jar' caused some trouble. The winner happened to be going out with the sister of the person holding the jar, but the argument was settled in his favour by offering the organiser a dip in the jar. The Swindon Fencing Club display proved a good draw. The Trampoline Club followed, starting with a dive through a burning hoop. The Pet Competition proved impossible to judge. Dogs, cats, rabbits, and even a lamb defeated the adjudicator, who eventually drew the winner out of a hat. The school had hoped for a thousand visitors, but far more turned up.

During the morning breaks, you could buy biscuits from the school tuckshop. My favourite and best value biscuit was Abbey. You got three for tuppence. If you wanted a chocolate biscuit there were Penguins. It was a difficult decision to decide which colour to choose: either red, blue, green or yellow. It was years before I realised that all Penguins were the same, regardless of the wrapper's colour.

Our woodwork teacher was Mr Batten. He was very fussy about the quality of our workmanship and he made sure when we planed a piece of wood it was perfectly flat and square. We learned about different types of wood and practised making mortice and tenon joints and dovetails. I got an 'O' level in Woodwork and enjoyed making things at home for many years later. I still have some of the things I made.

I was quite good at Technical Drawing. I even bought my own drawing board and tee square. We kept our drawings inside cardboard tubes. It was a favourite prank of the lads to break other boys' tubes so we used the strongest we could find. The best ones were corset tubes but I didn't know what they were originally used for or where the lads got them from. Anyway, they didn't provide enough support to prevent them from being sawn, drilled or crushed in a vice so they got wrecked anyway.

Mr Still was our chemistry teacher. He loved to demonstrate the electrolysis of water so that he could make a loud 'pop' at the end by igniting the hydrogen. He also liked to place a small lump of sodium onto a beaker of water and watch it ignite. Occasionally, he would accidentally set fire to things.

Sex lessons were part of Mr David Garside's biology classes. I don't remember much of what Mr Garside taught us, but one lesson had a long-standing influence – that you must wash your willy every day. He taught us a phrase I had never before heard: 'manual masturbation'. He didn't say anything about an automatic version. That must be coming soon. David Garside's car had a personalised number plate – we decided the letters stood for Dirty Garside. We didn't need sex lessons because we were well-informed lads who already knew how babies were made. To test my knowledge, a doubting girl once asked me if I'd ever heard the word 'period'.

I replied, "Yes, you mean the menstrual period."

But I probably didn't know what having one involved or why girls queued outside the senior headmistresses office when they were 'on'.

The school motto, displayed on the covers of our exercise books, was *omnia experire bona contine* which means try everything and continue with the good. The sort of thing I was wanting to try was not taught at Headlands. It took me the next six years to try all of them and a further three before I started to be good.

We still had the 'Bittern' canoe and would paddle on the Thames either at Lechlade or further upstream from Hannington Bridge. The canvas ones were being superseded by the Kayel kayak. I built first a single one for me and then a double. The Kayel was a tougher boat than the canvas on wood ones. We bought a kit that comprised shaped pieces of plywood, copper wire, fibreglass tape and epoxy resin. To build the boat, all you had to do was stitch the plywood together with wire and paste the tape over the joints with the resin. It sounded simple, but often the plywood shapes didn't always seem to fit together properly. Once assembled, the canoe was painted with three or four coasts of marine varnish, with thorough sanding down in between to produce a smooth glossy finish.

Dad 'launching' Kayel

A few doors away from our house in Downton Close lived a girl called Shirley. She was writing a book and sometimes came around to our house to borrow a hole punch. That's how I knew her and that's all she was to me: the girl who borrowed the hole punch. But on the last day of March 1964, Shirley suddenly became part of my life. I was nearly fourteen. From that day onwards I couldn't help but notice her. She was no longer just the girl who borrowed our hole punch. Now she was a real human being, who smiled, often wore a pretty dress and always smelt nice.

We were going on a school canoeing trip to the upper Thames at Hannington Bridge. The farmer there said we could use his cow shed to keep the school's canoes in. Mum was driving our blue Vauxhall Victor estate. On the way we stopped at Blunsdon to pick up Guy, the doctor's son. He sat on the front bench seat so I had to squash up between mum and Guy. Turning around I could see Mary and her friend Alison. Sitting in between them, shining out like a beacon, was Shirley.

We pitched two tents in the field above Hannington Bridge. The tents were for changing our clothes, in case we fell in: one for the boys and one for the girls. This was where we launched the canoes. On later visits, we would paddle down the weedy Upper Thames as far as Lechlade. On this day we were staying near the bridge because we had with us some newcomers to the sport. Shirley was a newcomer. Since I was already an 'expert' canoeist, I would be her teacher. I took out the double canoe with Shirley as my pupil. She immediately took my fancy, and she was the best-looking girl there. That day I never stopped thinking about her. Soon we were speaking freely to each other, as if we were old friends.

Next morning the sun was shining brilliantly. We were going to Hannington Bridge with Mr Bolton for the day to clean out the cow shed. I had just been on my bike to buy some things for mum. When I approached the gate, I saw that Shirley was standing in the garden wearing her best clothes. She always dressed that way in the morning. That day, she seemed the most beautiful sight I had ever seen. She had come to borrow the hole punch. Mum asked me,
          "Would you like Shirley to come to Hannington Bridge with us Mark?"
I almost ran Shirley over in surprised delight as I rode down the garden path.
          "Yes. OK," I replied, refraining from showing my eagerness.
Inside, my heart was burning with desire for her to come with us. Mum asked Shirley if she wanted to go. When she replied, "Yes," I was overjoyed. Mum told Shirley to go and change into some old clothes and to get something for lunch.

We met Mr Bolton, dad's woodwork teacher, in his yellow Ford Anglia. He said he was going to install some windows in the cow shed. I asked if I could go with him and to my relief Shirley went in his car too. We climbed in, with Mr Bolton driving and dad in the passenger seat. Shirley and I sat on the back seat, separated only by a few pieces of timber. As we arrived at the cow shed I suddenly realised how miserable I would have felt if Shirley had decided not to come with us, and how joyful I felt that she was there.

On our return journey we stopped to see progress on the house we were having built at Blunsdon. We talked about going canoeing together the next day. I asked dad and he agreed that the two of us could cycle out to Hannington Bridge. That evening I felt myself progressively wanting to get nearer and nearer to Shirley. The next day Shirley and I cycled to Hannington Bridge. This was the first of about seven consecutive days when we cycled the seven miles there together. My bike had three-speed Sturmy - Archer gears and a speedometer on its straight handlebars. The best part of the ride was descending Nell Hill out of Hannington village and my target was to reach 40mph, the highest speed shown on the dial. I took a photo with my Brownie 127 to prove that I had done it but sitting up to take the picture slowed me down to 38.

Over the next couple of weeks, I went to Shirley's house or she came to mine most days, including on my 14th birthday when Shirley and her mum gave me a present. We went swimming at Milton Road baths together every Tuesday for four weeks in succession. On one Friday afternoon I went delivering groceries with her dad. If I wanted to recall how I felt during these happy weeks, I just had to listen to Peter and Gordon's 'A World Without Love':

Birds sing out of tune
And rain clouds hide the moon
I'm OK, here I'll stay
With my loneliness
I don't care what they say I won't stay
In a world without love

At Hannington Bridge we would not launch the canoes until about an hour after arriving. Before that, we just sat talking. Sometimes we just sat. Sometimes I put my arm around her. But I was too shy to do anything more adventurous. By the seventh visit, words of the song, 'Code of Love' by Mike Sarne kept running though my head.

Number 1 you find someone,
2 you hold her hand,
3 you kiss her on the cheek,
Number 4 you squeeze her,
Number 5 you tease her,
6, 7, 8, 9, 10 too late to say when.

Like a damaged record it seemed to get stuck on the line, 'Then you kiss her on the cheek.' But I never really kissed her until Saturday May 9th, after over a month of visiting the cowshed together.

It was a cool Saturday when we cycled to Hannington Bridge. After paddling canoes a short way up river and back we put the boats away early. We played "wrestling" for a while on the cowshed floor. It was fun and a good way to get warm. We both enjoyed the physical contact of the game but to me it was different to wrestling with boys. Afterwards, Shirley lay down on the groundsheet that she always brought with her. I lay beside her, and put my arm around her. This was no longer like wrestling with boys. I kissed Shirley on the lips. It was the first time I had ever kissed anyone on the lips. We lay in the same embraced position for the whole of one and quarter hours. It was challenging to match her breathing rate, so as not to breathe in the breath she had just exhaled, while we were lying face to face. I will always remember that first kiss. I wanted to remember it. I mentally recorded what I saw and how I felt so that I could always recall the sensation of kissing a girl for the first time in my life. I will remember it for the rest of my life. Not because it was sensational but because it was my first proper kiss.

When we finally broke apart, Shirley went outside and we both straightened our clothes. It felt bitterly cold cycling home after being so close together. I ached from Shirley lying on my arm for so long. It was the worst journey home from Hannington Bridge I had ever had.

Sometimes at Hannington Bridge, there was a man by the river who always wore black swimming trunks. We never saw him swim. He just watched us while we paddled the canoe. We kept away from him. Children were always wary of men who watched children. The word paedophile hadn't been invented. In those days, if you spotted a 'dirty old man' you kept away from him. We looked out for each other and took responsibility for our own safety.

On Thursday 7th May I went with a party from dad's school to London. Shirley and her friend Sandra sat in front of me on the Rimes coach. We visited the Planetarium, Madam Tussauds and the Zoo. I took a liking to Sandra. One of my friends was hoping to go out with her. I took a photo of Sandra, Shirley and Mary sitting on a park bench in Regents Park. I thought Sandra was great but I never got to go out with her. I was too slow. I knew her for over a year later and missed every future opportunity of chatting with her.

The journey home was the most enjoyable ride I had ever had on a coach. For the first few miles I sat on the seat next to the back one. Shirley, Sandra, two other girls and two boys were on the back seat. Sandra was not feeling well so I swapped seats with her and sat next to Shirley. From the back window we displayed pictures of the Beatles to passing motorists. This was fun but not as good as what went on for the rest of the journey.

One of the boys started to tease me and Shirley for holding hands. David, who was in the seat in front of us, kept peering between the seats and shouting 'Yoo Hoo!' at us. We tried to quieten him down because Shirley's mum was sitting in the front of the bus. Shirley rested her head on my shoulder. This provided another subject for others to tease us both on the bus and later at school after Brynley's sister told her brother who then spread it round school. From then on, people kept calling me 'Shirley'. One day someone wrote her initials next to mine in a heart on the blackboard. Unfortunately, there was also a really ugly girl in our class called Susanne who had the same initials as Shirley.

Mark with Shirley & Mary

Nearly every time I was at Shirley's house, her mother would sing this song:

"On top of old smokey
All covered in snow
I lost my true love
Through courting too slow."

On Saturday May 23rd my sister Mary, Shirley and I spent the day in our caravan which was still parked outside dad's school. At the time I thought we were having fun being together but it turned out to be the last time Shirley showed any interest in me. The following week Shirley said that she had to see some friends she hadn't seen for a long time because she had been seeing me every day instead. I tried to get her to stay with me but it was useless – I had lost Shirley through courting too slow – the very words Shirley's mother used to sing to me. It was many weeks later before I guessed she had been trying to give me a hint. After that I went to Shirley's only twice more: once for tea and once when we went to see stock car racing at Blunsdon stadium.

After the summer holidays, we had to go for dinner from Headlands (my school) to Merton Fields (Shirley's school). Every Friday lunch time they had a disc club. I don't think the word 'disco' had been invented then. We ate outside the doors to the hall. From there, we could watch the girls dancing and listen to the music. They played songs such as 'Baby Love' by Diana Ross and other songs from the brand-new Tamla Motown label. Herman's Hermits 'I'm Into Something Good' and the Four Seasons 'Rag Doll' were the ones that reminded me most of Shirley.

I tried to get Shirley to go out with me again. After a sudden idea, I wrote her a letter before registration at dinner time and sent it via my friend's sister Valerie, who was in the second year. I wrote that I had a wonderful time doing the washing up with the girls. Janet, who I also took a fancy to when we went to dinner, later passed me a reply. Unfortunately, Brynly and Malcolm ripped it open when they snatched it from me.

Dad bought at new house at Sutton Park, Blunsdon. Well, it wasn't a house at first, just a plot of land on a new estate, so from time to time we would visit the site and watch the house take shape. After we moved in in 1964 it was a few months before the road was properly surfaced. After a heavy rainstorm we were even able to launch a canoe outside our house.

Although I had my own bedroom in the house at Blunsdon, the area that was really my own was the loft. Some of the floor was boarded and detailed drawings of our Heron sailing dinghy mounted on large sheets of cardboard were pinned to the rafters to make a ceiling. There was a beam across the space which I utilised to support a bench. I enjoyed making things with wood. This was also my private place where I could write secret thoughts. I never felt the need to discuss my feelings with others and nobody asked me to do so. It was enjoyable to write down my thoughts without fear of retribution or repercussion. The writing made me feel more comfortable and it was satisfying to read later on. I had acquired an unused green Headlands Grammar School History exercise book so I used that to record my thoughts.

In the loft I would also fantasise about sex and write essays beginning with me meeting a girl and building up gradually to us having sex. By the time the story approached its climax I became impatient and finished the story in a couple of lines. I hid the essays underneath the fibreglass loft insulation. I hope nobody found them!

Forest of Dean Walking Tour
On Friday 10th October 1964 I left school early. When I got home I was told Shirley was going on the trip too. It was a pleasant surprise because I thought that the only people going were 1st and 2nd year pupils. Shirley would be the only other person of my age. Mary, mum and I walked to the bus stop and joined the others who were already on the bus to Cheltenham. As we got on I smiled to Shirley. She did not know I was going either. I had to sit downstairs at first but I could see Shirley through the round mirror that the conductor used to see who was on the upper deck. Shirley and I waved and mouthed words to each other. After we passed Cricklade I moved upstairs and sat on the empty seat nearest to Shirley, but it was two seats away from her and on the opposite side of the bus. Soon afterwards we both changed seats and sat together on the row next to the back. Shirley told me the names of other people on the bus.

This was the first time I had heard of Teresa, who for a short while sat on Shirley's lap.

During the bus journey, every time we passed a horse there was uproar from most of the girls saying, "Where?" as if a horse was something that was never seen in Swindon. Towards the end of the journey a man, probably in his late twenties moved to the seat in front of us. He turned, grinned and asked Shirley her name. Shirley blushed but turned her head away, then escaped to the lower deck of the bus. Older men would try openly to 'pull' teenagers but Shirley was street wise and knew how best to respond. After getting off the bus we walked four miles to the youth hostel. I accompanied Shirley and commended her response to the incident. We were about a hundred yards in front of the party. As it started to get dark we began to drop to the back where we joined Dennis and some girls. I was holding Shirley's hand pulling her up the hill and she in turn was pulling Avril. It started to rain. Shirley put on her yellow cape. I held her hand under the cape. I felt good.

We arrived at the youth hostel just in time for supper. I sat next to Shirley. She didn't eat very much. After supper I played dominoes with the boys. The girls stayed in their dormitory until 8.30 when they came out wearing their best clothes. Shirley kept going in and out of the room so I didn't get a chance to talk with her. At 9.30 the boys decided to say goodnight to the girls who by then would be by the dormitory door wearing pyjamas. Teresa and Avril were the only girls who came to the door. Shirley's excuse was that she had a tear in her pyjamas. I later discovered that it was just a small tear on the knee.

In the morning we walked back into Cheltenham along a muddy road. I enjoyed helping Shirley from slipping. After that we caught a bus to Gloucester, where we met a lady teacher who took us round the cathedral.

I can't remember what happened during the tour on a day to day basis. To cut a long story short, Shirley drifted away from me whilst at the same time Teresa and I became very close. The day I remember best is when we stayed at the youth hostel in St Briavels castle. After supper, Teresa and I walked outside the castle walls and kissed enthusiastically. Whenever I think of St Briavels castle I can recall that scene. I've been back since and it brought back fond memories of Teresa. A few months after the walk I wrote that the kiss was cold and unenjoyable, but that I felt we had to do it. Strange how our memories work.

I passed Teresa's house on my cycle journey home from school so after the walking holiday I sometimes called to see her. Her parents didn't get home until five so we had nearly an hour together alone. We kissed and I daringly put my hand under her blouse, but her chest was as flat as mine.

My elder sister Dorothy thought she behaved like an obnoxious teenager. I don't remember that, but then none of us took much notice of her. Neither did mum or dad. She was always the black sheep of the family. Dorothy must have been a difficult daughter but I was mum's favourite child. Dorothy worked in a public library. The adult books she often brought home were left in her room and when I was alone in the house I would flick through the pages to find the "juicy bits".

Generally, mum and dad seemed to be incapable of discussing things to do with sex. They never raised the topic and I never asked. They certainly never talked to me about 'the birds and the bees'. If it was mentioned I would have reassured them that I'd learnt all about that at school. It would have been at least as embarrassing for me as for them to talk about sex. When Mary started having periods she tried to talk to mum about it, but was told not to talk about them. The nearest mum got to giving Mary a sex lesson was to warn her once, saying, "No hanky panky," but otherwise, conversations were shut down with an imperative, "Don't be so silly."

On Saturday nights Dorothy went out to a club, but I didn't know who she met or what they did there. One day in May 1965, mum told me that Dorothy was going to get married and was having a baby in September. I guessed that the club was the sort of place I would like to visit. Soon after Dorothy's announcement she left home and sometime after that she got married at the Registry Office. I suppose mum and dad went to the wedding but I wasn't invited. It wasn't until after the wedding that I got to meet Dorothy's husband, Terry. Dorothy's sudden marriage and disappearance was a huge shock to Mary and me. The first Mary knew about the pregnancy was when dad appeared at Sunday breakfast and announced that she was going to be an aunt. Mary didn't understand; she sat counting the months from May to September and could not understand how it was possible. When asked to explain, mum dismissed the question in her usual way:
     "Oh, don't be silly!"

A daughter getting pregnant outside marriage was a difficult situation for parents to face in those days. It was frowned on and in their position it must have been an embarrassment. They wanted Dorothy to go to an unmarried mother's home to have the baby, where you stayed for 6 weeks then gave the baby up for adoption. Dorothy just couldn't do that so she got married, which set the path for the rest of her life really. Mum said it would kill grandma to know about the scandal but as it turned out she was supportive and wrote Dorothy a really nice letter.

Shirley's friend Sandra used to say hello to me as I cycled past her coming home from school. I was proud that she greeted me in such a friendly way. I longed for a time when I could speak to her alone and ask her for a date. The time never came. Every time I passed her house I looked out for her but she was never to be seen. And she never will be there, or anywhere. When we came back from school holidays dad told me that one of his pupils had died. He explained how one evening, whilst she was watching television the girl cried out, rushed to her father's arms crying, "Oh daddy" and then died. It was Sandra. Other girls may grow old and rickety but Sandra will always stay 15, beautiful and friendly. In my mind, she will be in either of two places: Penhill Drive or London Zoo. Her red and white striped summer dress, her brown coat, her friendly nature – lost but not forgotten.

I kept a copy of Sandra's obituary from the local newspaper.

> *COULSON – July 17, 1965, at 69 Inglesham Road, Penhill, Swindon. Sandra, aged 15 years, dearly loved daughter of Mr, and Mrs. F. H.Coulson and dear sister of Carole, Susan, Jennifer, Jasmin and brother Jim. Funeral Thursday, July 22, service at St Peter's Church 8.45 a.m., followed by cremation at Cheltenham. Flowers to Co-operative Chapel Chapel of Repose. Phone 4759.*

Summer holiday:

In the summer of '65, we went as a family with dad to the school summer camp in a field near Beaumaris, Anglesey. We arrived early to help set up the camp. This included building the toilet facility, which involved digging a trench about one foot wide and two feet deep. A box shaped structure with a circular hole was built over the trench and a square tent erected above. I never liked using it and could go for several days without needing a poo.

One of the girls at the camp was Glenda, a pleasant and attractive lass. We enjoyed our trip to the fair at Benllech one evening, but I made no further progress in our relationship, perhaps because I was too shy.

Glenda

On one of the days, dad organised a canoe trip from Red Wharf Bay intending to paddle up the coast to Benllech or beyond to Moelfre. We set off in three double canvas kayaks with me in my own wooden Kayel. Once we got out of the sheltered bay the waves were quite large and the doubles were shipping so much water that they became unstable and capsized. We must have been spotted because a rescue helicopter appeared above us. Everyone except me were winched into the helicopter but I missed the ride because I was the only 'expert' canoeist. It was only by application of my superb skill as a canoeist that I avoided being capsized from the colossal downdraft from the rotors. Against that, everyone else got a free ride in a helicopter. To make up for my disappointment I sprinted to the shore and surfed onto the beach hoping that anyone watching would see me as a hero escaping from a dreadful ordeal. The waterlogged canoes soon drifted ashore by themselves. A teacher loaded the boats onto the Land Rover, taking extra time to fasten securely because he said he needed to drive fast. He could have saved time by fastening them as normal and then driven at a sedate pace. Instead he raced along the sandy lanes back to the camp site. Like me, he wanted to be a hero in the drama of a daring rescue.

Monday 5.11.65
Feeling in a melancholy mood, I wrote the following paragraphs.

"Two years have drifted by since I last saw Teresa, before Thursday that is. I have only kissed a girl once since then. It was with Glenda at Beaumaris summer camp in summer 1965 and it was nothing either. Two years without a girlfriend will probably (I hope) seem an awful long time in the future. I hope it extends no further or is not repeated.

"I repeated part of the walk almost two years later to the day. St Briavels was the same: St Briavels, where I had that cold kiss that led to so many more. St Briavels, the start of my last relationship with a girl. And Welsh Bicknor, where I had a last but foolish try for Shirley. And Symonds Yat, where Shirley and Teresa sat equal distances on either side of me. Those were foolish days where I carelessly missed many wide-open opportunities. I hope never to be so slow to recognise opportunities in the future.

"Denise used to go to Merton Fields School when dad was head teacher there. She knows a lot about me, as I found out as table captain of her table. I may have been too slow and missed an opportunity again but with luck there will be future opportunities to meet her. She spends most dinner hours with two or three friends in the library. I can't think of a way to start talking with her there. Perhaps next week I'll have some inspiration. Last night, at the Headlands Association dance, my excuse was that she was always with her friend Linda and would not dance with me. Given two more dances I think I would have plucked up enough courage to ask her, but then the dance ended. But there's next week…

"Eunice is nice. I went to the dance and back with her in our car. We had to wait for dad to pick us up. I think I was quick enough to start chatting with her but doubt I will get another chance to see her. It's a pity because she lives only 150 yards away from our house.

"I went to a new trampoline class at Penhill last Thursday and Teresa walked in to the hall. She was much more developed than two years ago: now she sported two nice little mounds under her tee-shirt. After a while I went over to her and said,
     'I haven't seen you for a long time.'
As I spoke I could see that her reply would be unwelcome. She didn't even turn to face me. It was hardly worth waiting for her inevitable reply.
     'Goodbye,' she said.

It didn't disappoint me. I was pleased that the truth about our relationship had at last got through to me: that although I had fond memories of two years ago I never really wanted her. I went home that evening satisfied with the outcome."

The 1965 school summer camp was based indoors at a school in Beaumaris. There was a record player in the hall but we only played about two records. One of them was this song by The Animals. It was inspired by the Vietnam war that was dragging on at this time and entitled 'We Gotta Get Out of This Place':

> In this dirty old part of the city
> Where the sun refused to shine
> People tell me there ain't no use in tryin'
>
> Now my girl you're so young and pretty
> And one thing I know is true
> You'll be dead before your time is due, I know
>
> Watch my daddy in bed a-dyin'
> Watched his hair been turnin' grey
> He's been workin' and slavin' his life away
> Oh yes I know it
>
> (Yeah!) He's been workin' so hard
> (Yeah!) I've been workin' too, baby
> (Yeah!) Every night and day
> (Yeah, yeah, yeah, yeah!)
>
> We gotta get out of this place
> If it's the last thing we ever do
> We gotta get out of this place
> 'cos girl, there's a better life for me and you

One of the activities I participated in was sailing a Wayfarer dinghy. This was bigger than the GP14s that I was accustomed to and also carried a spinnaker. I quickly became accustomed to the boat and on the last day we had a race in the the Menai Strait. We were leading up to the outward leg where we rounded a buoy and headed back to Beaumaris. For the return leg, I selected a course to take the best advantage of the wind but was dismayed when other boats passed us. I consoled myself with the thought that being locals, they must have had the advantage of knowing about the tidal flow.

During the half term holiday in February 1966 I decided to take a bicycle trip on my own to Somerset. On Friday 18th I didn't get up until 7.30 for a start so I could not possibly reach Beer Youth Hostel before dark. Then it started to rain and it looked like I was in for a dull cycle ride. So it was a bad start to the trip. My leggings worked well and so did my cape, but they kept in the sweat so I got wet anyway. I was 15 miles from Yeovil when I heard, "Pff, pff, pff" every time the wheels went round. It was only a puncture and it was getting on for a lunch time stop anyway so I pulled in to a barn and mended it whilst eating lunch at the same time. Three miles further on the "Pff, pff, pff" started again forcing me to re-tyre to the side of the road again. This time only a wall sheltered me from the wet wind but I was still warm from my exertions. After another four miles the all too familiar "Pff, pff, pff" started again. Now only a thin hedge separated me from the elements but I was still warm from the anger that fate was dealing me. I decided to do what fate obviously was trying to tell me, which was not to go to Beer, so I diverted towards Street Youth Hostel instead. Five miles further on and –yes you've guessed it – only by now I had run out of rubber solution. But now it was fate's turn to help me and she did this by planting a friendly Automobile Association patrol man right where I stopped. He kindly gave me some more rubber solution. There was no barn, no wall and not even a hedge for shelter here but I warmed to the thought of only having a further ten miles to ride.

I was surprised to find that the cycle shed at Street Youth Hostel was full of manure – the smelly mixture of hay and brown stuff that cows produce. Then I discovered why. The youth hostel was closed. Glastonbury was three miles away, Wells six miles after that and Crascombe Youth Hostel another three, so I had another twelve miles, or one hour's cycling to do. At Glastonbury I bought a puncture repair kit for my tyres. At Wells it was me who was tired. At Wells it got dark and the last three miles seemed to be a long way. I had a good supper and slept well that night. The next morning turned out bright and clear. It was going to be a good day for cycling. My front tyre was flat.

Some cycling trips were like that.

Setting off cycling in 1966

Later that year, Malcolm and I cycled around Wales. Headlands school was offering £10 for the most adventurous summer trip but we failed to qualify.

Malcolm and I both participated in the town sports in the mile event. I finished in a highly creditable 2nd place behind the town champion while Malcolm laboured in 4th, still good enough for a point though. I just managed to achieve my target time of five minutes for the mile, a pace I never succeeded in beating. Headlands school won the annual sports that year.

I passed seven 'O' levels; most were grade E but I got grade A in Geography. That was because of an earlier field trip we had to Llanberis when I learned all about glaciation.

In my school report, my form teacher Mr Millin (who also taught me maths) wrote,

"Chemistry is his weakest subject & I would not advise a career along these lines."

I went on to pass 'A' level Chemistry, took a degree in Colour Chemistry and followed a full career in the chemical industry. Was this me being defiant of adult advice?

Number one in the charts was the Beatles 'Paperback Writer'. The biggest hit of the year was Tom Jones with 'The Green, Green Grass of Home'. The Beatles had a hit with 'Yellow Submarine/Eleanor Rigby' in August and later in the year the Beach Boys "Good Vibrations' reached number one. I liked playing records in our lounge'. Two tracks stood out – a Monkees LP with Daydream Believer, Saturday's Child and Sweet Young Thing.

> Oh, I could hide 'neath the wings
> Of the bluebird as she sings
> The six-o'clock alarm would never ring
> But six rings and I rise
> Wipe the sleep out of my eyes
> The shaving razor's cold and it stings
>
> Cheer up sleepy Jean
> Oh, what can it mean to a
> Daydream believer and a
> Homecoming queen?

I never remembered 'the shaving razor's' line but the chorus kept going round and round in my head and the only way to stop it was to replace the tune with another. The trouble was, that would also get stuck in my head. Later, I found one song that could 'overessnride' all others without getting itself in a continuous look. It was 'We Can Help You' by The Alan Bown:

> We can help you, we're gonna help you,
> We can help you today, tonight
> We can help you
> We're gonna help you
> We can help you today, tonight

At the end of July 1966, we had our last family holiday staying at the cottage in Anglesey. Grandma came with us too. The Thomas's sheep dog had recently produced a litter of puppies so we bought one. We called her Sian, which is the Welsh equivalent of Mary. On the afternoon of 30 July instead of going to the beach, we sat in the Thomas's darkened lounge and watched TV. I didn't normally watch football matches but Hefin was a soccer fan. England beat West Germany 4-2 in extra time in front of a packed crowd at the old Wembley Stadium. It was pleasing to see England win the World Cup but I wasn't surprised. After all, football was invented by the English wasn't it?

The mock 'A' level exams showed that there was a risk of me failing to achieve passes in all three subjects. I was pleased with what I had recorded in my Thought Book and it helped to reduce my worries, so in November I wrote the following introduction to it.

"The purpose of this is to produce something to show for two years of study should I fail my 'A' level GCEs. It had to be something that I could not do if I had left school. I decided that a sort of autobiography would fulfil the above requirement and also relieve some of the worries.

"Really, through there should be no worries ('Wot, me worry!') but a sort of despair. At the moment I have not that worry and so will continue when I have."

The discotheque:
The New Yorker Discotheque was in Milton Road, Swindon. It was often raided by the police but somehow everyone knew when that was going to happen. A new experience for me was the ultraviolet lights that made white blouses see-through. Zoot Money, Chris Farlowe, Georgie Fame and Geno Washington & The Ram Jam Band all played there. 'Michael (The Lover)', by Geno Washington still reminds me of the place. One evening in February 1967 I arrived at the discotheque at about 8.45pm after parking my bike in a nearby car park. The dull but dazzling ultraviolet lit dance hall surprised me. Two of the walls were painted with a New York scene. A band was playing on a platform at the end. There were pillars on the other side and steps leading down to the coffee bar. Some of my friends were standing near the steps – Martin, Brian and Stephen. Pete and Ron arrived later. After a while we decided to dance. Martin told me of how on a previous visit he had danced with a girl, put his hand on her shoulder and after that was well away. Rather unlikely I thought. But within a few minutes I was doing even better: I was snogging in the middle of a dance. What a place! It started when I put my hand round her during the dance. It was as if I had known her for weeks, but at the time I didn't even know her name. She was called Lesley and she lives at Wootton Bassett. It was so enjoyable that I could not find the words to describe the scene, after all I only got grade 'O' for English and that was after a re-sit.

It must have been about midnight when I met Lesley and her friend. Lucas, who was the main singer that night, had just come on but I was not interested in him. I was searching for two girls we had seen earlier on and seemed to be friendly. I was beginning to think they had gone home when I saw them sitting on seats behind the pillars. I tapped Martin's shoulder and led him to the girls.

I went up to the prettier one and shouted in her ear asking if she wanted to dance. She couldn't hear what I said but we danced anyway. We found ourselves dancing in front of the loudspeakers. I was not enjoying the dance because of the loudness, but then I put my arm around her and kissed her. Her lips were very active. We moved towards the back of the hall to dance further away from the speakers, but we didn't dance very much. We went and sat down. I don't know how two hours had passed but it became time for Martin to go home. The girls had no intention of leaving – their parents were away and they didn't want to get home until dawn. Eventually we left them and I went home at three but couldn't get to sleep.

I wrote,
"My heart aches. All day I have had last night on my mind. 24 hours ago, I was content; now I want to re-live every moment of the evening: her warm body, her friendly lips, the atmosphere in the discotheque. There must be better ways to relieve this tension.

"It took me a week to get that evening off my mind. Now the feeling's back again. In six hours, I will be back at the discotheque. I wonder what the night has in store for me. Tomorrow I will want to re-live tonight."

During that second visit to the disco, I failed twice to get a girl to dance with me, but it was not all bad. It was a good dance, but there was no fun to be had. Maybe I should have tried Martin's way. He was crazy. He said he walked up to a girl in town whom he's never seen before and asked her to go to the disco with him that evening. And she went with him! I needed to try something original. So that night had nothing 'in store' for me, but I still looked forward to future visits. I thought about cycling to Wootton Bassett to stand outside the school at four o'clock and look for Lesley but it would be a long ride for nothing.

I met two girls at the trampoline class – Maureen and Kathleen – twin sisters by their looks – and I was hoping to get better acquainted with them the following week but the class was cancelled because Notts Forest were playing Swindon Town. Furthermore, there was no class the week after that either, so Maureen and Kathleen had to be taken off my list of 'probables'. Anyway, Kathleen had cold ears when I danced with her.

The YHA Local Group Sunday walk would have been a lot better if a few girls had been there, but even so, it was enjoyable. I had an interesting discussion with Martin. He's funny. He thinks he's so clever with girls but he doesn't have a girlfriend. When I pointed that out to him he got quite cross.

After Easter 1967 Dad was to start a new job as headmaster of a school in London. The headmaster that was replacing him visited us and brought with him his daughter, Katherine. She seemed quite sweet to me. I day-dreamed of taking her out, but was sure that if I could have made the dream reality it would have been disappointing. She was very pretty but seemed rather narrow minded, just like my sister Dorothy used to be.

Of my thoughts, I wrote:
"Back to my problems: I haven't any. I like to think I have but they're really only imaginary. Perhaps I like feeling fed up because it makes me look forward to the future: the next dance, the next girl, etc. I think 1967 is going to be my best year so far. Looking back over my failures I think that given the same opportunities, I cannot possibly make the same mistakes of being much, much too slow, too shy and too content with my present way of life. I look forward to a memorable summer. Seventeen is said to be the best age in a person's life. I intend to make it so with mine. My life has already changed greatly during the past six months and there are still many improvements to be made.

"Where have girls gone? Another nine weeks have passed since the disco! That must have been a freak bit of luck. And last night I was the same old slow nut I used to be. I thought I couldn't possibly be too slow any more but look at me now. The old Mark again. I'm giving up trying now. That is, unless there is a band like Lucas playing again. Turn the radio up full blast when it's playing a soul record and put an ear close to the speaker. With a little bit of imagination, you can almost believe you are in the discotheque. Why waste six shillings? Forget girls! Remember the enjoyment you get out of canoeing, cycling or sailing instead! Next week I think I'll go youth hostelling or cycle all through the night. That ought to dispel these feelings."

Aged 17
It was my 17th birthday. I wanted to do something special. I knew I could cycle all day and cover 12 miles an hour continuously. Lands End is 240 miles from Swindon so I could cycle there in less than a day. That would be something special. I planned the route carefully and told mum the details.

After cycling home from school, I packed my saddle bag and set off. I got past Bath before dusk and was feeling good as darkness fell over Somerset. At around midnight I found a barn beside the road and rested there for about an hour. There wasn't much traffic about and to save batteries I only put the lamps on when traffic approached. I was well into Devon when I was stopped by a police car. I thought he'd spotted me riding without lights. The policeman asked me my name, age, address and where I was going then let me ride on. But he kept stopping in front, letting me pass then going ahead again. This silly game of leapfrog was annoying because I had to keep putting my lamps on and off. I later learnt that mum was awoken late in the night by the front door bell ringing. She opened the bedroom window to see a policeman standing outside.

"Do you know where your son is?" he called up to her.

"What time is it?" mum asked. The officer told her.

"I think he must be somewhere near Dartmoor by now", replied mum. The officer must have been satisfied by her reply because he departed and my leapfrogging partner left me alone as well.

The last 50 miles were hard work, but I arrived at Lands End at 3 o'clock, two hours before the youth hostel opened. It was a bit disappointing after all that work with nobody to tell what I had just done. Eventually, the hostel opened, I went in, cooked a meal and went to bed at about 8. The trouble was I couldn't get to sleep for ages. The return journey took me more than two hard days. It seemed to take forever.

Another break I took was to go camping and canoeing at Widemouth Bay near Bude with Ron, David, his sister, Geoff and his girlfriend Jane. I travelled with Ron in his mini. We spent the days canoe surfing and the evenings at the pub. How happy a few pints of beer made me! I think I've fallen in love with unromantic evenings. Well, there I was drinking away nine pints of dark mild and talking to this couple from Sheffield. He was a great bloke. She was – well – I wish I were him! If she was younger and he was not, I would have – how can I put it – wouldn't mind her! All I have to do is run the Beatles' song 'All You Need is Love' through my head and I remember the scene. We talked about his job in the steel works, how easy it is to earn £30 a week. And the words of the Beatles song express my needs exactly!

Malcolm and I applied once more for the £10 offer from Headlands school for the most adventurous holiday. This time we won and were rewarded £5 each for our efforts. On 25th July 1967 we set off on a cycle tour of Scotland that took us to John o' Groats. For much of the tour we cycled our separate ways. Altogether, I cycled 1,300 miles. The longest leg was 146 miles from Lavendon, where we stayed with grandma, to York Youth Hostel. We had set off at 5am and arrived at 5pm. We travelled together for the first six days and parted company at Inverkeithing, so that Malcolm could take the coastal route via Aberdeen. We met at Strathpeffer Youth Hostel at the end of day 10 and continued our separate ways apart from 15 minutes together on day 11 at John o' Groats. I arrived home on 10th August, having caught the train from Kendal back to Swindon.

I kept a log of the whole holiday. One memorable part of the adventure occurred during my ride to Aviemore. An easy gradual climb up Glengarry brought me to its summit of 1,508 feet, the border between Inverness-shire and Perthshire. Then I dropped down to Dalwhinnie. A few miles further on, about three miles before Newtonmore, I stopped for lunch. A blue Bedford van pulled up when I had almost finished my break, the occupants offered me a cup of tea. I accepted and went to the van with his wife and two other people. They did not give me tea to drink: they gave me coffee, with steak, vegetables and potatoes followed by rice to go with it. Such was the kindness of some people in Scotland."

Postcard from John o' Groats to Blunsdon, dated 5th Aug 1967:
Dear All,
Hope you had a good holiday. I arrived here at 3.25 pm from Helmsdale. I haven't decided yet where to stay! If I go west I will never get home. If I go south I will repeat much land already covered. That just leaves north and east! I have covered 791 miles since leaving home. The weather has been mixed but is usually on the dull side. Scotland is a very beautiful place. We ought to go there next year or the year after.

Best wishes, Mark

After reaching John o' Groats, Malcolm turned back south but I continued westwards along the north coast of Scotland. I left the guesthouse at Greenfield after a hearty breakfast and cycled along the narrow A road with passing places to Bettyhill. It was a new experience in cycling: having to use all 10 gears up hills and shooting down them, hoping that there was nothing coming up on my side of the road. After this excitement came the dull moor of A'Mhoine. Those 10 miles were just a tiring push against the wind. At Tongue I decided to stop at the next store and buy some food for lunch. Three long hours later I had lunch at Durness 36 miles away. Continuing along more interesting roads I arrived at Scourie Youth Hostel at 5 p.m. At the time I thought that if an overtaking car gave me more than two feet of clearance the driver was being generous. Scourie Youth Hostel is a school normally and is only used as a youth hostel during the summer holidays. Although in such a remote position this part of Scotland has a very mild climate and in fact, palm trees grow there. There were also many wild raspberries growing at the roadside. I found the northwest part of Scotland an extremely beautiful part of Britain. I think Malcolm missed the best part of Scotland by going directly south.

My favourite youth hostel was Carbisdale Castle: a magnificent place worth 4 shillings bed night fee just for the visit. There are two galleries of painting and sculpture, and hundreds of rooms. There are beds for 200 hostelers. It is the most magnificent youth hostel I have ever visited."

My second longest ride was 109 miles from Loch Lochy to Loch Lomond. At North Ballacuilish there were two ferries, each capable of carrying six cars if tightly packed together. As I approached the ferry there was a long queue of cars, the last of which was expected to wait for nearly two hours. I simply rode past the queue and boarded the next ferry. The charge was 6d, another advantage of cycling. I had lunch beside a small waterfall between Bridge of Orchy and Tyndrum. I reached a maximum altitude of 1,036 feet and then dropped down to Crianlarich. From there to Inveran I had an extremely fast ride, at times travelling faster than cars ahead of me. This was because the wind was behind me and the road sloped gently downhill and also because the cars had to slow down for the bends. The ride beside Loch Lomond was pretty but rather long. If there had been a headwind I think I would have found it monotonous. From the road the youth hostel looked more like a stately home. With 250 beds, it must be the biggest hostel in Great Britain. England's biggest is Holland House in London, with 190 beds."

My final day's cycling took me to Kendal in Cumbria. Ullswater looked pretty in the still wind and with the surrounding mountains shrouded in mist. After a stop for refreshment in Patterdale I tackled the Kirkstone Pass. I had to walk up most of it but when I came to a signpost indicating a 1:4 hill I mounted my bicycle. Not long after, I found myself at the top of the hill. The road down to Ambleside is called the Struggle: it was steep, narrow and twisty so I had to keep my brakes on all of the way down so that when I reached the bottom the rear wheel rim was too hot to touch!. After looking round Ambleside, I continued to Windermere, where I went directly to the station and enquired about trains to Swindon. I cycled to Kendal and took the train from there. My bicycle cost half adult fare so altogether the cost came to £4 13s. I caught the 21.20h train, changed at Carnforth, Crewe, Birmingham and Bristol and arrived home for breakfast at 7.30 the following morning."

Thoughts during Autumn 1967:

"The emotional season of spring is long gone and summer, my favourite season, came and went. Now it's dark before eight again, the blackberries are out and I will soon have to start wearing a coat to go to school. I've given up counting the days, weeks and years since being with Teresa and Shirley. So much for my expectation that this would be a memorable summer: it will be, but not for the reasons I expected it to be. What made the season memorable had nothing to do with love: it was my cycling trip around Scotland. This year I have cycled from Lands End to John O' Groats (and back in a roundabout way). I hardly spared a thought for girls during the whole of the journey! Not once did I feel an urge for sex. I must remember this about cycling. It has nothing to do with the saddle of my bike, although parts do go a bit numb sometimes! The main thing about cycling is that it is very relaxing mentally. It's satisfying to know that every mile you go is due to your own efforts. It does you good both physically and mentally. You don't have to think, but you get to thinking.

"I've just finished reading 'Fanny Hill'. Here's an extract:

I lay then all tame and passive as she could wish, whilst her freedom raised no other emotion but those of a strange, and, till then, unfelt pleasure. Every part of me was open and exposed to the licentious courses of hands, which, like a lambent fire, ran over my whole body, and thawed all coldness as they went.

"I wasn't impressed by the book. I can't see how I can put any of its ideas into practice! All it seems to amount to is descriptions of sexual acts strung together by a flimsy story about a beautiful and misguided girl. Maybe if I connected all the rubbish I've been writing I could sell it, get it banned and make a fortune. Let's get busy!

"Three years have brought great changes to my life. I used to be a shy, stupid little weakling. Now I'm just ... ditto ... No, actually I'm quite proud of myself. I've learnt to taste life as expected of a 17-year old.

"I think a lot. I think how good things are going to be. I think that sex is just around the corner. I think how clever I shall be when I get that girl. I think how easy love will come. Always thinking but never doing! Will I ever go to bed with a girl? Will a girl ever like me? I don't know – I've never tried!

"Always thinking, never doing – that's me – everything's great in theory but there's no practice. There's no such thing as 'in theory'. If something should work 'in theory' either it works or the theory is wrong. You might as well say,

'In theory, this book ought to be a masterpiece.' In fact, it's far from it. You might as well say, 'In theory, this pen will write a masterpiece all by itself if I let it go.' Sometimes when I ought to be revising for my 'A' levels I write down my thoughts, like I'm doing now, because I can't concentrate on my work. I once had a theory that it is better to revise a little, however slowly, than to not revise at all. In other words, if a job's worth doing, it's better to do it badly than not at all. Sometimes it works, sometimes it doesn't. I think I theorise too early, before I have all the facts. But if I did have all the facts it wouldn't be a theory would it, it would be fact. So how do I know when I have all the facts? If I don't know if I have all the facts it might be a theory but it could be a fact. So my theory is that there's no such thing as a theory.

"Half term's coming up next week and I'm taking my driving test. If I fail I wouldn't mind going on a cycling trip to compensate for the disappointment.

"The solution to a problem usually comes to me when the problem isn't there. The problem might be how to start chatting up a girl but I can't think of what to say. Later on, I'll think of something I could have said, but it's too late then. If I wrote it down first I might remember what to say when the situation arises. Sometimes I think that if I could see the solution written down the problem would be solved. I could get better exam results. I could find a girl more easily. At least I might find a girl. At least I would start looking for a girl. Usually though, the words don't look as good on paper as they seem in my head. Anyway, girls aren't on my mind all of the time. Sometimes I can go for a whole ten seconds without thinking of them."

November 1967:
I filled that old History exercise book that I acquired when I was in the third form. I started it at the end of Summer 1963 as an emotional outlet. Not that I needed one, but I liked it. My lack of a girlfriend was partly made up for by having something to 'talk' to. I was able to say almost anything I felt in any way I wanted to. It did not have to make sense, as long as it sounded good and gave me satisfaction. Entries in it were few and far between as I rarely had any sweet memories that were worth writing about. Then, one night at a dance, something that I rarely visited, I met this girl. That was what started me off. I began to write more frequently, at first with great emotion (which, unfortunately I was not able to bring out in my writing) until I reconditioned myself that it was not for me. But I carried on writing. I liked to see something of my thoughts in writing. I liked making up theories about things such as why I failed to find a girlfriend. I thought I theorised too early, before having all the

facts before me. But if I did have all the facts it would not be a theory, would it? It would be fact. How was I to know if I had all the facts? I could not be sure if something was fact or theory until I knew I have all the facts. Sometimes I just confused myself.

I was bored – couldn't decide what to do. The phone rang. It was Martin. He was bored too. He came round. We decided to plan a party. Who should we invite? Firstly, we tried Jeff. He worked in a camera shop in Havelock Street on Saturdays and had the reputation of being clumsy. I don't know how many cameras he'd broken. Jeff wasn't in so we plodged round in the rain to Paddy's. I'de never liked Paddy much. He was big headed. By the time we reached his house we decided not to invite him, but suddenly he appeared behind us so we had to invite him anyway. Nigel lived somewhere on the Greenmeadow Estate. You went down a hill opposite the Rodbourne Arms and turned right at the bottom. His house was the one at the bottom with latticed windows. We couldn't find it. We tried phoning some girls. Being with Martin and Paddy I was more confident talking to girls than if I was on my own. But none of the girls agreed to come to a party so the plan was off. But I was no longer bored.

In a daydream I've bought an old fishing boat on the south coast and decide to organise a boat warming party. Martin and I go to the harbour a week before and get everything ready. Word goes round the 6th form social room and all the good looking girls decide to come along. We decide to head for a quiet creek rather than have the party in the harbour. Soon, it starts to get dark and we take turns at the helm. When it's my turn to helm I scan the sea in all directions but there is nothing but sea in all directions. The girls are frightened but they trust me to sail the boat safely to land. They bring me cups of coffee and I make love to them in between taking sightings from the start. After a brilliant piece of navigation I calculate where we are but discover that we have insufficient fuel to return home. Instead, we head to a nearby French port, where we are confined by bad weather. Every night we have fantastic rave ups, with the local inhabitants joining in too. Eventually, we have to return to school, sadly because every boy has been to bed with every girl. We're all quiet in M4, each of us absorbed in his or her loving memories. Others ask us questions but all they get is vague answers. They don't know what happened and we're not telling them. We exchange loving looks which the others don't understand. In my daydream, there's a colossal finale. It's so good I haven't even thought of it yet! I guess I never will.

Colin never had more than one pint (in practice I think it was really only a half) when he was driving his scooter. Ron and Dave both thought three pints was quite a moderate limit. Ron drove quite normally on three but he sometimes pretended to be a bit jolly. At the end of autumn term party, I noticed that Martin could not have had more than three when he started acting strangely. Mike had been in a pretty queer state since he fell off a ladder whilst putting up Christmas decorations in the school hall. During the party he acted like a semi-conscious duck and got off with fat Penelope. The following Friday when we were at the Shield he disclaimed all knowledge of nearly everyone at the party. He certainly didn't admit going with Penelope.

January 1968:
The Christmas holidays seemed to have been wasted. I had a quiet Christmas and a shocking series of exam results left me feeling miserable about going back to school. I went to the London Boat Show and afterwards visited the West End and visited the Cameo Royale cinema showing a double X programme: 'She Made Her Own Private Hell' and 'The Virgins'. The films were rubbish. What a waste of time and money.

A colleague of dad had gone to America for a month or so. His two daughters, Fiona (aged eleven) and Melanie (aged thirteen) stayed with us. I took some photos of Melanie. I considered that in a few years' time, Melanie would be fantastic. She could be my most glamorous girl ever.

Swimming made me feel better. I resolved to concentrate on fitness this year and go in for canoeing, cycling, walking, cross-country walking and athletics. I'de always thought that to be able to work well mentally you've got to do plenty of physical work as well. So I started the physical part. I hoped I could keep it up. Monday swimming, Tuesday weight training, Wednesday cross-country running, Thursday weight training.

I went to see 'Bonnie and Clyde'. It was the best film I've seen for a long time. I decided to see it again. 'A Man and a Woman' was my other favourite. I also enjoyed 'Grand Prix' and 'Quatermass and the Pit'. Whenever I saw a crane on a building site again I was reminded of that film.

My thoughts:
"Passing driving tests for both motorbike and car should open up new avenues to girls. It has not been so with the scooter nor with our current car. If I had a car of my own, just imagine the possibilities. The scooter is a Lambretta LD 150. It's dad's really but I have exclusive use of it since he bought a newer one. You can't really see any of the working parts. If you remove the side panel you

can see the metal parts of the engine and with a spanner you can begin to dismantle the gearbox. The mystery of what the inside of the gearbox looks like is almost as exciting as discovering a girl's sexual parts. I've got the Lambretta and all the tools required to get inside those secret parts. I've also got the tools that boys are born with. All I need now is a girl!

"It should be a dead easy thing to get a girl. For instance, a few weeks ago, when I was in the library, I saw a girl sitting alone on a bench. I worked out a plan that could not fail. By the time I left the library, two other lads were talking to her. Instead of dithering thinking about it, I should have gone to her straight away. The chances are that she's less intelligent than me and that my lack of experience is more than made up by my ability to think quicker than she does. I shouldn't think so deeply.

March 1968:
I bought a long-distance racing canoe. It was 13'6" long, 23" wide and had a red fibreglass hull, plywood decking and a foot-operated rudder. It was unstable but fast and lightweight - ideal for long portages. I decided to race it at the Leamington Spa Long Distance race the following Sunday. I positioned myself at the start line behind an overhanging tree but an extra fast sprint got me clear of it. I was pleasantly surprised by the relative ease of a good start and kept with the three leading boats. The bow seemed very low in the water. The first portage was about 400 yards after the start. I lifted my canoe out of the water with one hand, placed it on my shoulder and ran fast across a field and down a steep bank to the river. I decided it would be quicker to launch the canoe if I first put one foot in the river. Suddenly, I was in the water up to my chest and my paddle was drifting downstream. I'd lost the time gained from dashing across the field and the three other leaders were now ahead of me. I scrambled onto the bank, got in my canoe and hand paddled to pick up the paddles. The canoe now contained a pool of black muddy water. I stayed with two other competitors as far as the first turning point then overtook them both. On approaching the second portage I passed Ron (who had started in an earlier group). He'd lost his rudder and was travelling in a far from straight course. This portage was slower than my first but I overtook another competitor by launching in a difficult place instead of waiting for him to get clear. It was very shallow below the weir but I enjoyed a fast paddle to the half way mark. I was on my own for most of the return journey but enjoyed overtaking canoes in faster classes, including Mr Lancefield in his soft skin double. The third portage was made very slippery by repeated use and my seat fell out during the last portage, which was made difficult by a strong cross wind. With the end in sight,

I overtook a K1 that was being cheered to the finish by his supporters. I didn't have any cheering supporters but I was well pleased with achieving first place in my class.

I was equally pleased with my next long-distance canoe race at Stratford on Avon. After tailing a competitor along a twisty part of the river I was eventually able to pull up alongside him. That took a lot of work but when beside him I gave the impression that I was just pausing for a chat before sprinting ahead. It gave me the psychological boost I needed to win.

I took the dog Sian out for a walk in the rain. The weather reminded me of the Lake District and prompted me to arrange a youth hostelling holiday. Instead of suggesting the Lake District I decided instead to take a cycling trip with Malcolm to the Isle of Wight. Apart from the cycling, a highlight of the trip was at Sandown Youth Hostel when we stole glances at a most beautiful girl and her less attractive girlfriend while we played chess.

Throughout my 18th year, it seemed that dad I hated each other. We are always arguing. At times, dad could be very nasty. I didn't like the way he did things. He seemed to do things the long way round, get cross and blame whatever it is he was doing for it not working out. One of the tasks he did was to prepare the school timetable. It took him ages: always rubbing things out then writing them in again and blaming the lack of staff or classroom availability for his inability to work it out. It took him at least twice as long as necessary to do anything. Even going to the toilet took him twenty minutes. He just sat there reading the newspaper.

I spent a lot of time daydreaming. 'A' levels were dangerously close but I could not stick with revising for long enough. I was in the library one afternoon and daydreaming rather than working as I frequently did when Colin, who was sitting next to me, said in a loud voice,
> 'Get on with it then!'
I think I should have had someone to say that to me more often. I was easily distracted from working. When revising for my 'O' levels I sat outside enjoying the warm sunshine, but in practice learning very little. When Dave called and suggested we go canoeing at Lechlade I was easily persuaded to break me away from my studies..

Thinking of the past made me aware that I no longer seemed to have the warm memories to ponder over like I used to. Words used to flow from my mind to the page like magic. Many of the things that happened this year were of the sort that I would have written about a year ago. Now I was not inspired to write about them. It seemed I had nothing to write about. Despite the things I called 'problems' I decided that I must be better mentally balanced. I was not as moody, more stable and more certain of my feelings. My ideas were more set, less erratic. Instead of having occasional bursts of hard work I was working more steadily. But mentally I thought I was very lazy. Instead of living in a daydream interspersed occasionally by bursts of hard work I now worked at a steady, if somewhat lazy, pace. My hobbies were moving in a more definite direction too, with canoeing taking the lead. I began to socialise more with my schoolfriends. For example, I started enjoying lunch hours chatting enthusiastically to others in the 6th form mess room (room M4). In the past I found M4 was a very dull place to go. Now I was finding myself talking with an enthusiasm rarely displayed by me outside a pub. Inside a pub I could really enjoy a lively conversation: like at Bude last summer, where the evenings held warm memories for me. I felt part of the conversation, confident that I was not falling into a sort of rut that I would have to painfully dig my way out of.

Whilst revising for my 'A' levels I liked to listen to Radio Caroline or Radio London playing songs like 'Black is Black' by Las Bravos. I also had Caroline on when I was in the loft, which I made into a private den. In the summer it got really hot up there. Caroline's music and my sweat poured out in equal portions. The programme didn't seem to have any programmes. You just turned it on and music came out whatever the hour. It didn't matter whether it was midnight or noon, you'd get the same sort of music.

Caroline – the sound of the nation – CAROLINE!
You're listening to 259, radio Caroline!

Then along came the GPO and took Caroline off the air. Radio London was the first of these two to go. There were other pirate radio stations of course. I listened to the sad, final hour of Radio London, retuned the radio and heard Caroline paying them their tribute before they too went off the air.

Black is black, I want my baby back.
Grey is grey, since you went away, oh no.
What can I do, cos I, I, I, I, I, I'm feeling blue

I should have recorded an hour of Caroline – the tape could have become a collector's item!

Preparations for my 'A' levels became more business-like. I arranged my room in such a way that it was fun to work, a bit like a toy shop I suppose. All the pencils, pens and so on were arranged on a shelf attached to the wall above the desk. There was a filing cabinet to my right, with the periodic table pinned on its side. There were oodles of scrap paper pinned into a pad for scribbling aide memoires and other little notes that made revision fun in a childish sort of way. A radio was perched on top of the filing cabinet. But there was no freak-out music, no noisy advertisements, no jingles, no special effects. There was the Light Programme introduced by 'the oldest teenager in the business' - a sedate Jimmy Young with his recipes and telephone calls chatting up housewives. But from noon to 1 o'clock on Fridays there was Stu-art Henry. He would play 'Air on a G-string' by the Swingle singers and say in a smooth, sexy voice,

"And now, I want you all to rela-aax."
I did as he said.

"If you're driving a car, just pull into a lay-by and switch off the engine. If you're making your husband's dinner, leave it for a minute – he'll understand. If you're doing the ironing, put your iron down, sit, and make yourself comfortable. Now I want you all to rel-a-a- ax."
After the second piece quiet music ended Stuart would say softly,

"And now my friends, for the past two minutes and forty-five seconds you have been listening to the sound of Bobby Gentry and after that you heard Otis Redding."

"But now it's time to WAKE UP!"
Then louder, "THAT'S RIGHT – WAKE UP!"
Then followed the agonised squawk of 'Soul Finger'.

"Come on. Get on your feet again. Get your mind working. Get yourself moving. There's your husband's meal to cook. The kids will be home any second now!"

My 'A' level exams finished at last. I had passed three 'A' levels: chemistry (grade C), physics (grade E) and maths (grade E). School broke up on 12th July. My last day of school. For ever. It was just like any other Friday: I didn't even say goodbye to many of the people I had known for the last four years even though I knew I would not see them ever again.

Seven of us decided to celebrate by taking a camping trip to Weymouth. This was my report the trip:
"We drive down to Weymouth in Colin's mini-van, Paddy's motorbike and three scooters including mine, all fully loaded with camping gear. Top speed 40, slower on hills, not stopping well on brakes. Oil has sprayed all over my rear wheel. There is almost no petrol left. I just make it to the camp site. I

arrive shivering with cold but the sun is beating down and people are sunbathing. It's a family camp site – no single sex parties allowed. We find another camp site on the other side of town. The ground is a bit soggy but there are showers and bogs nearby. Evening comes and we all clamber into the van and go to a night club. We have no luck with girls but we meet an old drunk called Paddy, which is occasionally amusing but mostly tiring. We retired at 2 a.m.

"We spend day one on the beach and go to town in the evening. No luck with girls. We spend day two on the beach and go to town in the evening. No luck with girls. We spend day three on the beach again. It is boring and the town is disappointing. We try Bournemouth. It's even more depressing.

"On the last night we drink cider. Three pints of Cyder Royal, vintage variety. It's a great drink, really smooth and a taste like wine, and an alcohol content to match. We drink the first pint like beer, although it seems wasteful to consume such a delightful drink so fast. During the second pint we hear fantastic stories about people who drink two pints of this stuff. I'm no chicken, I go for three. I don't feel drunk or sick, but something in my body is telling me that there's trouble ahead. I take the third pint slowly. Colin's starting to look a bit queezy. It's 10.30 – time to drink up. Now the barman is collecting the glasses. He tells us more stories about Cyder Royal.
   'Finish your drinks now lads.'
Everyone still seems to be sober. Then suddenly Colin just drops his glass and it smashes on the floor. He offers to pay for the damage, but his voice is strangely slurred. The barman – he's a nice chap – says that's OK – please go before anyone else makes a fool of himself. I take my empty glass and place it on the bar. I wish I hadn't bothered – it took such concentration to put it down carefully. Now I need to be careful not to behave like the people in the stories we were told. Pretend to be sober and not act like the others. Paddy can't find his motorbike. Someone must have stolen it. We tell him to leave it until morning. Now I help Colin and Martin to walk down the road. Colin mutters,
   'How is it you manage to remain sober when everyone elsh is drunk?'
I feel flattered by that and try to maintain the appearance of the proverbial judge. Colin and I weave from side to side of the road. The tents now seem to swim towards us.
   'You're drunk!' slurs Colin.
Peter, Geoff and I play the role of sober members of the party, helping the others into their tents and making coffee in the back of Colin's mini. Geoff has gone to a neighbour's tent to apologise for the noise we were making. I affirm his apologies speaking in as sober a voice as I can manage. I feel as if I'm floating

on air rather than walking on the ground. I feel as if I could push people over like skittles. I push Martin, he falls easily and rolls on the ground. I push Bob but he just laughs and takes a step backwards. We listen to Steve's account of when he first went to bed with Vanj. I drink some coffee. It tastes sweet and sickly. Now there is nobody standing talking. My head is swimming. I feel ll. I grovel around on hands and knees. I spew up. Eventually, I make it to my tent, take off my clothes and lie on my air bed. Can't be bothered to climb into my sleeping bag. Peter congratulates me for taking the cider so well and how the coffee and the cider's delayed action made me sick but not drunk. Somehow I fall asleep. I awake early feeling as miserable and ill as I can ever remember feeling. I dare not stand or even sit up. Eventually I force myself to go outside. The campsite is a mess. I wash, try to eat and am pitifully sick. I start to pack up, stopping every now and then for useless attempts to recover. It takes hours to pack up the campsite and I am pleased to start up my scooter and depart. I don't look back, but keep going, the wind rushing past helping me to feel better. Pete, Martin and I stop for petrol at Salisbury and for coffee at Salisbury. I begin to feel well at last and we talk cheerfully. By the time I get home I am almost back to normal. Normal that is, until I get the taste of cider again. Little do I know that I still wouldn't drink the stuff forty years later!"

After the camping trip I launched a Kayel slalom canoe that I had been building at school for ages. It had rained a lot and there were floods. It was fun canoeing over the fields next to the Thames at Lechlade.

Paddling my Kayel slalom canoe

During the summer holidays, mum and dad moved from Swindon to Dagnall, which is a small village in Buckinghamshire and next door to Whipsnade Zoo. I think it was easier for dad to get to his job in London from there. Usually, he would drive to Berkhamsted and take the train to London.

Silverstone race circuit was about an hour's drive away from Dagnall. On several occasions, my cousin Stephen and I enjoyed watching and photographing various types of race meetings.

Silverstone

In July 1968 I cycled to Minehead Youth Hostel and toured anticlockwise around the coasts of Somerset, Devon and Cornwall. By Tuesday I had reached Perranporth and decided to slow down. I had a swim from the beach after treading on a remnant of the Torray Canyon disaster, which had spilt over 25 million gallons of crude oil into the sea. I spent 8 shillings shopping at Hayle and cooked myself an enjoyable meal of potatoes, tomatoes, onions and minced steak at Phillack Youth Hostel. When I reached Lands End the scenery did not impress me and I was feeling lonely. I contemplated taking a sightseeing flight from St Just airport. The price of 18/6 seemed reasonable until I observed that the time spent in the air was only about 15 minutes.

On the Thursday, the enchanting little creeks near Helston impressed me and I had an enjoyable lunch stop at the Shipwrights Inn at Holford.

Helston

I raced down the narrow roads to Gweek, braking as little as possible: it was a pity to waste the energy taken to climb the hills. Maintaining a fast pace, I crossed the hills to Devoran. The unclassified roads to the King Harry Ferry were like the main roads in northwest Scotland. The ferry across the River Fal cost 6d. I continued through Camels, Portloe and Trevesky to Portholland. The road signed "Unsuitable for Motor Vehicles' was little more than a clifftop track to a field path joining a road that took me to Porthluney Cove. After climbing a steep hill I arrived at the modernised Boswinger Youth Hostel at 6.15.

On the Friday, after through St. Austell and Par I crossed the Fowey via the passenger ferry. The fare was 6d for pedestrians and 3d for my bike.

Above the Fowey

By Sunday 21st I had run out of pretty countryside and felt like going home. I telephoned home but mum and dad suggested I should carry on. There was no particular place I wanted to visit so I kept cycling eastwards, giving Weymouth a wide berth and ending up at Southampton Youth Hostel. My dormitory was on the ground floor at the front of the building just opposite the hostel office.

The first thing I did was to have a much- needed refreshing cold shower (there was no hot water). Monday being wash day, I washed two pairs of socks, a shirt and pants. Whilst pushing open the kitchen door I bumped into a very attractive girl and we talked. She's a Brummy, mad keen on football and her name is Janet. Since she was moving to Portsmouth Youth hostel for a few nights I extended my stay to the maximum of three nights in succession. In the evening I played crib with a funny old lady, an amusing German the Brummy girl and her friend. As the days passed the girl seemed to became more and more beautiful.

Immediately after saying goodbye to her I set my mind on cycling to Portsmouth where she was staying. It was only 20 miles away but I had a lousy day's cycling because it felt much furthered. I met the girls again there. I was thrilled to see them at first. Janet seemed shy of kissing me and did not like to be seen in public doing anything 'sexy'. I went everywhere with Janet and her friends doing nothing in particular – swimming on two days, shopping and lazing on the beach., then cycled home.

Marlene was someone Mary met in France. She wanted to be my pen friend. I sent her a lengthy typed letter about my cycle tour of Devon and Cornwall. I told her about the girl I met at Southampton called Janet who lived in Birmingham and spoke with a Brummy dialect. I did not tell her about the fat girl I liked for over a year and that I that I had not had a girlfriend for over four months. Marlene never replied.

On Friday 9th August 1968 I set out again on my bike for a tour in South Wales. The weather was miserable so I waited until Stuart Henry's lunch time show finished and cycled in miserable rain to Milford Youth Hostel.

My cousin Anna and husband Milton lived in Wales. Mum bought their old 'sit up and beg' Ford Popular from them and I agreed to drive it home. It was a long journey down the A5 for a car with a 3-speed gearbox and a top speed of 55mph but I enjoyed it. Over the coming weeks, I learnt to master the art of double de-clutching down into first gear and relished alarming passengers by the angle it leaned on bends.

Rather than go to university I decided to get a job. After attending an interview in London I was successful in being offered a place in the Development Department at ICI Plastics Research Laboratories in Welwyn Garden City, Hertfordshire. My work at ICI was colour measurement. This included using state of the art equipment including a spectrophotometer and an analogue computer called COMIC (COlorant MIxture Computer). I was pleased with the expertise I developed with the equipment.

Colour lab COMIC computer

I wrote:

"John Keitch is my boss. He's old: must be at least 40, and he always wears a black suit. I like him. He reminds me a bit of my uncle Jack. Norman is a Technical Officer (TO) in charge of the Physical Testing lab. He's funny. He made a joke as he opened his payslip last month by saying, "Yipee, three figures this month!" My gross salary is £454 a year so he would have to earn three times as much as me to get more than £100 a month. Margaret works in the Colour lab and is quite nice to look at and to talk to. She comes from Plymouth and has failed her 'A' levels. Mike Parker comes from Leicester and he failed his 'A' levels too. Linda works in the same lab as me. She's not very pretty. She's self-righteous but can be fun. She's about 18 and has been here for a year. Norman's lab assistant is Julie and she joined ICI at the same time as Margaret. Julie works in the lab next to mine. She's pretty. She will be 17 next Wednesday, the 18th December 1968. Julie has a boyfriend called Jon. I don't despise Jon, neither am I envious of him. I like the way they are so happy together and am pleased that Jon is keeping Julie feeling that way."

ICI found digs for me in Welwyn Garden City and I went home to Dagnall for the weekends. Chris Wheeler already had a room at the digs. He also worked at ICI and we would return from work and Mrs Guiver would serve us both an evening meal at six o'clock and a bedtime drink after the 10 o'clock news.

Chris drove fast in a tuned-up mini-van. He introduced me to developing and printing in ICI photographic club darkroom.

Dad and I must have come to terms with each other by then – we could just about tolerate each other for a weekend. Anyway, he would often lend me his rail season ticket and I would wander around London taking photos. I would walk most of the time so I must have covered miles, but I got to know my way around the city very well.

Piccadilly circus

A place I particularly enjoyed was Speakers Corner in the northeast of Hyde Park.

Speakers Corner

London in 1968

I usually travelled between Welwyn Garden City and Dagnall in the Ford Pop or on dad's Lambretta. His scooter was better than the old one I had previously used but not very fast.

The training officer at ICI sent me on day release to study HNC Chemistry at Hatfield College. I hated the course and could not understand a lot of what we were told. I spent our lunch break eating sandwiches with one of the other students.

November 1968 thoughts:
"Now that I leave home in the dark, return in the dark, pay six shillings for a gallon of petrol and hate doing academic work, it's time to resume writing down my thoughts. The moody season is here.

"Vic Collinson is a bloke I met at Horrible Hatfield college. He comes from Melton Mowbray and talks about his parties, friends and car accidents. He drives a clapped out 1959 mini. He used to have a new sports car but since his accident he can't afford to insure it. He has a wife (so he must be quite old) and regrets getting married in some ways because his misses the swinging parties he used to go to when he was my age."

I went to Hatfield College on Mondays supposedly to learn more about chemistry. When my car had a puncture, I decided that this justified missing at least a morning from college. After changing the wheel, I went into town to arrange a repair. The garage could not guarantee to complete the job that day so I went to the department store in Welwyn Garden City and purchased their last remaining tyre lever and a puncture repair outfit. I enjoyed motoring to Hertford where I bought two more tyre levers and then removed the tyre in the car park. I couldn't locate the puncture in the flat tube so I bought a foot pump for 42 shillings and sixpence, repaired the puncture and replaced the original wheel on the car. Next, I decided to find the canal and go for a walk there. I located the River Stort but didn't feel like walking along it so I went to Chesham instead. Feeling depressed I headed towards Hatfield, wondering whether I should go to college for the afternoon. I stopped by a wood. It had three way-marked footpaths through it – 1 mile, 2 miles and 3 miles. I decided to skip college and take the 3-mile route, but reckoned that would only take me to 2:30 and I needed to wait until 7 before going to the ICI film society. Perhaps I could do two laps. Now my thoughts were consumed with how to waste as much time as possible. I wondered slowly round the 3-mile route. The weather was cold, wet and miserable. I tried hard to waste time whilst keeping warm and happy. Warmth was easy, happy impossible. It occurred to me that although I hated the work at college I was never unhappy there. Although I was thoroughly bewildered by the lectures, during the breaks I was very happy. Skiving off college had made me more depressed than I had felt for a very long time. Not since my 'A' levels had I felt this way. I started to feel better after eating a picnic lunch, as I wandered through the pleasant pine wood over a soft carpet of yellow pine needles. I reached the car at 2.45 and drove to St Albans. To me, St Albans is simply the place where the YHA headquarters is situated. I thought it would be best to do a proper sight-seeing tour of the town but I couldn't be bothered. I still had four hours to kill. I was feeling sexually pent up so I went into a bookshop to look for the dirtiest book I could find. Remembering one I'd seen at Ryde during my summer holiday cycling round the Isle of Wight I bought 'The Marriage Art". I also got a local paper to see what was on at the local cinema, and read it with a cup of coffee in the Wimpy bar. I didn't want an ordinary film because I was going to the film society later. There was nothing suitable.

The coffee was good but I drank it quickly so that I could read the book in the car before it got dark. I parked in a private place to read the book but soon got bored with it. I felt disgusted and annoyed with myself for the stupid way I had wasted the day and there was still two hours to go. I went to the public library and read the 'Practical Motoring' magazine. Time passed quickly there. I left at 7.20, collected my film society membership card from the digs and enjoyed watching an excellent film in the works canteen. Mike Parker sat next to me and asked why I wasn't at college (it finished at 8). I said I skipped practical to come to the film society. That was true, but it wasn't the whole truth.

I was glad when the day was over. I'd wasted time, skived college, disgusted myself, spent over three pounds and driven needlessly over fifty miles. It had ended in a satisfactory way and it had taught me a lesson, but I still felt bad about college. I ought to go but don't want to. Years later I had dreams of waking up, realising it was exam day and not knowing anything at all about the subject.

My landlady Mrs Guiver had the radio on nearly all the time. I was trying to concentrate against a background of 'Desert Island Discs'. When she nipped upstairs turned down the volume slightly to help me concentrate. The interference didn't used to distract me. After all, I studied for my exams against a background of music.

I received an invitation to a party:

YOU ARE INVITED TO A PARTY
AT THE 'THREE BEARS' COTTAGE
Firs Walk, Tewin Wood
- *NEAR WELWYN, HERTS* –
ON SATURDAY NOVEMBER 30
DICK, NICK, BOB, MICK, MIKE, KEITH
WILL BE PLEASED TO SEE YOU
AT 8.30 P.M.

I paid my twelve and six. Alec gave me the phone number of Jackie Panel so I called her and asked her to come with me to the party. She was nice and polite, thanking me for the invitation but saying sorry she could not go because she was going out with her boyfriend. I met a different girl at the party. Aged 20, she has short black hair, slim legs and small breasts. She's sweet and lives in Croydon. That's all I know about her. I drank six pints of beer and enjoyed myself. The booze ran out early, the lights went out at 3.30 a.m. She conveyed her wish for my hand not to wander further up her leg by gently squeezing my hand. I was lying uncomfortably on a sofa and did not sleep. In the morning I felt lousy and left at 9.30 a.m., getting home at 10.15 a.m.

We now had a Ford Anglia to replace the old Popular. We travelled to Llangollen at Easter in it to see the International Eisteddfod. We gave a chap a lift all the way from Weedon to Llangollen. I am often giving and taking lifts. Over the past couple of weeks, I have given four and accepted seven.

I kept searching classified ads in the local newspaper and found a Triumph Thunderbird 650cc with a sidecar. It was cheap so I bought it. One weekend I gave Mary a ride in the sidecar and she was scared. The next day I took the corner in the village too fast for the sidecar and went into the hedge. I removed the sidecar. This was a fast machine. One evening, I gave Chris a lift on the back as we were going to watch 'The Good, the Bad and the Ugly'. Since Chris was a fast driver I thought he would enjoy it but when I shouted for him to look over my shoulder at the speedo he replied shakily,
        'Okay, okay, keep looking ahead!'"

Thoughts in April 1969:
"These sunny days remind me of my frustration during the summer - the girls all so pretty but so hard for me to get. I feel pent up, looking for an opportunity, but not knowing what I really want. Sometimes it's sex, sometimes love, sometimes friendship or even just someone to go places with. I go to the cinema alone and feel left out. Sometimes I'm bored and feel like I'm wasting valuable

time. There's a lack of things to look forward to. I can't think of a situation where I might meet a girl.

"I saw the aftermath of two car accidents over the weekend. The first was at Luton where a red Ford Anglia had smashed into the back of a parked F-reg white Vauxhall Viva. Yesterday, there was a car with a smashed windscreen on the wrong side of the main road and a blue car on its side at the exit from a side road. Traffic had to weave around the wreckage to pass. People with blooded faces were sat beside the road. An ambulance passed me two miles further on.

"When the sun shines the girls look so pretty in their summer clothes. It makes me feel lonely as if I'm the only lad without a girlfriend. At lunch time today I sat on the fire exit stairway and talked to Julie. I like Julie as a friend – a sisterly sort of friend. She understands my solitude. She was surprised that anyone goes on holiday alone like I do. She thinks that when I get to university I will make friends. I hope she's right. Julie is lovely, but I can't imagine going out with her. She's more like the perfect sister. I'd like to talk to her about my frustrations but feel afraid she would be offended. Julie looked ravishing when she came into my room in the afternoon to talk to me again. She was complaining about Margaret leaving her with Ron Harris, a T.O. in the Colour Lab. She hates him. He keeps looking at her legs. I think he's strange too. He walks round with his left hand in his trouser pocket playing with a couple of marbles or something. His stock phrase is,
   'What's going on there then?'
I told Julie that I thought Ron is alright but that I can understand her feelings about him. There was a campaign a few weeks ago to encourage girls to wear trousers at work. Julie once told me,
   'You can see the men at the bottom of the staircase looking up at you. It's horrible.'
The campaign was unsuccessful."

Summer 1969:
I made a step forward with Susan. I asked her out. Unfortunately, she said she had too much revising to do. The following week I asked her if she was revising every weekend. At least she said she was. I was hoping to ask her to go out on Saturday or Sunday, perhaps on a trip to London. I didn't like going out on my own on Sundays – all I saw is happy couples. It just emphasised my loneliness. Whilst driving round Comet roundabout I spotted Susan on the other side of the road. I stopped at Wates' garage for petrol expecting her to pass whilst I was there. She didn't pass, so I raced along to the next roundabout and back through

Hatfield to the Comet roundabout. Susan was at the bus stop so I offered her a lift as if I'd just spotted her on passing. I gave her a lift to her digs in Handside Lane, Welwyn Garden City and we had an enjoyable chat, mainly about college. On the way we passed The Bull and I asked if she would like to stop for a drink. She refused, saying that she was tired after nearly eleven hours of exams. When we stopped in Handside Lane I asked if she would care for that drink on Tuesday. After what seemed a long pause but was probably only a second she replied, rather awkwardly I thought,

'Well actually, I'm going out with this bloke from work.'

Another awkward pause followed before I continued our previous conversation. She seemed keen to continue talking. I turned off the car engine and we chatted for another half hour before she left, thanking me for the lift. It was easy talking to Susan, but the conversation was uninspiring and impersonal. We didn't meet again.

One warm evening after a scorching day I cycled to Cole Green and rested in a disused railway cutting. Flies and other insects buzzed and crawled round me. The sun went down and it was cooler. Sometimes it was best being on my own. It gave me time to think.

I went to a party that Chris had organised and met a girl called Kath. Afterwards felt really bad about it. At the time, it didn't bother me that Kath was fat so I arranged to meet her again. I wished I hadn't. She was walking down the street as I drove towards her house and I thought, 'Oh no, that can't be HER!' Until that moment I had been looking forward to the evening but from that moment on I hated every minute of it. Kath prattled on about the television programmes she watched. After what seemed to take ages for her to finish her drink she asked where we should go next. I said I felt tired after the previous night's party and suggested an early finish to the evening. When we got to her house the front door was open and she asked me not to park in front. We stopped by a hedge and I walked her to the back door. There was an awkward pause so I told her my work telephone number, hoping that if she rang, I wouldn't be in. She must have realised my hope because she replied in a spiteful tone,

"Oh, Ta."

I apologised for my manner and told her to ring between 12.30 and 1 on Monday. I shuffled moodily back to the car and drove to The Beehive. It was too crowded so I drove back to my digs. Chris' car was outside and I didn't want him to know that I'd finished my date early. After all, it was at his party I'd met the girl so I went back to the Beehive.

The phone rang at 12.35 on Monday. It had to be Kath so asked someone else to answer it and say I was ill. On Tuesday, the phone rang at half past three. I answered.

'Hello,' I said. I spoke in a flat voice in case it happened to be Kath..

'Is Mark back yet or is he still ill?'

I recognised the voice of Kath's friend Sally but my flat tone had successfully concealed my identity. I would be pleased to talk to Sally.

'One moment, I'll see,' I replied in the monotonous voice.

'Hello!' I said cheerfully a few moments later, "It's Mark!"

Sally asked if I was better. She had seen me in the canteen at lunch on Monday so I told her that I was back at work on Monday afternoon. We had a very friendly chat. Sally agreed to explain to Kath that I did not think we would get on well together, that I was sorry and everything, but that was that. Sally was very nice to talk to. I told her how I felt when I saw Kath for the second time and that I must have been drunk at the party. We then talked about Sally's boyfriend Alf, who has a rally car, a Ford Cortina GT. The car is white with green stripes along the side – it's very fast. Just after the phone call, Alf himself came in and we talked about rallying. We laughed about the party. Alf's philosophy is that you go to a party either to pick up a bird or get stoned, but it's best not to do both at the same time!

Sally rang me the next day for a chat and because I had asked her to. She must have enjoyed talking to me, perhaps she even liked me. I'd like to ask her out but she's Alf's girlfriend. She knows I respect her relationship with Alf and that I'm not trying to pinch her off Alf, but that doesn't have to stop me flirting with her. Girls like to be chatted up even when they already have a boyfriend.

The Wednesday play was a dig on human nature. It was about a family who go for a picnic in Cheddar Gorge. They took a car load of paraphernalia including a frame tent, barbecued chicken, liqueurs, a toilet tent and a cine camera. The son did not enjoy himself, even when an attractive girl attempted to seduce him. She even produced her own 'safe' (a condom) for him to use. Also, in the play were other families with children, a group of rockers and a preacher. I imagined myself being part of that scene. It felt like being alone on a crowded beach. All around me were all types of people doing all sorts of things, including the things I wanted to do but couldn't, including some who didn't want to do the things I longed to do. I could not imagine how those lads with gorgeous girls in bikinis did not want sex all day long. I was not a part of that imaginary scene, so I left it. I was a loner, I behaved like a loner. But I wanted someone. Every time I saw an attractive girl I just let her pass me by. That evening, on two occasions

I passed a girl who I could have chatted with but I missed both opportunities. I was either too slow or too shy. I expected that I would behave in exactly the same way next time it happened. Either that or I'd make a complete hash-up of it."

Feeling lonely, I decided to hitch-hike to Devon. Mum gave me a lift to Elmscott Youth Hostel. The warden there was a really friendly chap. I met an English student from Oxford University who had been staying there for over a week and later on a young Frenchman. In the morning I walked northwards along the coast and watched an auto-cross meeting in the afternoon. It seemed rather dull after my regular trips to Silverstone. Before I could start hitch-hiking the following morning I needed to take a four-mile walk to the A39. I met a stray dog whose name tag showed that he lived in a place I had just passed. I stopped a car going in that direction and the driver persuaded the dog to follow him.

After a long wait I got a lift to Kilkhampton. Whilst I was waiting at the bottom of a hill a lorry came squealing to a halt and took me to Bude and from I caught a bus to Tintagel. There were some girls who were obviously going to stay at the youth hostel there too. They were an interesting pair: one was a drama student and the other studied bio-chemistry at Essex University. After our evening meal I had an enjoyable walk into the village with them. The drama student, whose name I could not remember, was some sort of fortune teller and agreed to read my palm. I was impressed that she accurately identified a lot of my background. She could not have worked this out from our earlier conversations. The following day I visited King Arthur's castle with the girls and then walked with them to Boscastle in the afternoon. We headed to the nearest pub and before afternoon closing time I had consumed three pints of beer and a Cornish pasty. We sat on the rocks near the hostel for most of the afternoon and then did some shopping. That evening and the following breakfast we cooked and ate together. It was enjoyable working together as a team. The following morning the weather was miserable and no-one fancied the idea of the long walk to the main road so we decided to catch the bus to Plymouth. The girls got off at the main road but and I continued with a nine-shilling ride all the way to Plymouth where I ate fish and chips then started walking along the road towards Bigbury. It was interesting to see a battleship being dismantled near the bridge but then a heavy downpour suddenly came and soaked my back before I could extract the anorak from my rucksack. The rain stopped almost immediately so I walked to a roundabout and started to thumb for a lift. After about five minutes I got a lift to a village six miles further on. From there a Renault took me to a turning from where I walked the remaining six miles to Bigbury-on-Sea. In the village there was a pub named after a pirate: the bar was dimly lit and very romantic but it depressed me. If I'd not been alone it would have been a fascinating place.

The following morning, I walked along a tidal road: the tide was in and the water at one stage reached almost to my groin. I found a dry piece of land, changed my wet underpants for swimming trunks and donned my jeans about 100 yards from the main road. I didn't thumb for lifts because I didn't expect anyone to stop on the hill for me but surprisingly a driver who was going to Torquay stopped for me. He gave me a lift to Salcombe where he was hoping to make a tape recording of seagulls. I arrived at the youth hostel at three and as it didn't open till five I left my rucksack in the cycle shed and walked to Snapes Point. It was a cold, wet and unfriendly place. I chose to walk back via what seemed to be a quicker way but the path was very slippery and occasionally I fell which was annoying. The cliff path, which seemed promising at first, headed in the wrong direction so I made the mistake of attempting a shortcut. When I through I was about level with the youth hostel I cut through woodland up a steep slope. There seemed to be some sort of a path but I soon found myself grappling with brambles and thorn trees. Peaty mud ran into my boots and half way up my soaking sleeves and thorns fell down my neck. The discomfort made me feel more impatient but I refused to go back the way I had come. After wading through waist high brambles and pushing aside numerous thorn branches I spotted a building I recognised as the hostel. After further infuriating scrambling I found myself in private tropical gardens. I kept out of sight and carefully escaped over a wall to the youth hostel, retrieved my rucksack from the cycle shed and signed in.

In the morning I planned to take a slow gentle walk back to Salcombe, catch a ferry to Kingsbridge and hitch-hike from there. After a long wait in town I had a fairly enjoyable but cold boat trip to Kingsbridge. I foolishly followed a road sign and ended up walking miles further than expected. Eventually after reaching the main road I got a lift in a mini which dropped me off at Totnes. A lorry came along almost immediately after I'd stuck out my thumb and gave me a lift all the way to Exeter. From the city centre I set off walking the two miles to the youth hostel but after about 10 minutes a Hillman Imp pulled up and the driver offered me a lift so I arrived at the hostel a few minutes before it opened. On the door was a notice reading 'Remove all Outdoor Footwear Here'. I was wearing ordinary dry shoes that I would normally wear indoors so I stepped inside with them on. I had barely moved a yard when a voice sharply reminded me of the notice. However, the warden turned out to be a pleasant sort of chap. I enquired about a canoe regatta which was advertised on the notice board and another guest called Keith talked about canoeing in what I considered a very patronising manner. I decided to go to the regatta so in the morning took a bus to the river with him. We looked round the maritime museum in the morning and then I had a paddle in Keith's Scimitar K1 kayak. It was a very unstable kayak and I fell out at first and it was very cold in the water. Next day, Keith arranged to lend me a boat for the Long-Distance race on Sunday. It was a slalom kayak and the paddles came from his child's boat. There was a Le Mans type start and I wasted time fitting the spray cover on which was not needed as the waves we tiny. The canoe pulled constantly to one side so nearly all of the time I had to paddle on one side whilst boat after boat caught up and passed me. I ran aground on a sandbank and emptied water from the boat. After returning to deeper water Keith came alongside me and we paddled together. After a while I drew slowly ahead of him. The two portages were slippery and tricky but I was used to that challenge so I passed a few other competitors at this point. My position in the race was poor but satisfactory considering the boat and paddles and the fact that I beat Keith.

The following day I decided to make for Swanage. At the Exeter bypass I met an American, or he might have been a Canadian, who I had met earlier. It was not long before a large car stopped and gave me a lift all the way to the outskirts of Bournemouth from where I took a bus into town and had lunch. I decided to go the post office to withdraw some more money, but the little blue book was nowhere to be found in my rucksack. I reported the loss to the post office then phoned dad and asked him to send me some money to the youth hostel. The incident spoilt my afternoon. I continued to Swanage where I had a fairly enjoyable evening visiting several pubs with other guests of different nationalities.

I had to hang around in the morning waiting for dad's letter which arrived on the second post. I caught the bus to the other side of the ferry in Poole. I took a picture of the harbour with my Leica camera, the best one I had ever owned. It turned out to be the last picture I would take with that camera. I continued along the road for a few miles, caught a bus to the outskirts and hitch-hiked with three lifts to a village beyond Romsey. From there I caught a bus to Winchester and stayed at the youth hostel there. It was an interesting building called the Town Mill and was the first youth hostel in Great Britain. Whilst cooking my dinner in the members' kitchen I had an interesting conversation with Julie, a girl from California. She was going to London the next day and did not want to go by train or bus because she was on a tight budget. We agreed to hitch-hike to London together and then went out for a drink. She was attractive to look at and interesting to talk with so I was keen to find a quiet bar.

We returned to the hostel at 10.30, had a cup of coffee with the warden and his wife until 11.30 when I kissed Julie goodnight.

In the morning whilst packing my rucksack I discovered that my camera and light meter were missing. I reported this to the warden and phoned the police who arrived soon afterwards. Everyone in the hostel was gathered in the main room and all voluntarily allowed their possessions to be searched. Someone else who was in the same dormitory as me reported that his electric shaver was missing. I gave the police officer a full report and left with Julie at about 10.30. It was interesting to view the cathedral, law courts and museum but disappointing that I no longer had a camera to photograph it. It occurred to me that I could possibly have left my camera at Poole after taking that last photo so I phoned the police there with a description of the missing property and my name and address.

Julie and I caught a bus to the outskirts of Winchester and walked to the main road for London. I guessed that it would take less time to wait for a lift than normal since I had Julie with me. After about three minutes a lorry driver stopped and took us all the way to London. The three of us had an enjoyable conversation on the journey and reached London remarkably quickly. Julie and I walked round Hyde Park together and talked but due to my shyness, I didn't even hold her hand. Walking around the Serpentine seemed tiring. On reaching the lido I suggested that we take a swim. The sun was going down behind the trees, the water was cool and refreshing and there were few other people there. The swim rounded off our time together nicely. I was glad we went. Afterwards, Julie summed me up as being reserved but impulsive. We walked together to the nearest station and travelled by tube to Victoria. Julie phoned a friend of hers to ask if she would stay the night before flying to Paris. Meanwhile, I phoned home and checked that if she wanted to she could stay at our house. Her friend was able to accommodate her so unfortunately we had to say farewell forever. I gave Julie my address and she promised to drop me a postcard when she arrived in Paris. At last, we had a lingering kiss, we parted and I caught a train home. I never received that postcard.

Grandma, grandad and Sian

Driving on M1 motorway

Chapter 3: University years

My work at ICI Plastics went well. I developed an expertise on instrumental colour measurement and matching. I got on well with other employees. The Training Officer advised that to further my career I should go to university. I now felt ready for further education and expected to be able to return to ICI afterwards and develop my career with them. Due to my interest and knowledge in colour I decided to take a degree in colour chemistry. Two universities offering suitable courses were Leeds and Bradford. I had interviews at both and selected Bradford because it was more technological than academic. Harold Wilson was the university chancellor. I accepted a place at Bradford to study Colour Chemistry and Colour Technology on a 4-year sandwich course.

October 1969:
Freshers week began a week before the start of term. I was given a lift to Bradford by a friend of dad's. My luggage filled the boot and the back seat of the car. I was surprised to see that the M1 went beyond Sheffield all the way to East Ardsley where you joined the A650 for the last 10 miles or so. I was taken to Tong Hall, an impressive building on the southeast side of Bradford and five miles from the university.

Tong Hall

My accommodation for the first year at university was in the Lodge at the entrance to Tong Hall. This fine three-story brick building was rebuilt in 1702 and contained much of the original panelling, a large entrance hall and a grand staircase. All of the resident students were male and most were accommodated in the main hall. Ten of us shared the Lodge, which comprised a kitchen, a bathroom and five bedsit rooms: two students to a room. My room-mate was Craig. We met in the hall's games room. He had a beard and looked a lot older than me, not like a student at all. We shared the upstairs room overlooking the driveway to the hall. When we first met he seemed a completely different person to me. A year older than me, he seemed more mature. Craig came from Sheffield and he smoked. Each weekend he went home so I had the room to myself. Like me, Craig was studying Colour Chemistry and Colour Technology. Neither of us worked very hard for the first-year exams. Most evenings Craig visited the Greyhound Inn ('the Dog') that was 300 yards down the road. I just went there about once a week so I probably worked harder than him. Craig soon became my best friend and stayed so throughout our time at university and beyond.

Craig in our room

I don't know how the rooms in the Lodge were allocated but each pair sharing a room seemed well matched. Tiddles, whose real name I forget, was a pleasant chap from Bedford, but a bit childish. He studied maths. During the Freshers week we went sailing together. There was a strong wind and I let him take the helm because I had the impression he was the more experienced. I was wrong

– we capsized after about 30 seconds and that was the last sailing I did until many years later. Tiddles later joined the drama group and played a part in their production of 'Mutiny on the Bounty'. Ross had an attractive girlfriend, Gill, whom he'd known since their early days at school. I expect they got married later. Walt, a very honest Christian, left Tong after the first term to live in a grotty old farmhouse with Brian and Dave. The site of the farmhouse now lies beneath the M606. Milton played keyboard with a soul band. He was a 'way out, with it' type of person, friendly and great fun – like most of us in the Lodge were really – and played great music on the piano in the Hall. Trevor studied maths. He was okay, a bit childish at times, but weren't we all? He could get quite angry at times. Brian shared the other upstairs room with Nigel, a quiet lad from Sunderland. Tudor was a Welshman and a nice person. Steve, the one who played golf (and had a good par), studied chemical engineering, always dressed smartly and was a nice lad too.

Extracts from my letters to home:
I wrote voluble letters to my parents at home this month and copied the following extracts from them.

"I dozed off whilst listening to the Moody Blues at the University dance last night. When I'm at home, the noise dad makes when he goes to the loo at night wakes me up, therefore dad must make more noise there than the Moody Blues. It's not that the Moody Blues were boring, they were very good as were the Marmalade. The Scaffold were very funny and spent most of their time telling jokes. When Principal Edwards were on there was some fantastic lighting. They started with a girl dancing in the light of a stroboscope and then in light that made her seem as if she was in coloured bubbly water. Forthcoming dances will have Idle Race, Alan Bown, Windmill and Simon Dupre. Unfortunately, the girls at university are outnumbered 5:1 so for the dances girls from round about colleges come in so the balance is about right.

"On Thursday we had introductory talks and during the afternoon a storm of paper, paper darts and bog rolls descended from the balcony. This is the traditional welcoming for freshers. On the Friday I collected my grant cheque of £68.13s.4d, which is just a third of the £206 so they are paying it by the term. On Saturday I did some washing and I shall have to do more tomorrow but I've got loads of lecture notes to sort out as well. There's never a spare moment. I seem to have been here for at least a month.

"On Sunday I went for a trip to the Yorkshire Dales. We had lunch at Knaresbrough followed by an interesting ride through the Dales the long way around to Bolton Abbey. The Rivers Nidd, Wharf and Aire all looked interesting for canoeing in the winter. Our coach driver got lost three times and two of the other three coaches successively demolished a stone wall. It was a very interesting day with some spectacular scenery.

"I have joined the following societies and clubs so far: sailing, canoeing, trampolining, skiing, physics and materials, AESEC (I can't remember what that stands for but they arrange vocational work in other countries) and the chess club. The canoe club has a very small membership but owns about eight kayaks, all slalom or whitewater type. We are going tomorrow afternoon to Keighley on the Aire. The nearby rivers are excellent for canoeing in the winter so I might get a wetsuit if I don't get a motorbike and if I don't get a camera. We are going canoeing at the baths on Monday since the visit last week did not take place. Fortunately, there is a canoe club member with a car staying at Tong. There was a meeting of the club today and I was elected as a committee member as there has to be at least one fresher on the committee.

"I have been giving the subject of getting a motorbike a lot of thought. My thoughts at present are drifting away from the idea for the following reasons. It is not really very frequently when I do need one although there are comparatively few car owners here. The last bus back to the end of Tong Lane is at 10.30 p.m. There is a bus to Bradford at 6.20 p.m. going past our gate but that's just too early after supper on weekdays to catch. Coming back late there are usually four of us so we could take a taxi, the fare then being about 3 shillings each. A motorbike would not be of great use for coming home as the M1 is easy to hitchhike down and there are people from the university going to London at weekends in their own cars. Two of us went to the cinema on Wednesday and walked back in about an hour and a quarter. We watched 'I am Curious – Yellow'."

Later, instead of written letters I sent my parents audio cassette tapes, sometimes beginning with a recording of the Beatles song, 'Here Comes the Sun' (son). Dad replied by tape but didn't include music in his replies.

November 1969:
There was a bonfire party at Tong Hall. Bill and I were determined to pick up girls. When Bill started chatting to one I talked to her friend Jo. As the evening progressed my chatting up session was going well but then the coach came to take them home much earlier than I expected. Jo said I should see her the next week so that we could 'carry on where we left off'. I needed no further encouragement! In the morning I felt fine and had virtually no pain-in-the-heart

feelings about her. Then Bill said Jo's friend was talking about her and saying she was very popular. Also, he said that we seemed to be happy giggling away every now and then. That was it. From then onwards I just couldn't wait until next Saturday. I hardly stopped willing the week away.

One of the students staying in the main hall had an MGA in which he drove Mandy back to Ilkley after the party. I was told that their 17-mile journey, going through the centres of Bradford and Shipley, took them only 20 minutes.

The following Saturday I went round and saw Jo and we did carry on where we left off, just as she had suggested. She was a resident at the teacher training college on the edge of Ilkley Moor. Although it was against college rules I slept on the couch in her room.

Jo was fun and had a lot of energy. She never seemed to be unhappy. In fact, it was quite tiring trying to keep up with her smiling all the time. I liked the way she greeted me. She smiled, walked up and gave me a hug. It was not often I got a greeting like that. My concerns with Jo were that her breath smelt and she was fat.

I got a letter from Jo. There was a lot of 'hah hah tough' in it, which was how she talked. I found that irritating, but she was amusing. I did not agree with her serious stuff. I decided that if I got to know her really well she might be a good person to confide in. There were possibilities, but a lot of snags. I decided to wait and see what happened. The main snag with Jo was how my friends in the Lodge thought about her, as demonstrated by this conversation with Tudor:

       Tudor: Hey Mark, are you still going out with that blob?

       Me: If that's what you call her, yes.

       Tudor: Isn't it about time you packed her in?

       Me: Why?

       Tudor: Well, she's not exactly beautiful is she?

       Me: She's a very nice girl to talk to amongst other things and anyway, even if I wanted to leave her I haven't had the opportunity.

University life was at least as good as I had expected. There was never any time to be lonely. No longer did I need to rate my feelings as different grades of blue. I knew that I would look back to these university days as the best moments of my life. Life as a student was good and relatively uncomplicated.

Extracts from letters to home:

"Last Wednesday afternoon, I went to Scarborough and skied on the artificial slope there. It was harder than I expected, especially walking up the slope wearing skis. Later, we visited the coast and were fascinated by huge waves.

"On bonfire night residents from the Hall 'attacked' the Lodge with bangers. We 'defended' it by throwing buckets of water onto the attackers.

"On Friday morning there was a power cut so we ate breakfast by candlelight. The roads were very icy and at the junction of Tong Lane with Wakefield Road the back of the coach slid down the road camber. Yesterday was sunny so Jo and I walked about ten miles across Ilkley Moor to Keighley. There were good views. We got a bus to Bingley, walked to Baildon and caught the bus back from there.

"I enclose ten Green Shield stamps that I got with a gallon of petrol for my bike.
    'What bike?' you might ask. 'The one I bought'."

December 1969:

Jo always seemed to be happy. When we went for a walk across Ilkley Moor it was quite tiring to keep smiling with her all the time but she never seemed to tire. I liked her originality and individuality and the way she would agree with suggestions whilst at the same time preserving a strong will of her own. Jo could be nice when serious. Her friend Sue blew her mind when talking about a séance. When Jo became upset about it, she seemed quite cute. I wished she was prettier so that I could be proud to show her off. I was beginning to get the nickname 'blob basher'.

Jo agreed to stay with me at my home in Dagnall during the Christmas vacation. I had mixed feelings about this. I wouldn't be able to spend much time alone with her there. Also, my family might think I lacked taste by going out with someone looking like her. I seemed to pick them! I remembered the girl Kath I ditched in August and the goofy teacher at the party in Tewin Wood. It was not that I had bad taste. Even an ugly woman could be fun. The disadvantage was that it was embarrassing to be with an ugly girl in public. Kath was nasty as well as ugly. Except when I was drunk.

Extracts from letters to home:

"Mary, if you listened carefully to Radio 1 Club today you might have heard me. I nearly got a request in to Stuart Henry but he didn't notice. It was at Queens Hall which is the students union hall for the Margaret MacMillan College of Education for Women. They have some fantastic discotheques there. We got in in a crafty way, not being a Radio 1 Club member. Although there was a big queue outside we just waved our students union cards (the student pass to life) and walked in.

"I'm off to the Lake District in the morning to compete in the Levens White Water test on Sunday (26.10.69). I hope the union is subsidising travel expenses. We drove 55 miles to the River Swale last Sunday to find that the river was about a foot below its normal level. Normally, the River Swale is Britain's fastest river. We spent most of the time shooting a waterfall and then pushed or scraped down the river to Easby Abbey where there was a slalom course. The canoes are in really bad shape and covered in patches. Small wonder when you see the rivers. I shall almost certainly be buying a wetsuit kit before long. We might visit a place in the Lake District that makes them tomorrow.

"The walk to the end of Tong Lane is one mile but need only take 10 minutes. I will be walking to the swimming baths or canoeing on Monday 25th.

"The food here is good and plentiful. We have formal meals on Monday, Tuesday and Thursday where we must wear a tie and jacket, Tong Hall gowns and ties.

"Work is generally easy, sometimes ridiculously so. In a week I get 13 hours of lectures, 12 hours of practical and 3 hours of German. Some lecturers go at a remarkably slow rate over work I have already done at 'A' level. In maths we were shown how to work out $(x-y)^2$. The lecturer interpreted students' blank looks to mean they misunderstood when really they were bored. However, I was surprised to find how much organic chemistry I have forgotten. One of the lecturers could not even derive Beer-Lambert's Law and of course everybody knows that don't they? In case you have forgotten, it is the linear relationship between the absorbance and the concentration, molar absorption coefficient and optical coefficient of a solution.

"I have voluntarily taken on a four hours per week German course and had the first lecture today. It should be useful and interesting to learn but involves a lot of extra work.

"In practical we determined the melting point of urea to be 131^0C. Yesterday I dyed a bit of wool blue but I can't untangle it. Last week I did a red. Perhaps next week we might even do a purple! The normality of our potassium permanganate solution was 0.0999. The high orientation in thermoplasts means high strength and low moisture regain. State the Auf Bau principle. Do 10 back somersaults and four eskimo rolls. Write four pages of a letter. Go to the People Show, to the Ski Club AGM and then the dance. Make toast and coffee then go to bed. Ist nicht sehr schwer.

"Weeks go quite quickly now and there are a few odd moments but we haven't had any essays or anything to write yet, just a few practicals.

"I got my student kit from Barclays which is very nice.

"My industrial training commences in the first week of September. I might go to work in America for six weeks with AESEC.

"Canoeing on Windermere was very peaceful and pleasant. I tried on some wetsuits in a shop at Bowness. Camping conditions were ideal, there was no wind at all and it was warm. We camped at a beautiful site right beside the lake a mile up the east side from Newby Bridge. I borrowed a sleeping bag and an airbed so with a couple of blankets from Tong I was perfectly warm. In the morning I had two practice runs down the Leven white water course. The water level was quite low so the shoots were rather bumpy. In the timed run the course seemed surprisingly easier than before and technically not much harder than a long-distance race. I complete the one-and-a-quarter miles from Newby Bridge weir to the next weir in 9 minutes 22 seconds corrected to 7 minutes 12 seconds in consideration of a 2 minute 10 second allowance for low water level. That qualified me for a Silver Dipper award which is supposed to be one of the most valued awards for white water canoeing in this country. The other member who got a silver was division 2 slalomist Dave for his time of 7 minutes 25 seconds. I have been entered for the BUSF white water race at Llangollen on 14 December.

"The baths sessions on Mondays are proving quite valuable and my rolling technique is becoming more reliable. Last Monday, Trevor Eastwood, one of the River Inn canoeists featured in the Daily Telegraph and living in Bradford, gave us a demonstration and some tuition."

On Saturday 13th December there was a disco at Tong Hall. A group of student nurses from Bradford Royal Infirmary (BRI) came. I got talking to a pair of them – Hazel and Jane. Jane wasn't very talkative. She seemed shy. It was hard work keeping the conversation going. She seems unadventurous and had hardly been any further from Bradford than Hull. But she was nice looking and had a great kiss. We kept in touch by sending each other letters.

Now I faced a problem of a different type. Previously, the problem was that I did not have a girlfriend. Now I had two. My relationship with Jo was well established but I did not want to be seen with her. I had now met a more attractive girl but was not sure whether that relationship would last.

I recorded my thoughts as follows:
"I'm spending Christmas holidays at home in Dagnall. I am constantly questioning myself about Jo. Looks are important, as are the opinions of others. It's true that half the reason for taking a girl out is to show off to others. And I do feel awkward being with her when friends or relations are present. And the sight when she stands up can sometimes put me off her. Jo is coming to visit us there. I feel a little ashamed of showing her off to my family. Why do I persist in going out with her? The main reason I suppose is that I do not want to give up a little and be left with nothing. Then I think of her. She likes me more than I like her. True, she's got good points. Damn – why do other people's opinions matter so much? I don't want to upset her. I feel a little proud that someone likes me. I've never had a relationship like this before. And, putting it crudely, I need the practice! Jo will do virtually anything I ask of her within reason. Basically, the only argument against going out with her is the embarrassment in public and lowering of respect of self and from others. I would regret leaving her, especially in the evenings when I am alone and could be enjoying her company. I will wait for further opportunities to arise, such as with Jane. Unfortunately, Jane hasn't written. All the more reason to hang on to Jo. To go back to having no girlfriend from having two would be really disappointing. For now, I will ignore my inhibitions about beauty and tomorrow treat Jo as if she looked like Miss World's twin sister."

I did not go to Llangollen for the BUSF WW race because there were too many other things going on such as the Tong Hall discotheque (where I met Jane). I enjoyed a curry at the Kashmir (we called it the 'Kash'). It was the best curry I had ever had and it cost only four shillings.

January 1970

During the Christmas and New Year break, Jo stayed at our family home in Dagnall for a few nights. Nothing special happened although some weaknesses in Jo were identified, particularly by Mary, partly by mum, but mainly by me. After Jo left our home, mum said of her,

'She's very attached to you, isn't she?'

That made a difference. Someone had observed that Jo likes me. I took that as a compliment and mum's approval of our relationship. Jo did indeed seem to be attached to me. The trouble was, I thought it might take me a while to find someone else to be attached to me as much as Jo. I could not, for instance, foresee Jane spending a night with me at Tong. I wanted a relationship with Jane similar to the one I had with Jo. I could not have the best of both worlds though. If Jo was pretty, less childish and more original things would be near perfect. With her I could do or say virtually anything. I didn't have to bother with triviality. I felt completely mentally relaxed when I was with her. She didn't demand my undivided attention.

I returned to Bradford for the start of the new University term. The journey took about four hours and I brought so much of my junk from home there was not really enough room to store it all.

My 'Thought Book' reads:

"I'm meeting Jane on Monday at 7.30pm. I don't know what we're going to do. Go for a drink I suppose. There must be plenty to talk about after being apart for three weeks. Before the holiday I had doubts as to whether she would write to me since I had only known her a week before going away for three. The letters she wrote give an impression of her character – though comparatively simple minded, she's very nice just the same.

"The thought of going around with 'the blob' makes me feel miserable. I rarely see anyone as ugly as her. Come to think of it, Jane's not all that hot either. I seem to have two second-rate or one second and another third-rate girl instead of one first rate. Quantity but not quality.

"The advantage of Jane is that she has this fantastic kiss.

"I feel like writing Jo a letter explaining that I want to leave her, but what could I say? I can't say I'm leaving her because she's fat! We are both major events in each other's lives. Anyway, a letter would be a cowardly way out. I ought to see her especially. A few drinks beforehand would make it easier."

The Lodge seemed very quiet since four people have left. On one occasion I thought I was the only person in the building because everybody was actually working! There were two new inmates, both social scientists. They only had seven or eight lectures per week.

The bike's MOT certificate was not where I thought it was. Then the bike started on the third kick but the lights didn't work properly. I decided to ask Dave to have a look or take it to a bike shop and ask them to MOT test it as well. In the end, I found the MOT certificate and sent it off to tax the bike from 1st Feb. I did some work on it but it was still doing odd things such as running erratically and then cutting out. Once it stopped it wouln't start again. I took the bike to the shop and they got everything working so I could use it again. The repairs cost £3 which was not bad seeing as it got the bike on the road again. However, it was a terrifically expensive week. I decided I needed some motorcycle boots but did not want to spend more than £5 on them, so I bought some short ones for 85 shillings. The rain blew straight up my trouser legs so I decided to take them back and exchange them for full length boots. That evening I drove into town to meet Jane. I stopped at the traffic lights not twenty yards from where we were to meet and everything cut out. Verdict – dud battery not charging. The bike would not start so again I had to push it up the hill and park it near the university. First thing next morning I changed the boots (another £2 12s 6d) and bought a new battery (£2.4s 3p). On getting back on my bike with the old battery it started first kick! I finished my work for the day in 90 minutes and set off back to Tong. After about a mile the battery conked out again so I changed it for the new one. That seemed to be OK.

I spent most of the following Saturday morning working on my bike. I picked up a second-hand main gear shaft for £1 last Thursday. Spares are difficult to find for the Matchless. It was fairly easy to reassemble the gearbox but fiddly locating the selector and a number of springs. I completely reassembled the bike before testing the gears. The gearbox worked better than ever before. So apart from backfiring, which was occasionally embarrassing, the bike was in reasonable order again.

I used nearly all my spare half-hours writing letters. That was long enough to write a letter to Dorothy filling two sides of foolscap paper. I hoped she could read my handwriting! Altogether, I wrote six letters in a week.

Kirkgate, Bradford

Trolley bus

I loved Bradford. I enjoyed its fish and chips and its curries. The monochrome soot did not make the city monotonous. The black, narrow winding streets held a sort of romantic quality. Trolley bus cables gave a ceiling to the streets, making them feel cosy. I never tired of the view over the city from the university, which must be one of the best vantage points. On a perfectly clear day the chimneys and factory roofs made an interesting picture. Even the smell of the air had its own character. Outside the university main entrance, wafting up the hill from a nearby mill, there was a pleasant smell, a bit like oil paint, that reminded me of Far Cotton

Junior School art room. I suppose it was wool grease. The city did not smell of diesel fumes like in London, but more of fish and chips or curry, depending on which part you were in. There were always people going places, something which Swindon and Northampton seemed to lack. Even at nine o'clock in the evening there was always people moving about. The cinemas were always full. Queues at bus stops were not rows of blank faces but groups of people, all of different sizes and colours. Newspaper vendors had their own peculiar cry, which was often very melodious. One even chanted 'Telegraph and Argus' to the bars of a popular song!

It was disappointing to see that the city centre was being pulled apart. Historic buildings were being replaced by concrete monstrosities. Wool mills were being pulled down or burnt to the ground. Every week, the Telegraph and Argus would include a picture of another mill fire. I took dozens of photographs. Although the noise, smoke and smells of the mills were no longer there I could sense how it must have been in the past. In the centre, Collinson's Café had recently closed. It had been there for sixty years. The fine colonnaded building still looked impressive and I could imagine the rich aroma of freshly-ground coffee and the sound of the musical trio that once played there. It needed a staff of 40 to man the restaurant, self-service café, smoke room, party room, bakery and shop. The historic Mechanic's Institute had been demolished and now the site was surrounded by what looked like the biggest wooden box in England. Between the City Hall and Alhambra Theatre they were building a monstrosity costing a million pounds. It was to be the new police headquarters.

Darley Street

Bridge Street

Demolition of Listerhills

City centre redevelopment

The main block of the university was opened in 1965. It was near the top of the sloping Richmond Road and we were told that every year it moved half an inch downhill so by the time I reached 70 it should be a yard to the left of the photo I took.

University main building

The lower side of the main building was alongside Tumbling Hill Street, and it was here the pleasant smell of wool fat was easyiest to detect. Beyond, everything really was tumbling: the whole of the Listerhills area was being cleared for future development of the university. The Longside Hotel, which I remember as a rowdy pub where beer glasses where used as missiles, was gone for good.

I wrote about my finances:
"My spending problem is not really serious. At worst, I could live on next to nothing and take in sandwiches for lunch. We always have loads of spare jam and bread in the Lodge. If I didn't go out so often I might get more work done. I'm enjoying living slightly more extravagantly than usual. Since Wednesday I have spent very little apart from dance tickets that cost ten shillings. 'Chicken Shack' will be playing. They ought to be quite good. The trouble with these dances featuring groups playing 'progressive' pop is that they turn into a combined disco/concert with most people dancing to records in another hall whilst the supporting group plays to a handful of people. When the main group comes on everyone crowds into the main hall to watch and listen. The disco is one big 'cattle market' before the show if you know what I mean."

February 1970:
I had arranged to meet Jane in town at 7.30 p.m. The bus from Tong left me with 45 minutes to kill so I decided to have a few drinks to make chatting her up easier. Like me, Jane was a quiet person and not easy to make conversations with. I decided it would make a change to drink shorts. That would also reduce the need to visit the bog so often. For my first drink I bought a rum and coke for 4/3. It had no effect on me at all; it was the same as drinking coke on its own. I then went to the Old Crown. This was a building with character from the outside but inside it was little more than an empty room with a platform at one end holding a piano and drum set. There were two blokes at a table and four standing at the bar. I ordered a scotch (3/-) and added a very small amount of water then sat with it in a corner. The pub was like a scene out of a play with four men at the bar where the barman was reading a paper. I finished my drink and walked towards the agreed meeting place whilst eating an apple. I gazed idly into the window of a music shop as a number 8 bus came past. Jane wasn't on that bus so I started walking up another street and gazed into a decorating shop window.
        "What are you looking at?"
It was Jane. We walked slowly down the road. There was no time to catch the 7.30 bus to Tong without running so we walked aimlessly for a while and then turned up Leeds Road for about 400 yards and came back again. Steve was at

the bus stop. He gave us a dirty grin when I greeted him and we waited uneasily for the bus to arrive. Steve went upstairs in the bus and we sat downstairs. We did not say much and the journey passed fairly rapidly. Whilst walking down Tong Lane we talked a bit and Steve jokingly told of the 'dangers' of motorcycles. On arrival at the lodge, we went up to my room where there were about six people. I introduced them to Jane and they left us and fortunately they departed after about 10 minutes to go to the "Dog". Jane and I listened to a Leonard Cohen tape. When it had finished playing, we went down to the "Dog" and left at 10.15 to catch the last bus back to Bradford. I thought there was a bus at 10.35 but it hadn't arrived by 10.45 so we returned to the Lodge. When we got back I faced some dirty grins. Craig even started making sleeping arrangements in a different room but I wanted Russ to take Jane back in his car. So, she left with Russ at about eleven and said she'd meet me tomorrow at 7.30.

I was tired. After Jane had left everyone said, "Hard luck". Steve said I had no chance and Craig said he approves of her. No one would mind seeing more of her at the Lodge. In a week or so Jane was to start working more regular hours and would have the whole of the weekend off. I thought that, with a bit of luck, I might even get her to stay at the Lodge on Saturday night, although Steve may have been right when he said there's no chance. However, if I was successful I will have little need for the Blob any longer. I was afraid my relationship with Jo would not terminate easily. I'd arranged to go for a walk with her on the Sunday. It may be enjoyable. The last walk I had with her was okay. If she were a romantic type it might be more fun. If she wrote passionate letters to me instead of the rubbish that she usually wrote and talked about all the time I would feel better and more wanted. The trouble was she was not romantic. But then neither was I really. Passionate words could sound so pathetic and futile. It was quite off-putting when Jo laughed at romantic scenes in the cinema.

Friday 13/2/70 - Letter to Mary:
"I am writing this letter slowly because I know you are not a very fast reader. I got your letter last night when I got back from watching 'Topaz'. I've remembered some jokes to tell you but some of them are too rude even for a Rag Mag and anyway you wouldn't understand them.

"Here are the sick jokes:
  'Did you hear about the man who had constipation?'
  'He stuck a Smartie up his arse and it came out a Treat!
  'What's green and flies backwards?' (Sniff)
Al Capone is at the bar looking miserable. A friend asks him what was the matter with him.

'My woman died.'
'Oh dear. What did she die of Al?'
'VD'
'That's odd. I didn't think that women died when they had VD.'
'They do when they give it to me.'

"I enclose an article about Chicken Shack, who played at the university the other week. Actually, they weren't as good as the article makes out. For a start, Stan Webb's guitar was much too loud. When he played solo it was painful to the ear, even at the back of the hall. The drummer was good. I shan't be going to a dance on Saturday because we are having a party at the Lodge. Jane will be coming.

"My lecture is beginning so I'll finish writing now.

Thoughts on Sunday 15.2.70:
"So: I proved that Steve was wrong when he said I had no chance with Jane. Perhaps it was a bit unfair because she thought she was going to a party at Tong. She got a 'sleeping out' pass to stay away from the nurses' home. The party didn't happen. But the two of us had an amazing party together. I played a tape of Leonard Cohen and lit a candle. His slow, soulful songs and the romantic candlelit atmosphere matched Jane's fantastic kiss."

Like a bird on the wire
Like a drunk in a midnight choir
I have tried in my way to be free

Like a worm on a hook
Like a knight from some old-fashioned book
I have saved all my ribbons for thee
If I, if I have been unkind
I hope that you can just let it go by
If I, if I have been untrue
I hope you know it was never to you

For like a baby, stillborn
Like a beast with his horn
I have torn everyone who reached out for me
But I swear by this song
And by all that I have done wrong
I will make it all up to thee

I saw a beggar leaning on his wooden crutch
He said to me, "you must not ask for so much"
And a pretty woman leaning in her darkened door
She cried to me, "hey, why not ask for more?"
Oh, like a bird on the wire
Like a drunk in a midnight choir
I have tried in my way to be free

My relationship with Jo seemed full of deception. It was all false. She said in a letter that she did not want to share me with anyone. Little did she know that she was. As far as Jo knew I played chess at York, had some visitors and went canoeing. I did not go to York. I told Jo I went to see some films on sailing. I did see some films: it was with Jane at the pictures. I rang Jo and asked her to come over. She couldn't – she had some 'sitting in' to do. Stuck for suggestions, I rashly asked her to come to a party on Saturday, although Jane had already agreed to come. She agreed to phone me later and when she did, I made up the excuse that I was going to York to play chess and would not be back until late. I said we could go for a walk with her on Sunday instead. I was to meet her in Ilkley at 2.30. On the Sunday Jane stayed with me until 3 p.m. I phoned Jo and told her another false excuse. Why didn't I just tell her the truth? I knew why really. If I finished Jo and Jane finished me I'll be back to square one.

February 1970 Extracts from letters to home:
"At least my motorbike got to Ilkley and back without any trouble last Sunday. Jo decided to take an impromptu swim in a flooded stream on the edge of Ilkley Moor. We both found that highly amusing. Shortly afterwards it poured with rain and there was a piercing wind so we both got soaked anyway.

"We are expecting a 'raid' on the Lodge from the halls of residence tonight because they have not attacked us for the last two nights. Since there is no Rag Week this year we are taking Arts festival Week as the same to maintain traditions. Last Monday at 4 a.m. about twenty 'Gentlemen of Tong' went into the halls and removed all the ballcocks from the toilet cisterns (propping up the arms with pieces of wood) and arranged them on the Common Room floor in the formation of the word TONG. None of the residents knew, until morning of course… A childish prank, but fun.

"Last night I saw a performance of 'Moving Being'. The programme described it as 'a compound form of presentation which has its basis in movement and is primarily choreographic but which makes use of speech, sound, music, environment, objects, film and projection'."

Thoughts in March 1970:
"My feelings towards Jane have become stronger. I'm unsure about Jo as there are so many things that I don't like about her. Last weekend I was put right off her. As soon as I had arranged to see her on the same weekend as Jane, I knew I was asking for trouble. Having two girls in one weekend is stupid – its only value is in building self-esteem.

"On Monday I went to the pictures with Jane and was glad to be back with someone more respectable. Last night we went to her friend's party and I got to know more of Jane's character. Generally, my opinion of her has improved and I obtained some illuminating ideas and thoughts of Jane and her friends as well."

"The blob seems to get bigger every time I see her. Yesterday she looked massive. Ilkley College students were invited to a party at Tong Hall. I hated having to show myself up as Jo's boyfriend but as I knew several of the guests, I was able to create a reasonable impression. I took the precaution of having several drinks before Jo arrived. By the time I returned from the Dog, Jo had arrived. I caught a glimpse of her and as I dodged out of her line of sight, I accidentally sent Trevor flying and spilling his drink all down his front. When I finally approached Jo we hardly spoke. I left her to talk with her friends and chatted up another girl. Craig thought that behaviour was revolting. I started to tell Jo about Jane: I mentioned her name and read aloud a postcard from her. Jo seemed completely unaffected. She either didn't care or thought there was nothing serious about that relationship. I got the impression that if I'd told Jo that I've been sleeping with Jane, Jo would have not been ruffled. I said to other people, knowing that Jo could overhear, "You know Jane, don't you?" They denied it, either out of consideration for Jo or for their disgust in me. Jo and I went to my room and spent most of the time talking under the cover of my bedclothes. Occasionally, people poked heads through the door, muttered an apology and withdrew. They must have got the wrong impression of what we were doing! I was just talking to Jo under the bedclothes because I didn't want to see her. It was at this party that Craig met Mandy. He said that the only thing he didn't like about Mandy was her frizzy curly hair style.

"I have arranged to go camping with Jo during the Easter holiday following the Canoe Camping Expedition on the River Wye. It could be fun but I like her less every time we meet. I considered that it would be just as enjoyable camping with Jo as it would be with a male friend and better than being on my own.

"My affection for Jane grows. She is not ideal, and I wouldn't particularly want to marry her, but she is nice. She seems incredibly experienced. Right now, Jane is holidaying in Edinburgh. I've had a letter from her every day and have sent lengthy replies to each one. She says she misses me and would like to be back. I do wish she was here, although I don't have a big pain in the heart for her. It is a pity that I shall be away for so long at Easter."

"I've been canoeing at the swimming baths with the university canoe club. It was an enjoyable session with only a few people there. Ray lost two canoes off the top of his van on the way, smashing off the end of one of them. Afterwards we watched the late-night horror films at the university."

"I met Jane as soon as she returned from Scotland. She was in a nice mood but wore a perfume that smelt like tobacco and made me feel sick. We walked up Manningham Lane and around Lister Park. Jane knew the park like the back of her hand. The park attendant said hello to her. It was quite a sad evening as I would not be seeing each other again for three weeks. It was cold as we waited at the bus stop for half an hour until 11. Then we parted."

Extracts from my letters to home:
"It has been very warm recently. I went for two walks today: one just before lunch and another at two. The countryside around here is very pleasant. There was a party here last night and we have another end-of-term booze-up after the horror films on Monday night. There are three films: 'Quatermass and the Pit', 'Frankenstein's Ghost' and one more.

"I charged the bike's battery last week and it seems OK but misfires occasionally.

"The motorbike fared its holiday better than the last one but it still drops a lot of oil."

The last day of term was bright and sunny but I stayed in bed until nine and completed preparations for going away. Craig gave me a lift to Sheffield from where I started hitch-hiking down the M1. After five minutes I got a lift on a lorry but it broke down after five miles. I hitched another lift from the motorway hard shoulder and got a ride all the way to Luton on a lorry transporting tractors and was home at Dagnall by five o'clock."

Thoughts in April 1970:
"I did not receive a letter from either Jane or Jo this morning. Jo will have received my letter last Saturday, written her reply on the train yesterday and posted it later than yesterday's collection. Jane was expecting me to phone yesterday evening so perhaps she didn't bother writing. I was unable to be connected to her on the phone, although I tried for 25 minutes. The phone was either engaged or the phone code for Bradford was wrong, having changed in the morning from 0274 to 01274. Now I'm wondering if Jane wants to finish with me. Anyhow, I shall know by tomorrow, that is if I can contact her by phone or if I get a letter from her. Not that I would care if Jo didn't write.

"Whilst staying at grandma's on Saturday night I had a dream. The person in it I suppose was Jo and Jane combined. Her uncleanliness reminded me of Jo but she was reasonably pretty; although plump – about half way between Jo and Jane. I knocked on a door that was Ray's in Bradford. It opened and I was pleasantly surprised to see this girl there. She wore a blue V-neck sweater and a short grey skirt. Above the V was a medallion or cross or something. She was not tall: possibly a trace of Olga, a girl who had recently joined our course at university. She smiled and invited me in. I was in a large bed with her. Other people were in the house – my parents I think. She was lying naked on her back. I thought she looked quite nice. Then I was sitting and putting on a pair of socks. Someone came into the room. There was a large light, a warm room and people sat around a table playing cards. I walked past the table to a room behind the far wall. Something interesting or sexy was going to happen but I never found out what. I woke up, disappointed that it couldn't continue. Grandma had brought me a cup of tea.

"I must have told grandma about Jo and/or Jane and got talking about marriage because during our conversation grandma surprised me by mentioning her relationship with grandad.

She said, 'He doesn't do his dirty business any more'.
It was clear that she wasn't talking of his work as a cobbler!

"I want to do something creative. I'd like to write a novel. I would write about how I feel without incriminating myself. I'd base it on someone like me but more so, if you see what I mean. He would have similar characteristics to me but they would be more extreme. I'd like to write humorously.

"If I find myself without a girlfriend next term I ought to get down to some serious working. The compensation for not having a girlfriend is that I'll get more work done. When I started writing these thoughts I began with an introduction based on the idea that if I failed my A levels the creation of this would be a sort of compensation. I never finished the introduction and went on to pass the exams. I like to have compensations. If I got chucked out of university my compensation might be to hitch-hike around Europe. I like to think that if all goes wrong then I've got such and such to look forward to.

"Life is balanced. Bad luck is frequently followed up by good. If the worse comes to the worst there is the promise of something better to follow. Some people believe in life after death. I think it's rubbish, but Jane believes in God and in life after death. Jo in neither. Last term, I found this balancing force worked for me financially. The more money I spent, the more came my way. Not as a result of the spending, but by coincidence. I could live for next to nothing since my accommodation is payed for at the beginning of term. I could go out and buy a new camera and not face hardship from the expenditure. I don't accept comments like 'you don't know how well off you are'. Times aren't hard; people just make out they are. In this country, no one needs to be denied at least one luxury. You can't die from poverty here. Lack of interest or care in life can lead to unpleasantness."

Jo

"I have completed the 117 programmed learning questions that I had to do and don't feel like starting more work. I phoned Jane last night. Like before, it was engaged the first time so I let the operator ring me back when she got through to the number. The operator called at 9.15 and said she had the call for me. It was not Jane who had answered the phone but when I asked for her, she came quickly. It seemed strange listening to her voice. Her Yorkshire accent seemed very pronounced after so long without hearing it. Jane was not any different from usual though. When I said I had not heard from her since Friday she said she would write that evening. I said I'd ring again on Friday, same time."

Easter meet of Canoe Camping Club: River Wye from Whitney to Monmouth, 26 – 30 April 1970:

I arrived at Whitney-on-Wye at 2.15 p.m, pitched my tent and cooked a meal. The campsite was next to the Boat Inn so I spent the evening there talking with the people I met last year and Ron from the canoe club in Swindon. The following morning (Saturday) I left before Ron and drove to Hereford, did some shopping and wrote to Jo and Jane. I paddled for 65 minutes to the confluence of the rivers Lugg and Wye where I met most of the party having lunch. After a quick lunch I continued paddling with Ron. We camped near Hoarwithy and had a social in the evening three miles away but left after half an hour for the pub. I got a lift to the pub in Hoarwithy and another in the rain back to the campsite.

On the Sunday I continued down the river most of the way to Ross by myself. We landed near a pub so I went in, got a drink and sat next to two girls who were in a canoeing group from Bradford: Susan, who was studying catering at Bradford college, and Christine, who looked about 14. After the drinks the three of us went outside and ate our lunch. I spotted a dog trotting along the other side of the river and said to Susan, "That looks just like our dog." A short while later I recognised that the people with the dog were mum, dad, Dorothy and her two children. They had come out from Gloucester (where Dorothy lived) for the day. Ron, who had arrived later than me, was still having his lunch when the Bradford party set off but we caught them up near Goodrich Castle. They were arguing with a fisherman who apparently had deliberately cast his line directly in front of the canoes and complained. We paddled with the group to Welsh Bicknor Youth Hostel, in whose grounds we camped. In the evening I walked with Derek and Brenda (who lived in Dunstable) to the pub. The evening was more sociable than the previous one. I chatted with a group from Isleworth Canoe Club then walked back with Ron.

On Monday morning I was about the last person to get up but by 10.30 was on the river waiting for Ron. After a few miles I paddled on ahead to pitch my tent at a campsite two miles above Monmouth. I chatted to some people at Symonds Yat then shot the rapid to the right of the island. On previous visits I had gone to the left. There was just enough water and a few rocks to dodge making it more interesting than the soaking I would have got paddling the simpler way through the 'haystacks' on the other side. Ron pointed out a wrecked canoe stranded on the island as we passed. There was a strong headwind below Symonds Yat causing waves which soaked me and made the boat feel very unstable. At times it was hard to keep hold of my paddle. If I stopped paddling the wind would have blown me upstream. At the campsite I had to jam my canoe firmly under a tree route so it didn't blow away. After pitching my tent and unloading the canoe I paddled on with a girl from Cork University who was doing her PhD on Pollution in Cork Harbour. The empty canoe was easier to paddle and a lot drier. We landed at the rowing club steps just above Monmouth bridge. I collected my car from the car park, did some shopping and ate chips by the riverside. After Ron arrived and we had said goodbye I drove to the campsite where Derek, Brenda and two others of the party had arrived. I gave them a lift to Monmouth so they could collect their cars. The traffic made it a slow journey. After my evening meal I wrote a letter to Jane and the five of us went out to a pub in Brenda's Mini van. At 10.30 the lights were flashed to indicate closing time but no one left. We got our last order at 11.10 and left the pub at 11.30. It was an enjoyable and amusing evening.

I slept well that night and got up at about 9.30 and messed around until midday when Derek and Brenda left. I then meandered in the forest, along a track by the river, up a steep hill and back along the top of a quarry. After eating I went shopping in Monmouth and looked at the 'Nelson Collection' in the museum. I filled the car with petrol and parked in the cattle market car park. I had arranged to meet Jo at the bus station at about six. I did not feel like meeting her. The reason I had invited her here was because some time ago I had promised to take her camping. At the time I thought it would be fun. Now though, I felt the same as I did at that party when I spilt Trevor's drink whilst trying to avoid Jo. I went to the bus station at 5.30 and as I passed the café window I saw Jo inside with her back to me. I felt worse. I tapped the window next to where she was sitting. She smiled and I went inside the café. We left immediately and I drove us straight to the campsite. When we arrived, she went for a walk whilst I read a pamphlet I'd picked up from the museum. Jo returned and started to read it too. I cooked a meal of minced beef, peas and potatoes whilst Jo watched without comment. It was not fun. After eating we walked the two miles to the pub. It took just half an hour.

I quickly drank four pints, which was more than I would normally have. We left at 10.30 and walked back to the campsite not talking much.

We got up late. I had been lying thinking of how to spend the day, filling time as much as possible. I did not want another night with Jo. I had fulfilled my promise to take her camping and now I wanted to go home. I got up, heated some water, washed and cooked scrambled eggs; all the time being watched by Jo. I did everything in efficient camping style, largely ignoring Jo. We made sandwiches and packed up. It had been snowing quite heavily.

I drove at a sedate pace and we visited Raglan Castle, an interesting place and a worthwhile visit. We continued to Tintern by minor roads, had a drink and visited the abbey. I then drove us to 'The Scowles', a place near Bream which Ron had said was worth seeing. It was interesting wandering around the collapsed mine shafts, passages and holes. As I roamed around the site Jo just stood where I had left her. She did not like the place and said it gave her the creeps. Now my planned day had ended and I wanted to go home. I drove to the landmark of Speech House, where we stopped and ate our cheese sandwiches. I talked about what to do next, occasionally mentioning the things I had to do at home and it soon came around to a point where I could tell Jo that I felt like going home. She did not seem disappointed and I kissed her gratefully for making it easy for me to say. I felt considerably more cheerful once I knew I was not going to camp another night with her. I was glad that she did not mind. I wonder if she felt in a similar way.

The return journey was uneventful. I took Jo to Berkhamsted station, leaving her at about seven. Her subsequent letters made no mention of our night camping, although she had rarely referred to past events before. I'm sure she was not disappointed – she said at the time that she had enjoyed it. Now what of the future? I guess I'll continue to let it hang a while.

And hang it did. I didn't see Jo again.

Thoughts on Friday 8.5.70:
"Maybe it's the photo that did it. Maybe it's the fact I bought a dance ticket just for myself. Whatever it is, I find myself missing Jane. I enjoyed last Wednesday afternoon with her. We went to Shipley Glen. It was a hot day but on the hill a cool breeze was blowing. Jane was completely against the idea of having her photo taken but I managed to sneak a few shots, one of which came out good enough for printing. I bought a new camera during the holiday and joined the Photography Society last week. Since then I have been doing hours of work in the darkroom. I printed a 10x8 from the suitable negative and took strong delight and care doing so. It seemed to bring me closer to Jane in a way. I was supposed to phone her afterwards at ten but was unable to due to the phone being engaged.

"The dance ticket is for tomorrow. It is a long time since I last went to a dance without a girl but Gordon encouraged me to go anyway. After buying the ticket I asked myself, 'What if any of Jane's friends are at the dance?' Since then I have had a sort of guilty feeling of disloyalty and a wish to go out with Jane instead. It's a lot nicer going out in the day when the weather is fine than in the evening. Anyway, I'm going to ring her up after she finishes work at eight.

Birthday letters from grandfather and grandmother, dated 8.5.70:
"It was very nice to receive another letter from you and we are glad to hear of your activities in canoeing and your purchasing a camera. Yes, we remember Manningham Park quite well and if you continue the walk past the museum you will come to a small gate which leads you out into Emm Lane just opposite the College gates.

"I am sending you a cheque for half-a-guinea for your birthday which comes round next Tuesday and we hope you will have a very happy day and get a lot of presents. I am sorry this is small; but with so many people, we can't do more. But it comes with lots of love from us all. Unfortunately, I can't get into town – I haven't been since last December and I'm beginning to wonder if I shall go again! So I couldn't get you a card! We are so glad to hear of your news. Our daffodils are over but there are some narcissi still out and the tulips. The gardener takes a real interest in the garden. Now I must close with lots of love and good wishes to you.

Grandfather

"Another birthday. I'm afraid I forget just how old you are? I expect you are now entitled to a vote. So many happy returns to you. It does not seem so long since you were quite a small boy.

We had a long thunderstorm yesterday so the atmosphere is much clearer today. The grass looks beautifully green and fresh. Have you made any plans for your holiday? I expect you will be taking a long walk soon. We have a few bright coloured hyacinths out and some pure white daffodils which are really lovely.

Hope you keep well and do well at school. I suppose you have not finished your O and A levels yet. Even Mary is talking about hers. She is planning to be a secretary; so has a lot of hard work to do. Take care of yourself especially when out biking etc.

Have a nice day and best wishes from Grandma xxxxxx"

Thoughts on Tuesday 12.5.70 - my 20th birthday:
"Inebriated maybe but my thoughts are clear. I've been to the Dog, drank two pints of Double Diamond, a Tong special (martini with cider and vodka) and a Pernod with vodka all in 45 minutes, but I'm not drunk. Jane didn't turn up

yesterday evening and I couldn't contact her until just now on the phone. As expected, when I asked her the reason she replied, "I don't know." What this means is that she doesn't want to tell me why. I told her how disappointed I was. She says she likes me. Instead of meeting me she "just went to a youth club with friends". I asked her if she did not want to see me again. She didn't actually say, "I don't know" again but that is what she wanted to say. I'm glad I had those drinks before talking to her. It enabled me to say just what I felt whilst still being able to think clearly. If I had been 100% sober I would not have done better. I told Jane just how I felt. Anyway, we'll meet on Thursday at 7 and sort things out.

"I am sure that Jane is honest. She's just not really sure of me. I like to believe she likes me sexually. I think she believes that I like her for herself, not just for her body (in my present state I rate her assets as 40% body, 40% herself, 10% character...). Jane is going to be working nights so I won't be seeing her so much.

Letter from grandfather, dated 22.5.70
"It was very nice to get another letter from you the other day. It is good to be remembered by our grandchildren. And thank you for the photographs. We remember the one of the market; but the other one we could not remember, except for the chimneys and smoke!

"We went to the hospital yesterday afternoon when grandmother had a little operation; but they do not want to see her again and the operations seems quite successful. I am about the same: very tired but maybe I shall rest more now that the operation is over.

"I hope you have done well in your German exam.

We remember Richmond very well. We went to a hotel there; but it was not very good! I hope the weather keeps fine for your camping.

"The bookstall I mentioned was Powers. You are fortunate to be at Tong Hall. We did not know the district when we were in Bradford and it was a very pleasant surprise when you went there. I am sure the rhododendrons will be nice. Our azaleas are just coming out and the cherry blossom, the apple blossom and the red flowers and the yellow (I can't think of their names) are lovely. When the driver of the ambulance came yesterday, he stood and said, "What a wonderful garden."

"Now I must close and we hope you do well in your exams and your sport. Mary took the first in the long jump yesterday. We had a girl of 17 at Hanover who won the world championship in both the long jump and the high jump in one afternoon and had a full-page photograph of her in the Daily Mirror! But she is over 60 now.

"Grandmother won't write today. She is in bed, just a little tired after the operation."

Thoughts on Saturday 30.5.70:
"A week ago, I felt completely different. I had no trace of how I am feeling now. It bothers me. It's not like the feeling I had after that discotheque in Swindon. It's a feeling deep inside and makes me breathe more deeply. The thing is, it started not when I left her, but when I was still with her.

"A week ago, I was trying to revise for the tests we had the following Tuesday. Monday was a Bank Holiday and was also a day off for Jane. As it was a fairly nice day, I arranged for her to come to Tong in the afternoon for a walk. She found her way with no trouble, which surprised me, indicating that I had been underestimating her abilities. I met Jane at the end of Tong Lane and we walked to Drighlington. I admit that on the way I was leading her to a secluded spot that I had identified the day before, by deliberately going the wrong way. The ploy did not work and as the walk continued the path faded so we turned around and went to the Lodge. We played records and a Leonard Cohen tape, but the tape jammed. I started talking about how things were not really as they ought to be. We had known each other for six months with practically no progress in our relationship. Perhaps I was influenced by my failure to seduce her during the walk. I must have got carried away as I began spouting out by saying how different we were, not having the same interests and having opposite opinions on many aspects. Jane disagreed. That started me off pointing out her faults and accusing her of having no interests. I asked what her objective in life was. Tears started to form in her eyes. I listened as she told me about her family. As Jane spoke, I stroked her hair and my feelings towards her became stronger all the time. Then I realised. I had fallen in love with her.

"I kept thinking of Jane all day long on Thursday and hoping that she can stay with me on Friday night. When I went to bed the thought that she might refuse really troubled me. When Friday evening finally arrived, I became increasingly worried as the time we agreed to meet passed. I became convinced that Jane had no intention of coming back with me that night.

"Mum and dad had been visiting me and wanted to meet Susan. We went to town, had a curry and returned to the car at seven, the time I had arranged for us to meet Jane. I wanted to meet Jane before introducing her to mum and dad so they agreed to wait. The number 8 bus arrived with Jane just before 7.30. She said she had waited ages for the bus to come. Mum and dad were still waiting and the four of us went to Manningham (Lister) Park. After my parents had left, Jane and I walked round the park. Jane was in a passive mood, not giving anything away about her feelings. As we headed down Manningham Lane she talked about what she was going to do that night and the following morning so it was obvious that she had no intention of coming back with me to Tong. We had a drink at the Queen's and Jane became 'nice and sweet' to me. I tried again to persuade her to 'come to Tong' (a phrase which was becoming all too familiar) with me. She refused but we left the pub in time to catch the 9.30 bus. Jane playfully resisted going to the bus stop so we got nowhere near it in time. I was getting miserable and said I was going to drown my sorrows. The next pub we passed (the Yarnspinner) was overcrowded so we crossed the road to a grotty hotel that was full of drunks, ruffians and dirty-mouthed women. There was some sort of horse-play going on at the other side of the bar. The setting suited my mood admirably! In fact, I was slightly aroused by it all.

"A woman who seemed to fancy Jane and kept admiring her legs said to her,
            'How old are you love?'
            'She's thirty-five', I replied and the woman left us.
An old man stumbled past us muttering to himself. I said loudly that I agreed with him wholeheartedly and Jane laughed. There can't have been a bus at 10 o'clock so we sat and waited on a subway wall. We were amused by cheerful sly remarks spoken by passers-by.

"I told Jane that I wouldn't see her back to her bus stop because I was going to catch the 10.20 back to Tong. She seemed most lovable as I was still pressing for her to come with me. She came with me to 'my' bus stop and we were sitting there when the 10.20 bus came and went. I really wanted Jane to come back with me. I said she could sleep alone in Craig's bed and that I wouldn't touch her all night if that's what she wanted. But her mind was made up not to come as strongly as mine was for her to do so. I agreed to walk with her half way to 'her' bus stop. I still wasn't going to give up trying! We reached the far corner of the Town Hall – about the half way point – and stopped. Jane kissed me really lovingly (her kiss is always very special) and hugged me tightly. It was like a dramatic scene of a love story. She clung on even when I said I was going to catch my 10.30 bus. I played the scene lovingly, but not passionately, because this was not where I wanted to be passionate. She promised to phone me at 9.30 in the morning and continued to hold me tightly until I gently pushed her away from me and started walking briskly away. It made a perfect scene: if it were a film, she would come running behind me, calling my name and fall into my arms. I did not look back as I wished for the imagined scene to become reality until I was sitting on the back seat of the bus and it pulled away. As I walked slowly down Tong Lane my imagination continued to compose the love film. In the film, Jane gets back and tells Hazel all about the evening. Hazel persuades Jane to get a taxi and take her to Tong where she meets me as I walk down the lane and we fall into each other's arms.

"Returning to reality, when I got back I made myself some toast and coffee, did a good hour and a half of work, went to bed at one o'clock and fell asleep quickly.

"Jane rang in the morning. I said I was sorry if I had made her miserable. She said she was mean to me and that I didn't deserve it. The following Monday I received a letter from her saying the same heart-warming words in her brief unsophisticated manner.

"I counted down the days before I next saw Jane. When we met on Tuesday evening she told me that she was extremely tired and wanted to go to bed without even getting undressed. As predicted, she messed about before going to bed. I'm getting better at predicting Jane's actions but my speculation of what she might be doing with other blokes upsets me. She told me that she spent the other Wednesday at Baildon Moor. Six blokes wanted to go out with her. At the pictures she was moody, restless and miserable but refused to tell me what was bothering her. She assured me that it would neither bother nor concern me but she preferred to keep this to herself. I considered that day another successful step forward. It was difficult to get her off my mind.

"I took a picture of Jane at Shipley Glen. It was very nice up there and only a tenpenny bus ride away. Jane didn't like having her picture taken but I managed to snatch one before she covered her face with her hand. It is my favourite picture of her."

My favourite photo of Jane

I found the reason the bike's battery wasn't charging was a bad connection in the ignition switch. The bike seemed to be working OK but I lost a clutch cover cap. You could see the clutch belting round at 5000 rpm half an inch from my foot. Next day, the engine packed up. It sounded rough as I drove to go canoeing at Bingley. On the way back, it stopped after half a mile and then repeatedly at ever decreasing distances. I ended up putting the bike in the back of Dave's van. I checked the timing, points, etc. but got a weak spark. I gave up trying to find the fault and managed without the bike for a while. Craig now a van so I sometimes went into town with him.

Thoughts on Thursday 4.6.70 - Jane tells me she has another boyfriend:
"I suppose it must be the pressure of exams approaching that makes my mood the way it is nowadays. Or maybe it's Jane. My mood changes rapidly. Early afternoon was much like any other day and I enjoyed a light-hearted

conversation. Later I began to feel slightly depressed and sorrowful. It is a feeling that continually, sometimes continuously, possesses me. There is little to divert me. I seem to be either wasting time, seeing Jane or trying to work. Normally, I have more diversions such as canoeing or photography but there's no time for that. I find revising is very dull. It makes me realise how much I don't know. If I stop revising I think of Jane and become hot and uncomfortable inside. It feels as if I am in a state of shock. Yesterday I tried to tell Jane how I felt but it was an inappropriate time as we were walking down the lane to the bus but I needed to tell her. I had rehearsed it too much in my mind and it came out too fast so I had to repeat it.

Very rapidly I said, 'The-only-thing-that-stops-me-from-loving-you-is-the-fact-that-I-don't-want-to-dissapoint-myself.'

That was the truth. I feel I have got too emotionally involved with Jane. It's like walking close to the edge of a cliff. Jane said she should not have told me about the other boys. Perhaps she is right, but better to have been told than for me to find out. Just think how upset I would be then. I expect she likes me better than them. But I can't help thinking that she might be thinking of someone else when she gives me one of her fantastic kisses. To share that, as well as her thoughts, her mind and her body is a feeling that abhors me. I must stop myself from giving her my whole heart in return for just a part of those things.

"Jane told me that tomorrow she is going out with a boy who has a white sports car. He doesn't work because his father supports him. He's supposedly going to London on Saturday to find a job. He believes that everyone should be allowed to do just what they want. Jane doesn't agree with that because if so everyone would be idle like him. His car is not an MG.

"Jane spoke of the difficulties of meeting me when she's working nights. I said that she doesn't have to miss sleep to go out with me but she replied that I'm always at college during the day. But it doesn't seem an inconvenience for her to go out with someone else.

"In a way I'm honoured. Jane admits to getting fed up easily but she's stuck with me for six months. She's promised to come and stay with me at home in Dagnall. She promised not to let me down again. She sticks up for me when I get moody. Okay, so I'm her honoured boyfriend. But I'm jealous.

"Last night I set out to prove a point to my conscience – and succeeded. After being with Jane in the afternoon – and she wouldn't stay longer because she said she was going to talk to a friend called Paula – and why I accepted that I don't know – I decided that if I tried to work I would get depressed thinking about her. So, I went to Mara's Disco to prove that if Jane can do it so can I. My miserable mood cleared up after the first dance and I felt a lot better after teaming up with my friend Dave. We had a second dance with a pair of mediocre girls and I started chatting up my girl to prove my point. I did well: we went for a drink after the third or fourth dance and chatted happily. She was called Susan, came from Wakefield and was taking her 'A' levels in a fortnight. They had to meet the parents of her friends Gillian at eleven so I walked them to the Town Hall. When we kissed goodbye, I knew I had to be thankful for Jane. Susan's lips were hard and tight. I had to restrain from kissing her the way I do Jane.

"The evening worked. Now I needn't feel peeved about Jane going out with other blokes. I went out and deliberately picked up another girl. Maybe Jane played a more passive role when she met those blokes. I've been wondering whether to tell her. It might make Jane feel less about me, especially as I had been with her earlier that day. Today I imagined asking Jane if she had ever been out with another bloke on the same day as with me and decided the asking would serve no useful purpose.

"I think it would be better if I stopped my romantic, although honest act with Jane. It would be better to regard her simply as a girlfriend again. It wouldn't change anything. We'd get on just as well together and I wouldn't be missing her whilst trying to revise or when I can't see her because she's working nights. I would avoid tying myself in knots. I'd like to hear more about her other boyfriends. And I'd like to sleep with her next week.

"I feel that Jane would make rather a good wife, although there would be hundreds of snags. A lack of common interest of any standing is just one of them."

Letter from grandfather, dated 24.6.70:
"It was very nice to receive another letter from you and we are glad you are enjoying your stay in Bradford. We wish we were back there again, although our garden here is lovely. We hope you have done very well in your exams. And I envy you your visit to the Yorkshire Dales. We stayed at a very nice cottage near Kettlewell and I was on my bike and had some hair-raising rides over the moors and down again! I hope your motorbike is alright, though I should not like to ride where I went on my push bike! I hope you get a nice job for the holidays. It would be nice to work at the Zoo!

Mother is getting on really well. This morning the nurse came to give her a bath and, for the first time, she went up the stairs, got into the bath and came down again! It is dull and much colder today; but still very fresh and nice.

With lots of love and good wishes to you from us both."

Thoughts on Sunday 28.6.70
"Again, so much has happened since I last wrote and my feelings are different. I am surprised by what I wrote last and feel I ought to modify it. Some of the ideas are slightly in bad taste. For example, I said that I like Jane equally for herself and for her body. It must have been true then. I have always thought that I liked Jane more than she liked me but my writing doesn't show that.

"The other day I told Jane that I love her. I haven't told her before because I like to say precisely what I mean. It's only recently that I have convinced myself that I do love her. According to the dictionary definition of the word I have loved Jane for a long time. But surely love is something you know when it happens and that it's obvious in itself. There must be varying degrees of love. So, to what degree do I love Jane? It's impossible to quantify. All I can say is that I love her quite a lot.

"Last week was great and Jane agreed. Monday and Tuesday weren't so hot but the other two were brilliant, especially Thursday. On Monday we walked round Lister Park and went to the pictures to see 'Winning'. Jane had been working the previous night so she went back to her bed and me to Tong. On Tuesday, Jane came to Tong. Sorry, I was wrong when I said Tuesday wasn't hot. This must have been the day I started to love Jane. We walked towards the golf course, lunched at the Dog where we talked about the other guests, guessing what they were like and what they did. We must have been the most loving couple there. Jane was not keen to go for the last bus but her conscience or something told her that was best. We walked down the lane quickly. We were in two minds about whether it would be better for her to stay or go. The bus solved the decision for us by arriving soon after we reached the bus stop. I think we were both sorry to part but she felt she ought to go. I asked if she would come tomorrow night and she replied with a promising, "Perhaps".

"We arranged to meet the following evening after she had caught up on lost sleep and visited her home. I met her at seven at the usual bus stop and we went to the ABC cinema, this time to watch Marty Feldman in 'Every Home Should Have One'. Afterwards we walked around and caught the 10.20 bus to Tong. The journey seemed to take longer than usual, perhaps because this is what I had been wanting since Easter. At the lodge we had coffee in the kitchen with some of the other lads. Conversation was good and after washing up the mugs we slipped away quietly. I avoided bidding goodnight to avoid possible ribald comments but I think that disappointed them. In my room we listened to music, expecting Craig to arrive soon before he went to Ilkley to see his girlfriend Mandy. At about 1.30 we heard Craig's car and a few minutes later he knocked and tried the door. I went down to the kitchen and we had a cup of coffee together. Nigel and Craig's friend Steve were there. We had an enjoyable discussion, shook hands and said goodbye. It was a while before I got properly back to bed.

"In the morning, Jane suggested a visit to Leeds. We walked across the fields to Drighlington and caught a bus from there. In the city we visited a museum, looked in a few shops and went to the pictures. 'Lord of the Flies' and 'Doctor Faustau' were both good to talk about afterwards. We returned to Bradford by train and went for a drink. The Yarn Spinner was too crowded so we walked across the railway bridge and down to a pub at the bottom of Leeds Road. On the way I told Jane I loved her and she muttered, "I love you" in reply. Then I was sure that I did love her. She agreed to come and stay with me at Dagnall in a fortnight and I agreed to drive to Bradford and fetch her."

June 1970 Extract from letter to home:
"When you come to collect my belongings from Bradford I could escort you back on my motorbike if you don't mind cruising at 50 mph and stopping every hour or so. When I went to Bingley on it on Sunday it overheated and lost half of its power. I shall make a few adjustments but it looks like being a very wearisome journey. If you don't mind travelling in convoy please bring a petrol can as my reserve tank is insufficient to go from one service station to the next."

When I drove my motorbike to go home to Dagnall it got precisely half way, that is to Loughborough, when the engine faded and gave up completely at the exit road. I readjusted the valves, which had come loose as predicted, and adjusted the ignition timing. The whole assembly had become loose. I found there was not a drop of oil in the clutch housing. I'd poured a whole pint in before discovering that a large pool of it had formed underneath. The drain plug had fallen out! Next, the kick starter just slipped round on its spline and refused to grip no matter how hard I tightened it. After much pushing I finally got the ting going but hellish clanking noises came from the engine and seemed to get worse. I drove the bike slowly into Loughborough. After two miles it gave up completely so I pushed it the final mile. I found a motorcycle shop.

The mechanic suspected big ends. I decided to leave the bike with him and continued home with mum and dad in the car. It was the big ends and a replacement would cost £21. To pay for the work done already and bring the bike home would cost a further £10 and I would still need a second-hand engine. The dealer wouldn't offer anything for the bike in part exchange for another so it remains in Loughborough.

Jane stays at Dagnall:
I spent the following week doing jobs at Dagnall. Jane and I wrote to each other every day, frequently telling of our love for each other. I looked forward to the following Monday. On the morning of the trip I drove dad to Berkhamsted station so that he could take the train to work in London. From there I drove to Bradford, not stopping until I reached the city. I arrived at Bradford Royal Infirmary where Jane worked, dead on time. I walked through the hospital towards the nurses' accommodation at Field House and met Jane at the entrance. We drove back by a route to show Jane the special places of my childhood. We passed through the Peak District, joined the M1 at Pinxton, left it again at Northampton and visited the waterways museum at Stoke Bruerne. Jane was tired, having not slept since the previous day.

During her stay at Dagnall we visited Whipsnade Zoo, London and Windsor. One of the most memorable parts of the week was a walk along a muddy path near Chesham. We were of course sleeping in separate rooms in my parents' house. On the last night of her visit Dad was working late downstairs. I started to creep towards Jane's room but slipped back to my room quickly when I heard a sound from downstairs. I felt miserable when she left on the train the following morning. During the following two weeks I got a job selling hardware door-to-door. Many of the goods were of inferior quality and I was a poor salesman but it filled in time. Each morning before going out I wrote Jane a letter.

Thoughts on Saturday 25.07.70 - Jane is worried about something:
"I wish Jane was here now. While we were talking on the phone she sounded like an ordinary girl who was worried about something. She didn't know what she wanted and was neither happy nor displeased when I told her I could see her tomorrow. I committed to drive the 400 miles to Bradford and back and it might not be worth it. Dad is concerned about me putting too high a mileage on the car. I wanted Jane to come back here so I could spend a night with her. Jane admitted that something was worrying her but she won't tell me what it is. She was very firm about refusing to say. The obvious thing is that she is worried about missing a period. Surely it's a bit early to worry about that. Perhaps she

is worrying about her family or maybe she feels the way I do now. She's surprised that she's not excited with the anticipation of us meeting. I feel the same. It's barely worth going all that way just to see Jane for a weekend. But if I don't go I'll be extra miserable. So, I lose if I go and lose if I don't. I'll go and expect to find that her worries will have disappeared by the following day."

Thoughts on Saturday 8.8.70 - we got engaged:
"I feel sad. Jane left this morning. Now I have to face an indefinite period of up to eight months before we can be together for more than a short visit. Even a short break is difficult.

"We are engaged to be married. It seems a bit silly when you think about it. I've known her for only seven months and we intend to marry in three years' time. It was only three months ago when I wrote 'I find myself missing Jane'. Only six weeks since I decided I love her. And what about the snags I've talked about? The differences of opinions and interests? I think these things don't matter. It doesn't matter if Jane doesn't want to go canoeing. And differences in opinions add variety. Little things such as likes and dislikes in clothes are unimportant. We have never had a proper argument and Jane has never annoyed me in the way some, like mum, dad and Mary do. I think Jane and I have a better relationship than do Mary and her John. I imagine some marriages are love-hate relationships. A long time ago I recognised that Jane has some very desirable asset as a wife. She's tidy, doesn't grumble or moan, and makes love in a way that I am sure must be better than average. I could describe hundreds of instances that show she is better than most women in things that matter. I don't have to. The only important thing is that I love her a lot, assuming there are degrees of love.

"At £25, the engagement ring was a little more expensive than I anticipated, but my expenditure for the past two weeks (including the purchase of a photographic enlarger) was less than expected. A lot of people would criticise me for spending that much on Jane. In a strange way it is satisfying for me to realise that although over £100 of my money has gone this year I'm not disappointed. I spent over £25 on a camera and £50 on a motorbike. There are many other ways I could have spent that money less usefully. Jane's ring is a surety that she won't just walk out on me.

"The thing I find difficult to grasp is the thought of getting married. With the ring, the jewellers gave me a booklet titled, 'The Wedding Book'. I can't register the fact that its content is aimed at people in my situation and not others! I must get used to being engaged and that I have a fiancé. It is like the first time

I kissed a girl or my first experience of sex. In each case I expected to feel different in some way but I did not. Dave once told me he was thinking of getting married. When we had finished discussing the merits and demerits of such a union Dave simply concluded that its advantages would be 'rather nice' to have. I tend to agree.

"Jane and I agreed it would be impracticable to marry while I am still at university, though we would marry sooner if we could. It might be feasible to marry sooner, if anything happens. Jane said that no one has to get married and that cheered me. When we talked about this our conversation drifted away from fear of pregnancy and towards fear of losing each other. When I suggested that during our long period of separation we might meet other partners she started crying. The more I tried to reconcile the situation the deeper I got into the mire. She ended up thinking that I did not trust her. This worried me because I had to agree with what she said. In reality I didn't trust her, especially since she has told me more about the boyfriend called Steve. I was shocked to learn what must have gone on behind my back. But then I think about my own disloyalty through my relationship with Jo. That makes me equally unfaithful."

Thoughts on Sunday 16.8.70 - I discover that Jane is pregnant:
"Well. Today's Thursday (20th August) and I'm not thinking what I expected I would. The worry is not the triviality I expected but practically the worst imaginable. Everything I wrote turned out to be the opposite to what I expected. My experiences of the last few days exceed everything that has happened to me so far in my life. Instead of being a boring 'nothing ever happens' sort of person I'm now faced with the a most distressing situation, a mess even. What is the worst thing that Jane could worry about? Being pregnant. But worse than that. Not by me.

"Last Sunday I drove to Bradford, met Jane after work at BRI, took her to her house to collect her things and drove back to Dagnall. She seemed so nice that I already felt the 340-mile journey was worthwhile. We had the house to ourselves because dad was abroad and mum was staying at Lavendon. I asked Jane what it was she had been worrying about but she firmly refused to tell me. She did not tell me in bed and I did not persist asking. On Monday night she was still clearly worried and I decided that I needed to find the reason. I asked if it concerned me and she said it did. I asked if anyone else was involved and she said yes. Was it Steve? Yes. Now I could guess what was coming but Jane would only tell me in yes/no answers.

So, I asked her directly, 'Are you pregnant by Steve?'
Her answer was affirmative.

"She cried a bit and said she would be happy if it was mine. Then she told me everything I asked her and she said she would do anything I wanted her to. My first reaction was to feel extremely jealous, that someone should steal from me what was mine. I was slightly cheered but a bit surprised when she confirmed that I was the first person she had been to bed with. She told me about the very day it happened with Steve. She said that Steve is a womaniser, having about a dozen girlfriends including the one he lives with. She met him whilst out with a couple of friends one evening. Jane visited his flat one day when she was working nights simply because he invited her and she accepted. She said she was not going to let him get his own way but he was too strong for her.

'Why didn't you just push him off?' I asked.

'He's strong, you know,' was her reply.

Jane said she left immediately after that, much to his displeasure.

"I can't really say it served her right. I could if it was me that made her pregnant. She made a series of mistakes and this is the result. I still love her. Perhaps more so now that we have a deeper understanding of each other. We have talked a lot over these past few days. Now we probably know more about each other than anyone else does. And that's what marriage is all about. And we will get married in three years' time.

"Mum phoned to say she was coming home and asked if I was alone. I told her that I wasn't.

"Who've you got there then?"

"Jane."

"Oh. Where's she sleeping?"

"In my bed."

Then I hurriedly added, "And I've got a sleeping bag in the study."

Well, that was true and fortunately mum didn't ask where I was sleeping.

"We then went to bed together almost immediately and I set my alarm for 12.30 a.m. The idea of getting up at that time was strange so I kept checking to see how much time we had left. When the alarm sounded I shut it off quickly thinking there were others in the house. I gathered my clothes and went to the study and was soon back to sleep in my sleeping bag. In my sleep the tightness of the bag around me felt like Jane's arms around me. I wished they were."

Thoughts on Thursday 27.8.70 - Why marry?

"Why do I have to marry her? All this time I've been thinking it was a good idea. It would be much simpler if we didn't get married yet. I want to marry her. I thought marriage was the simplest answer to our situation. Now I think it would be best to have the baby adopted soon after birth. Jane could live here at Dagnall during the later stages of pregnancy if she wanted. After adoption, she could return to work and complete her nurse training. Then we could marry as already decided in three years from now. Jane probably won't want to have the baby adopted, or it might be difficult to arrange. She might agree to adoption now, but when it arrives we could both feel differently. The idea of bringing up the child of the man who took my girlfriend made me feel sick. Perhaps I will see the baby simply as Jane's and overlook who fathered it. To hate the child would then be hating a part of Jane.

Extract from my letter to Jane

"It was good seeing my old friends yesterday. I spent most of the afternoon sitting in the lab talking. They never seem to do any work there either! I gave Paul a lift home to Hitchin and met his wife and five-month old baby. Personally, I don't think I've seen such an ugly baby before but that doesn't seem to matter. They seem happy enough. Afterwards we went to Julie's flat just around the corner. She got married three weeks ago and they've got quite a nice flat. We talked about a lot of things like how well they were managing but if I was to write down all the thoughts I had yesterday it would take too long.

"I didn't get to sleep for a long time last night thinking how well it could work out for us. I know I'm always comparing and I shouldn't really but I think we could make a better pair than most couples. Last night, when I did eventually get to sleep I had weird dreams about you and me. I can't remember much about it but there was this big old house with lots of strange people in it and we couldn't get away from them. We went into a large room that was almost empty. It had dark wooden walls and furniture. I kept locking doors to keep these weird people out but they kept appearing from other doors and wandering about. All the time these people had sick disapproving looks on their faces.

"I was trying to devise a way by which I could be with you as much as possible with the least financial problems. One of the solutions I thought of was to get married soon and for you to live here in Dagnall until Easter by which time the baby will be born and I will have accumulated some money. Then we could get a house or flat in Bradford. During the summer vacation I could get a job in Bradford and save enough to see us through to my next period of industrial training. It would work, but it would be difficult. I think my parents would agree to it but I don't like the way it involves them with you and the baby staying here. I like to live life my way, which is different to that of my parents. Living with them is bound to have some effect which I don't like. On the other hand, it would only be for a short while and it would be a fairly simple solution. If you agree with this suggestion I will discuss the whole plan with them. I thought about all of this last night and at the end wondered why I was giving so much thought to something which doesn't have to be my problem. You know I have a selfish reason for everything. The selfish reason is love, not just because I love you, which I do a lot, but because of love nothing else matters. I don't suppose you understand what I'm getting at but I can't really explain what I mean. It's not just because I care about you a lot, that would be the unselfish answer. It is simply because love exists. Just remember that I love you a lot and you needn't worry about me leaving you. It's the thought of you leaving me that worries me and the day I dread is the day you stop loving me.

"I think I've said too much again, like I did the other day. I make you worry more by saying all these things than I would if I said nothing. I tend to write letters for the benefit of straightening out my own thoughts rather than to convey a message. The only message I have is that I love you and I don't want to lose you."

Sunday 30.8.70 Extract from my letter to Jane:
"I have been to Wells-next-the-Sea to fetch Dorothy and Mary home from holiday there. In the evening Mary and I went into town for a drink. Before we went I told Dorothy and Mary that we were engaged and they were pleased. Mary was envious. When we were at the pub I decided that it would be an ideal situation to tell Mary about you. I thought about whether I should tell her for a while and decided that it was best I did tell her. So I decided to tell her in the order that everything happened so by the time I reached telling her that you were pregnant she understood the picture clearly. She feels sorry for you because I suppose she can understand by now how easy it is for a girl to get into a mess. However, it might be difficult to tell my parents for instance in the same way as I told Mary. They wouldn't understand so easily. But if I did tell them I'm sure they wouldn't think all that badly about you, in the way you think they would. If you went to a home perhaps I wouldn't tell them. Going to a home has a lot of advantages but also disadvantages. I don't know anything about such homes but questions that occur to me now are how you keep paid for and where there is a home you could go to? If you went to a home in London that would be good in a way because I could see you at weekends and even some evenings. One thing that worries me is about going into a home is the

psychological effect it might have. It may not have any effect at all of course but I don't want you to change. I love you just the way you are, the way you think, your ideas and outlook on life. That is what I fear might be changed in you or indeed in anyone who is shut in a home, away from life in the way he or she knows it. You may think this is all rubbish but it does bother me a bit. I love you more than I can say, as you are now. You are different to anybody else I have ever known and as you are so precious to me I'm naturally concerned if you should change in any way. I'll always love you; you can depend on that. A home is probably the simplest answer but don't go there just to suit other people. It is you that really matters and not just me and if you think living in a home would be sheer hell, you shouldn't go. On the other hand, you may like the idea and if so I shall be very glad if it brings you closer to me. I hope I haven't confused you by saying all these things but you did ask me what I think!

"I think adoption is the right answer now. I can't stand the thought of bringing up the child of the man who went out with the girl I love. But perhaps when the child is born I would see it as its mother's and forget about its father. Then to despise the child would be to despise part of you and I could never do that. You too could also feel differently when the child is born and what is the mental effect on a child without proper parents? Yet despite all these points I still think you should have the child adopted. As you say, it's not practical to keep it and when I go to Bradford at Easter it will all be over. In three years it will be almost forgotten and we can be really happy together. A little suffering now will be worth it later on. Don't worry too much: it'll be all right in the end and I'll still love you as I do now."

Autumn 1970:
Due to his poor exam results at the end of Year 1, Craig was demoted to the ordinary course and had to stay at university to repeat some work. My first industrial placement was with Laporte Industries Limited laboratories in Luton so from September 1970 to March 1971 I stayed at home in Dagnall, which was 10 miles away from work. I regularly walked our dog Sian, especially in the nearby woods of Ashridge.

Sian

I visited Jane every third weekend, borrowing mum's white Hillman Imp to drive there on Friday and sometimes clocking up 800 miles before getting home early Monday morning. I would stay at her parent's house, sleeping in Jane's bed while she slept with her mother. Her father slept in a room on the second floor and did not socialise with his family at home so I had not yet met him. Jane had told me little about him.

Jane and I wrote letters to each other every day. I kept most of hers.

Thoughts:
"My daily letters to Jane have made her worry about me being angry with her about something. I wasn't angry but a bit bothered that she hadn't replied to questions I'd asked or given any opinions on what I had said. Today I got a letter from her containing no less than 16 pages of written notepaper. Most of it was describing a book but it was still a very nice long letter. It has made me feel more cheerful. Over the past few days I have been miserable. My imagination got carried away with what Jane might be doing or thinking. I couldn't decide whether I needed sex or love most. I felt that I might feel a lot better if I had sex. I wondered how important sex is in our relationship and concluded that it is quite important. The relationship is still beautiful without

it for a while. I would be glad to see Jane, with or without sex, but sex is the best way we have of expressing our love toward each other.

"In the letter I wrote to Jane yesterday. I said that what I miss most, next to her, is a good old hearty laugh. I want to be able to laugh until my eyes water. I remember evenings at Tong when we really laughed. I was truly happy. Even when I'm alone with Jane I can't say I'm really happy because I'm dreading the thought of when she's not there all the time."

"I wish it was three years from now and then we would be married. I think it's bad to wish time away like that seeing as I expect to look back on these few years as being the best in my life. I've been reading what I wrote three years ago. It doesn't really seem all that long ago. It was the year I cycled around Scotland. I promised myself that I'd return to Scotland some time but still haven't done it. I shall have to go with Jane some time. I think we should go to either Scotland or the Channel Islands next year. After all, if we're not going to get married for three years we may as well have some good holidays together. It's been four weeks since I saw Jane now. She must be showing signs of pregnancy now. In her letters Jane doesn't seem to show her feelings very much. It is her actions that show the most, though her little things mean more than what they would with most people. This is an extract from one of her letters:

'We can get married when you like but I think Easter is a bit soon. I'll need a while to recover you see! But I don't really see why we can't get married next year, late next year anyway. After all, I'll be twenty next year and that's ancient. You can't go anywhere when we're married because I won't let you. If I get pregnant again it doesn't really matter. We'll have to start our eight boys sometime!'

"I can't decide whether being married whilst being at university will help or hinder my academic work. I could get more work done if we were married. Most of the time I wasted when not working at Tong was spent messing about, talking or going to the Dog. If we were married you could tell me to get on with my work. I'd get loads more done!

I felt that mum didn't trust me at all. She still considered her children to be as pure and innocent as when we were aged seven. When I asked her if it would be alright for Jane to stay the weekend after next. She replied,
        "Yes, I think we should be back from holiday then."

One of my favourite singers was Bob Dylan. When his LP 'New Morning' was released I drove into Dunstable especially and hurried home to play the record. It was always exciting to buy a new record.

One of the tracks was 'Sign On The Window':

<blockquote>
Sign on the window says 'lonely',
Sign on the door said 'no company allowed',
Sign on the street says 'you don't own me'
Sign on the porch says 'three's a crowd.'
</blockquote>

I was amused by the oxymoron 'Bargain Basement Upstairs' printed on a sign in the window of the record centre.

Dunstable Record Centre

My favourite Bob Dylan track was 'Three Angels':

<blockquote>
Three angels up above the street
Each one playing a horn
Dressed in green robes with wings that stick out
They've been there since Christmas morn
The wildest cat from Montana passes by in a flash
Then a lady in a bright orange dress
</blockquote>

Saturday 14.11.70 Extract from my letter to Jane:
"Something I read this evening bothers me. It read, "Most people fall in and out of love several times before they find their life partner but they always think it's the real thing every time." The thing that bothers me most about this is that a lot of people will use this argument to put us off getting married. Its author might say to someone he loved and wanted to marry that he wouldn't do so because he felt he hadn't loved a sufficient number so far. He might regret that decision for the rest of his life. Anyway, you needn't worry about me saying that. I've never loved anyone as much as I love you. I can't see how that can be an argument against marrying you. It is the main reason.

"I had some weird dreams last night, right up to the moment I awoke. It was a combination of thoughts on my mind before I fell asleep, mixed up with other things. The part I remember best was really strange. I was going to go on this spaceship thing and I didn't want to. I knew I would never come back. I kept finding things wrong with the spaceship. With just 30 minutes to blast off I asked my mate to give me 15 minutes alone with Jane. I really thought I was going to die in half an hour. A bit later I was standing by the door inside a blue Bradford bus as it was moving away. You were standing on the corner of the street. I shouted something to you and was upset because it wasn't what I meant to say. It was too late to say more because the bus moved away. Next, I was looking across a valley at veteran cars racing madly on the hill opposite me. They were travelling terribly fast along a narrow bumpy track, turning around and going back the same way. They were bound to be crashes, but I didn't see any.

"You asked why I think my thoughts are so important. What a person thinks tells a lot more about him than what he does. A person may think one thing and do another. What he thinks is the more important part. When I say 'a person' here I'm meaning myself. If I see my past thoughts I can see what sort of person I was at that time. In my writing, the only person who can 'pass judgment on', as you put it, is myself. If anyone got hold of these writings the only person they could incriminate is me.

"You also asked about Teresa. I went out with Teresa for quite a long time when she was 12 and I was 14. I would cycle to her house after school before going home. She was a nice girl. I don't know why we stopped. I suppose we just got fed up with each other.

"Talking about fainting in church, I fainted once during school assembly. I was singing a hymn merrily when in the middle of a verse I found myself floating gently to the feet of the children around me. When I came to I was in a horizontal position being carried out along the isle with rows of faces staring at me. From then on, every time we had to stand up in assembly I had cold sweats. I struggled to stay on my feet. Once, I walked out, pretending I had an appointment at the dentists. If I had stayed any longer I would have passed out. The moment I got out of the hall I was alright, proving that the feeling was purely psychological."

During her final months of pregnancy, Jane lived with a family (the Greens) in a bungalow at Huby, near Harrogate. We continued to send each other letters every day. On my visit to see her there on 21st November I bought Jane a black teddy bear. She preferred to say that we 'adopted' him.

Here are some of the things Jane wrote:
     'I've decided to call the teddy Timothey. He's sat here now and he's ever so cute. He doesn't look like a Timothey but that doesn't matter. He's my furry friend. He talks to me and smells of mothballs. Mrs Green thinks Timothey is a lovely teddy and her daughter likes him as well. He's sat here now and he's my very favourite teddy. Timothey does have an e in it I think. Well it does now because I've asked him and he said he wanted an e in it. He's sat here now and he's lovely. I've just sniffed him and he still smells of mothballs but not as much as before.
     'Timothey sends his regards and says he's being as good as I always am.
     'If we go on writing long letters we can always paper our walls with all the letters so you can always have a look and see what you wrote.
     'Startrek is rubbish. It's so far-fetched and daft but seeing as it's you I'll let you watch it if it's still on when we're married. Not that we'll have a television but you can always go and watch it in a television shop window on one of their tellies.
     'Did you know Harold Wilson was in Bradford yesterday? I never saw the nice man. I think I'll vote next time because he's a lovely man and better than Mr Heath.'

I numbered the pages of my letters. By 24th November I had reached page 484:
"Dearest Jane,
It's now just twelve hours since I left you. All this afternoon I've been thinking of 12 hours ago and all this afternoon of 24 hours ago. I just can't say how much I wish I was with you now and how much I love you.
I got back at about a quarter past four this morning so only had about three hours sleep. It wasn't difficult to wake up though, but I've felt tired all morning.

I stopped at a service station at 2.30 and had an ice cream. It was harder to stay awake whilst driving than last time when it was two hours earlier. This time, there was no rain and it was warmer, so for a lot of the journey I had the window wide open and sometimes put my hand outside for fresh air. Once, whilst thinking of you, I must have dozed off for a second or two. I was following lane markings and when I came to my senses couldn't understand whether I was still on the motorway or had taken a slip road off it. There was no other traffic so I stopped where I was. There was grass immediately on my right. It took me a few seconds to decide if the road on the other side of the grass was the opposite carriageway or the one I was supposed to be driving on. I decided the latter, drove over the grass carefully and continued on my way, now much more alert than before. I tried lots of different ways to stay awake. Eating helps a lot and I wished I'd taken some apples. Imagining what would happen if I crossed the central reservation or went onto the hard shoulder into a parked lorry helped to keep me awake. I listened to my tape recorder but someone seems to have run down its batteries! I wished you were there to talk to.

"Another person in your situation might find it alright but you're different. It's a pity that what are such good qualities of yours are responsible for making you miserable. I mean that perhaps if you weren't such a good person it would be easier for you. It's just not fair that it should be that way. I don't want you to change; you're so wonderful the way you are. What I was trying to say on Monday is that you could modify a few details to suit the situation without really changing yourself. I so much want you to be happy but I seem to be fighting a losing battle. Maybe you prefer to be miserable, but there's no need to worry about anything like I do. Perhaps you do have reason to be miserable but I can't think of anything you ought to be worrying about. Can you?"

"I can't explain what I mean but I don't expect you or anybody else to understand my impracticable mind. Why do you want me to change my views? What should I change? You should accept me for what I am and not try to change me to 'think like everyone else'. I can't change what I believe to be right. I don't see how I can change anything I don't want to and I'm satisfied with what I believe. I love you ever so much: just remember that and even if I get a mixed-up mind don't fuss."

That weekend I drove 640 miles. I accompanied Jane to church in Harrogate. She was brought up as a Catholic and would normally go to church every Sunday. I was staying overnight at Jane's parents' house in Bradford. In the evening I felt depressed.

Jane wrote in her letter:

"Why weren't you happy last Sunday evening? Didn't you enjoy going to church? It was probably me. I'm enough to make anybody miserable and I'm sorry. Everything is my fault you know. I always seem to cause problems for people and I don't mean to. I don't deserve you at all. I cause nothing but trouble for you and make you miserable all the time. I'm glad you put up with me though because I don't know what I'd do without you, ever. I love you so very much and I miss you like mad. And never mind perhapsing you'll not come and see me until Easter. That would be awful and you shouldn't even think about it. In all that time I'd go mad so you needn't bother doing it. Surely, every three weeks is better than not until Easter."

My reply:

"The letter I got from you today was such a nice one that I feel sorry that I write you miserable letters sometimes. I suppose the reasons I was unhappy was for a lot of little things. I didn't mind going to church. I think it was a better mass than the one at Dunstable we went to. It was nice talking to you in that pub as well. Then I started to think about having to go home the next day and then we started talking about Steve. That upset me a lot. You implied that he wanted a baby. That makes it better in a way but it did upset me, especially as you wouldn't answer my question directly. If you say anything more about it in your next letter please don't say more than a few words. You know how it makes me feel and there's no point talking about it any more. That's the past and it's finished with. We may as well forget about it, but if I've wronged you in any way by what I've just said please don't hesitate to defend yourself. I was disappointed when I found that I had lost your house key. I felt awful when I had to return you to Huby and spend 16 hours without you. I could get in the house at Bradford. It wasn't your fault I felt miserable. I wish you wouldn't keep blaming yourself. If it wasn't for you I'd be a completely different person – always fed up and with nothing really nice to look forward to. You don't cause trouble for me. There may be some awkward or complicated situations for me to work out but not trouble. Without you my life would be duller than I can imagine. You don't make me miserable all of the time. Some of the things that you have to put up with sometimes disappoint me so I become miserable but it's not you making me miserable. Sometimes you make me very happy. All the time I'm with you I'm happy inside. To me, you're the most wonderful person imaginable and it makes me very pleased indeed that you should want such a selfishly dull person as me.

"I couldn't stand it not seeing you until Easter but I'm sure it must make your life much unhappier having to live your life in this monotonous way. Three weeks is better than three months and you needn't worry about me not coming. I'm going to continue coming to see you whether you like it or not!"

Jane replied:
"I won't say anything about Steve if you don't want me to and one day I'll tell you all about it but I don't feel like telling you just now. It's difficult to tell anyway. I suppose you don't have to know Steve to understand. Anyway, I won't say any more about him. I agree with you about what's done is done and that's that but everything else past shouldn't be forgotten. I can't forget all the horrible things and remember the nice things. I just can't do that. I remember everything I can whether I want to or not."

In between seeing each other, we both wished time by, longing for the third weekend when we would see each other for a brief period. But the weekends passed too quickly and it was time to wish ahead another three weeks.

Letters from Jane on 9th and 13th December 1970:
"I wish it was Friday, but it's not so far away now. Then it will be another three weeks that I'll have to wait but I'll manage somehow. I love you ever so much and I miss you. You shouldn't be so far away from me because I don't like it and I miss you so much.

"It seems so silly only seeing you for such a short time. This weekend was shorter than ever as well [since I'd travelled by train]. You should take Friday and Monday off or not go back at all and then I'd be happy, honest I would. It's just that I'm always thinking about when you have to go back and it's never very far away. You won't have to come and see me many more times will you because it will soon be over and done with and I can't wait till that time comes; it will be great and I will come and see you if you want."

As the months went by, Jane became bigger and bigger as 'Fred' as we called the baby developed inside her. Jane was frequently depressed, bored, miserable and felt neglected.

The following extract from Jane's letters show how she felt.
"Fred keeps kicking me tonight and I dread to think what he'll be like when he gets bigger. I bet I won't be able to sleep for him moving about. I didn't realise having a baby entailed so much. It's daft. They should just leave you alone and let you have the thing in peace. Half of what you're supposed to do is unnecessary and I've no intention of doing it. Mrs. Prentice has got to have

iron injections every day and she's having a fit about it. She didn't take her iron tablets for ages so that's why she has to have injections. You should stay with me and make sure I take my iron tablets every day!

"It's funny to have something growing inside you and it keeps reminding me it's there and it's alive. I just hope I don't like the thing too much when it's born but I'm bound to feel something for it and I'll never forget you know. Maybe it's difficult for you to understand but I just can't forget and why should I?"

"About me being miserable. Today I don't feel miserable but I can't help it if sometimes I do. I've nothing else to think about and usually I'm bored. I can't really help punishing myself either. I can't think I haven't done wrong because I have and what you do wrong you get punished for and I can't forget that. I don't feel as bad as I did about it all if that's any consolation to you. When I'm in a self-pitying mood (like last night) it's worse. Other people do things and get away with it but I don't.

"The headmaster of my school is leaving next year so I'm going to apply to the headmistress because it was such a lovely school and I want it to be like that again and for everybody to enjoy school, it's such a nice place. I want a few of the old teachers that have left to come back as well. Father Burke, the school chaplain was good as well. I could easily tell him my troubles and he'd understand."

"I think God is very unfair sometimes and it's too much even for my mother to come and see me. I wouldn't mind if she didn't have the car but it's not difficult for her to get here. I haven't written to her yet either and I don't think I will. She can go mad. She won't even bother to tell Anne how to get here or bring her next week when she comes here. She's awful my mother and I don't care what anybody else says about her. She's done some rotten things to me. I just want to go back to Bradford and do as I like again. I'm so fed up of everything. Nothing ever improves and when you do come I'm rotten to you and you don't deserve it. Maybe if I didn't have so much time to think about things I wouldn't feel so bad but at the moment I'd had enough. This time next week Christmas Day will be over and it's going to be a funny Christmas. I won't be able to go to church and I'll feel awful if the Green's relations come or we go there because I'm sure they don't want me dragging along."

I did not visit Jane that Christmas because I was staying at home with my family. Jane stayed with the Greens and her mum paid them a visit. Jane's letters show that she resented her mum's behaviour:

"She was all upset when she left and put her arms around me and asked me if I was alright and she said she loved me then she went. I just can't tell her anything and that's the trouble. I answer what she asks and that's it and I don't feel I can tell her anything else. What does it matter anyway; she's not interested in how I feel and never has been so why start now.

"I can't tell my mother I'd appreciate a few more calls. Why should I? If she wanted to come and see me she'd come but she doesn't want to so she makes excuses. I've never implied that I'd like her to come more often but she must realise that I'm bored and there isn't much to do. Before I came she said she'd come often and take me out somewhere. She shouldn't of said that if she didn't mean it. She's not bothered if I'm unhappy. She knew when I was working at hospital that I didn't like it very much but she'd of gone mad if I'd left. She also knows I'm not dead keen on going back but she wants me to go back whether I'm happy there or not. I'm not trying to put all the blame on her but she's never bothered whether any of us have been happy or not. As long as no-one finds out about all this and it doesn't upset her world too much she's not bothered what I do though. You were there that morning she said I was getting out of it by going away and it was her and Belinda that would suffer. She said that to me before as well and it's a horrible thing to say. She says she loves me but she wants me out of the way so people don't find out and say something to her. It's so daft really. It all depends as she sees it on what other people say and how it will affect her and Belinda. I'm not bothered what anyone else says but she can't understand that. Maybe it's as well she doesn't come often because I never know what to say to her when I see her. We all just sat there on Saturday with Belinda discreetly looking at my tummy to see how fat I was."

Letter 101 from me dated Sunday 27.12.70, page 657:
"When I started numbering my letters I never expected to write more than 100. I remember thinking of 100 letters and it seemed an awful lot but it isn't really. It won't be long now before I will never have to write to you again, except perhaps very occasionally. I shall miss writing to you then but it will be much better being able to see you. How often will I be able to see you? Will I be able to spend a night with you or have I to wait years? I love you ever such a lot. In a way I'm worried about the future because I want it to be just fine."

January 1971

Extracts of letters from Jane:

"I've just drank a glass of Ribena and I want some more now.

"I just drank a glass of Ribena and I've nearly drunk all the Ribena now so you'll have to come very soon and bring me some more. Timothey sends his regards and says he'll let you take his photograph and not run away like me.

"I had this horrible dream last night. I can't remember much of it now but I had the baby and it was about one year old and it was ever so big and had teeth and horrible teeth and it was an awful baby. It was in the playroom here. It was a boy as well and everyone thought he was lovely but really he was ugly as ever and so big."

I also had a horrible dream that was repeated on several occasions. In the dream I am driving along at night when suddenly the lights all go out. When I put my foot on the brake pedal it isn't there and I frantically search around for it in the dark with visions of brick walls, ditches and cars about to come at me. It's every so worrying and I kick ever so hard trying to find the pedal so that it hurts my leg. Last night I was sat up trying to find the handbrake as well but I couldn't find that either. After a while it slowly dawns on me that I'm not in a car after all and I'm very relieved.

Letter 113 from me dated Tuesday 12.1.71, page 718:

"I shall enjoy reading our letters in 18 years' time and I shall save all yours. I shall still be loving you just as much as I do now, I'm sure. I think I should make a big box to put all yours in because they take up a lot of room on the bookshelf. I know you say I shouldn't but I keep finding myself comparing girls with you. You seem to have all the good points that are bad points in most people. If I started to give examples of what I mean I'd be here all night. You're such a good girl that there's no one in the world to compare with you. I'm sure I would never ever find anyone that I could ever love as much as I love you. I'm not even going to try to find anyone else, ever. I promise you that. It just isn't possible for me to love anyone else more than I love you."

Whilst living at home I would borrow mum's Hillman Imp to visit Jane every third weekend, typically clocking up 600 miles on each trip. I suggested to Jane that we could go on a boating holiday together at Easter after the baby was born and taken away. She generally agreed with the suggestion but appeared to show some concerns.

Letter from Jane dated Friday 15.1.71:
"You seem to think I'm going to say I'm not going on holiday at the last minute or that my mum's going to stop me from going. I can't help what my mum thinks and I won't say I'm not going either so don't think I will. Do you believe me? I hope so because I mean it."

My reply:
"When you say 'wouldn't mind' going on a boat at Easter do you mean that you like the idea? I hope you do. I told mum that I was thinking about it and she thought it was a good idea. I would be extremely disappointed if you were to say that you can't go on holiday with me at Easter."

Letter from me dated Saturday 16.1.71, page 731:
"You didn't seem very cheerful when I rang you up either. The phone call reminded me of when I rang you up several months ago. It just didn't seem right somehow. I hope you're OK and not worrying too much again.

"I posted eight letters today enquiring about boating holidays. The more I think about it the more I like the idea. My only worry is that you'll change your mind. Please don't do that."

The following weekend we spent what was perhaps the best and most memorable weekend visit I made to Jane while she was pregnant. I decided to go that particular weekend because Christine, the girlfriend of Michelle, a student at Bradford, wanted a lift there. We had a pleasant non-stop journey of three hours and talked most of the way. I left her at Michelle's house and went straight to Jane's mum's house in Victor Road. Her mum, Jean was at home for a while until the doctor said she could return to work. I was invited to stay there and given a key. I visited Jane at Huby and returned to Victor Road at about one o'clock. Sambo the dog barked at first. He was sitting on a chair in the kitchen. I stroked him and he jumped down into his basket. I covered him with a blanket and he snuggled down like a child."

I woke up at 9.45. This was late as Jane was expecting me at 10.15. I had breakfast of corn flakes and toasted teacakes prepared for me by Jane's younger sister, Belinda. Jean had gone to to stay with a friend who had a Boston Terrier like Sambo called Pup. We didn't know the friend so when Jean made the visits she just said she was going to Pup's. Perhaps Jean had a lover. Jane was neither disappointed nor surprised when I arrived late. We had already decided to go to the seaside, but first we visited Harrogate. It was wet and misty, but not cold. I bought some fudge from the shop I had found before that sold a huge selection of the delicious sweets. I also got some green mints for my journey back home. We set off towards York and Bridlington, stopping on the way to fill up with ICI petrol and buy some apples. At York I parked not far from the Minster in a 'Trust the Motorist' car park and we agreed to be untrustworthy and not pay. We visited an olde-world, Dickensian style pub and visited the Minster and bought some iced buns. At Bridlington we parked by the promenade. It was slightly misty, the sea greenish-grey with moderate waves. The harbour was so picturesque that I couldn't have captured it adequately even if I'd brought my camera. There were about 20 fishing boats bobbing up and down in the harbour, their bright colours contrasting with the grey sea and sky. Bright orange nets were sprawled across their decks. It could have been a scene for a jigsaw puzzle. Pulled up half out of the water was a sad old boat, missing its propeller and in need of care and attention. The town was not very busy. I bought sticks of rock for Belinda, her friend and another as a souvenir, and some flowers for Jean. We ate chips in the car and tea in a café. It was getting dark as we drove to an empty carpark near the coastguard's house and we sat there listening to the sea, not wanting to leave. On the way back we stopped at a small pub with a little dog that greeted us by jumping into the car when we stopped. The Hull Brewery beer was very bitter. It was a nice pub and when we left everyone said goodnight, reminding me of the time when we went to bed together at the Lodge. We stopped at another pub in Stamford Bridge. As we neared Huby, Jane seemed disappointed to be ending the day but there was nowhere else to stop.

Sunday was a sunny day and after picking up Jane we drove along the minor roads heading northwards until we reached a wide track leading off the road. There was a man collecting entrance fees. It was Brimham Rocks. I parked overlooking a steep drop. The strong wind made it difficult to open the car doors and we didn't spend long walking around the rocks, but I felt warm and comfortable when I held Jane in the shelter of a rock. We returned to the car and Timothey the bear and headed towards Richmond, stopping at the Crown in Grewelthorpe on the way. It was a real old type of pub and the scene might have been from 50 years ago. It had wooden rafters, a very tall bar with little behind it and an open fire. All the guests were men, swearing colourfully as they played dominoes. The barman, who had a patch on one eye, shouted at a customer for leaving the door open. There was biscuits and cheese on the tables and the barman gave us each a pickled green tomato, but Jane couldn't eat hers. When we left I took care to shut the door properly.

Our next stop was in the large cobbled square of Masham where I bought some fig rolls and a packet of mints. I don't know why I bought the mints because there was already some in the car. When we got to Richmond's cobbled square it started to rain. This time I bought chocolate covered cinder toffee. Jane likes the way the cinder goes soft when it's left standing for a while. I took Jane to show her where I once went canoeing near Easby Abbey. We walked over the disused railway bridge, where you could look between gaps below your feet and see the buff coloured water rushing below. We followed the river downstream by car and stopping in a layby. We listened to Pick of the Pops on the radio, but the reception was poor.

"I want some fish and chips", said Jane.

So, we went to Harry Ramsden's at Guiseley. It was a longer drive than I expected but the food was as good as always. This was the one and only Harry Ramsden's, so famous that customers from far and wide visited the restaurant in coach loads. You could buy take-aways or eat in the adjoining 'palace', an oak-panelled restaurant with chandeliers, which was said to have been based on the Ritz Hotel in London. It held the Guinness world record for being the largest fish and chip shop in the world, seating 250 people and serving nearly one million customers a year.

We continued driving towards Bradford and started talking about our friends. I asked Jane what her friends thought about me.

She said, "They like you because you're helping me and I'm such a miserable person."

Then she cried. I almost did too.

We walked around the streets of Bradford. Whilst crossing a road we passed a woman with a very cute little dog. Jane stroked the dog and the woman offered it to us, saying it was an unwanted present. We wanted to say yes, but there was no way we could keep it. The dog wanted to sit and stay with us. Then as the woman jerked it away with the lead, the poor thing yelped. Next we visited the Turf, a pub near the corner of Manningham Park. The park keeper, who Jane knows, was there and they said hello to each other. A man opposite us was sat alone and looked very sad. A glass of Guinness stood on the table in front of him. We felt sorry for him.

We started back towards Huby through Shipley to the traffic lights where the way ahead leads to Harrogate and Huby and left to Baildon Moor. On our last visit to Baildon Moor we made love there in the car.

"Left or straight on?" I asked Jane

"Left" was her reply.

Her reply made me feel excited. At the turning leading to the track where we went before I asked the same question and got the same answer. We stopped, well away from the road. It was past midnight when we left. We didn't want to part even after reaching Huby, so we stayed a long time in the car outside the gate. It was 2.15 when I departed to start my long weary journey home. At 5.30 I was driving through Dunstable. There was not much traffic on the yellow lit streets, the road was clear and all the lights green. Milkmen buzzed from door to door in their three-wheeled floats like bees collecting nectar from flowers. Boys with bikes stood outside brightly lit newsagents waiting to collect and then deliver the morning papers. Was it morning or is it still night time? I had driven from one day to another: from Sunday night to Monday morning.

Thoughts on 25th January 1971:

"I had only two hours sleep last night but what a lovely weekend! I suppose it wasn't a lot different to any other time but this one wasn't spoilt by being bored or cold. We went somewhere on both days and enjoyed it there. I rang Jane earlier this evening and she was happy. I forgot most of what I wanted to say but it was nice to speak to her. She sounded near and it made it seem as though I'd only been gone from her ten minutes. 24 hours ago we were wandering around Bradford. It seemed so idyllic there, like I was in a sort of dream. In fact, the whole weekend was like that: a sort of story in itself, and that is why I originally wanted to write about it. I decided I'd write something when we were at the harbour in Bridlington. I didn't have my camera with me and it was so picturesque I wanted to record the meaning of it all. I doubt if a photograph would have been able to do that anyway. The brightly coloured fishing boats bobbing up and down, with orange nets lying on the decks were pretty. Everywhere I looked on many an occasion this weekend could have made a wonderful painting. The harbour, that old pub and the sad man in the bar at The Turf all made great impressions on the romantic side of my mind.

Normally, I would spend all my evenings writing letters to Jane. The postal strike prevented any further letters and made phone calls more difficult, and it made me feel sad. Britain's postal workers had demanded a pay rise of 15–20%, and refused a lower offer. Their demands were not met so the country's first national postal strike began on 20 January and lasted until Monday 8 March 1971, which was after the baby was born. During this time decimal currency was introduced in the UK.

I booked a cruiser from Chertsey to hire from the week beginning 26th March. It was good to have something definite to look forward to. We only had five weeks to wait. The baby was due at the end of February so Jane was bound to be out of hospital by then. When I told Jane that I'd made the booking she didn't believe me at first. From our earlier discussions and letters, I expected the baby to be taken away from her soon after its delivery. We knew that it was important for the baby to be taken away quickly and before a strong emotional bond developed between baby and mother. Jane and I could then look forward to our new lives together. The boating trip would make a good start.

The baby girl was born on Saturday 6th March 1971, two days before Jane's twentieth birthday. Mrs Green told me that evening when I phoned to talk to Jane. I felt worried. I couldn't sleep at night thinking of her in hospital with the baby. The next day I went into town during my lunch break and sent Jane some flowers with the message,

'Congratulations and Happy Birthday. All my love, Mark.'"

I was nearly 200 miles away and unable to communicate with Jane either by phone or letter. Postal workers returned to work two days after the baby was born the day so at last I could send Jane a letter.

Here's the start of my letter (page 739):
"Dearest Jane,
I love you more than I will ever be able to say. I want to tell you over and over again that I love you. It's horrible not being able to tell you in person. I'm very glad that the postmen have decide to go back but they've left it a bit late. I'm missing you more than ever and every day I seem to be missing you more."

Jane's reply:
"Thanks a lot for the flowers, there ever so nice. My mum gave me some money for my birthday and then took it back again and said she'd keep it for me, she's barmy. She never asked what the baby was like or if she was alright or anything. All she's bothered about is me going back to hospital [to work] and I don't want to go back at all. I wish she wouldn't come and see me because she only makes me mad. She can't come and see me for four days and I'm glad. She rang nanny and grandad on Saturday and told them I'd had the baby and god knows who else she's told. Mrs Green said when she told the boys that Tony was ever so pleased about it and Richard asked why they couldn't adopt her and Jamie cried. Don't you think that's nice of them. Joe wanted to know why I'd gone but he seemed to accept it when she said I'd gone to hospital. He

knew I used to go on Mondays so her never asked anything else. Mrs Green brought Timothey last night because she said he looked ever so lonely all on his own. The baby is beautiful and she's ever so good. I'm going to call her Nicole I think. I'm not having any more babies because it's horrible it nearly kills you and I don't fancy going through it again. She's got long dark straight hair and loads of it and she's ever so tiny and gorgeous. It's not so bad in hospital really. There's nothing to do except feed the baby."

I did not feel angry with Jean for not asking about the baby. After all, Jane was not expected to keep it. But Jane's letter showed that she adored the baby, had given her a name and said we would not be having any of our own. I was worried and wanted to tell Jane so I started to write my reply to her letter, but after reading it decided it was best not to send it.

This is a reply I drafted but didn't send:
"I felt bad as soon as I read the bit about your mum not asking about the baby and that's exactly what I've done, or rather not done. Perhaps your mum thinks the same as I and is avoiding asking you because she thinks you'd rather not be asked. As I continued to read your letter I must admit I felt a twinge of jealousy. I wished it was my baby you were telling me all those lovely things about. Then you said you're not having any more babies. You may be joking but then you might be serious. How am I ever going to stop feeling jealous over this baby? You probably don't realise how much this child eats away at my 'pride'. At the moment I feel I won't be content until you've carried a child of mine. This sounds terribly selfish and that's why I probably won't send you this letter but I'm writing it in an attempt to rid myself of this horrible feeling. The last and least thing that upset me in your letter is that you're afraid of telling your mum about going on holiday with me. This is the most selfish worry of mine of all about this letter but you don't realise what psychological and financial disappointment will be involved if you don't come.

"I remember once saying to you, 'The only thing that stops me from loving you is that I don't want to hurt myself.' But I did start loving you and you did hurt me, just as I expected. The worst of these hurts was you becoming pregnant by some other man. Few things can hurt a bloke more than to be told that the girl he loves is pregnant by another man. I knew you would hurt me but I didn't know how. And wow, this hurts me in the worst possible way."

Jane looked after Nicole in hospital for a week. During that time, Jane developed such a strong bond with her baby that it almost broke her heart to know that Nicole was going to taken away from her. As soon as she was given the opportunity to change her mind about adoption Jane agreed to keep the baby. It was not what I expected or wanted to happen. I was very disappointed. I still wanted Jane, but I didn't want another man's baby. At first, Jean was reluctant to have Jane and her baby living with her at their home in Bradford but later agreed that for the time being they could stay there.

Now there was no possibility of Jane taking a boating trip with a new-born baby. I needed to console myself so a week on my own doing something enjoyable should help. Also, I wasn't going to waste the holiday I had booked and paid for. I went on the 'Silver Star' with just Sian the dog. The weather was dull and most of the time I was not happy, but the scenery and experience of living aboard a boat for a week was useful and gave me an idea that I would put into practice two years later.

Mum and dad must have thought it odd that Jane decided not to join me on the boating holiday. I had not told them about her baby. They knew we were planning to get married.

'Silver Star' on the Thames

I thought I should tell them the full story, so after returning to university I drafted them the following letter:

"Jane is a very honest person and cares more for other people than she does for herself. There's a lot about her you don't know. That's what makes it so difficult to begin. What I have to say will come as a shock to you. Since you saw her you must think that she has continued working at the hospital. If that were so it would be rash of her to give it up and marry me. At the beginning of last year, I liked Jane but she was little more than an ordinary girl to me. After a while I noticed that she is different in many respects to anyone I've ever known. Although at first impression she may seem to have a dull character she is far from it. That's because she hides feelings deep inside her. Last summer, when I promised to marry her I was only beginning to notice her inner self. I continue to learn more about her every time we meet.

"It was also during last summer that Jane told me she was pregnant, not by me but by a man called Steve. I'd heard about Steve from her before and can understand the chain of events which allowed this to happen. Jane never really cared much for Steve but she made a few mistakes and ended up pregnant. This probably makes her sound 'cheap' to you but she's not. However bad her sin may seem to you she did not go unpunished. Her entire pregnancy was full of guilt and misery. Jane decided at the start to have the baby adopted. The little girl was born on March 6th and Jane looked after her for a week in hospital. She is called Nicole. I don't understand the strength of maternal instincts but during that week of caring for Nicole, Jane developed such a strong bond with her that it almost broke her heart to see the baby taken away from her. Such a reaction might have been predictable but it came as a surprise to me. Her disappointment might have been even greater had not there been the possibility for her to change her mind about adoption.

"Over the last week I have given great thought about what we should do. Jane said that for my sake I should leave her. I suppose that would be your advice too. But I have no intention to leave her. Please don't tell me I've got to consider my own life first. It's not as though I'm sacrificing my career. Far from it.

"Whether to keep Nicole or not was a difficult decision for Jane to make. Keeping her would involve innumerable difficulties both financially and practically. But if she didn't keep Nicole it could be a decision to regret all her life. Steve said he wanted a baby but Jane has avoided contact with him. He lives in London now. Sooner or later he'll find out that Nicole is to be adopted and he might oppose it. Jane wants to keep Nicole and doesn't want Steve to have her. The best thing will be for Jane to keep her. I was surprised to find that her mother was open minded about the decision. It turned out that she is now delighted with Jane's decision.

"I think it should now be clear that if I am to marry Jane, now would be the best time to do so. Careful calculations show that financially it will be difficult but not impossible and there is no reason why this should interfere with my career development. Would I be wasting opportunities as a student? Opportunities of travel, fun, hobbies, meeting people? Perhaps, but isn't marriage more important than these things? Like Jane, I do not want to miss an opportunity that I may regret all my life."

I never gave the letter to my parents. In fact, they never got to find out about Nicole, even when they met her. This was when Nicole was aged 21, and it was at Jane's funeral.

For my accommodation in Bradford this term I rented a bedsit in North Avenue at the bottom of Oak Avenue. It was close to Manningham Park, cheap and not far from Jane's house. The building was a bit grotty but when my Uncle Jack and Aunt Mary, who also loved Bradford, visited me and appreciated its character I felt more comfortable about living there.

Over the following months Jane's life and our relationship carried on in a mundane sort of way. I got on with my university work and enjoyed canoeing with the club. Often, Jane and I would walk around Manningham Park, pushing Nicole in her pram. I took many photos of the baby. Looking back at what I wrote in my 'Thought Book' a year previously, what a contrast there was! At the beginning of that year Jane had never had sex and now we were pushing a pram around with her baby in it! Our feelings towards each other had diminished such that by the end of May I felt uneasy after arranging to meet her one afternoon. I no longer felt a wish for her to be with me. It was a strange feeling. I didn't like feeling that way.

Baby Nicole

Thoughts on Wednesday 2.6.71:

"I don't like staying indoors when the weather is as good as it is now. But what else can I do? Jane can't go anywhere with me, not even swimming. If I went on my own I would be miserable. What do my university friends do? Craig goes out with Mandy every day. Walt, Milt, Dave and others are living on the other side of town and anyway they wouldn't want to go anywhere. I'd like to go canoeing but the canoe club members keep themselves to themselves and I can never find a club member when I want to. I shall try hard to make contact next week. After that people will be finishing exams and going home.

"Wasting good weather is like wasting a good opportunity. At times, I'd be happier if it rained. I want to get out into the countryside. If I went alone I'd be wishing Jane was with me. I'd see thousands of people out together and that would make me feel worse. Even if Jane could come with me I'd be fed up of there being people everywhere. I could have a quick swim by myself. Why not? I'll go now."

Thoughts on Saturday 26.6.71:

"I seem to have reached a bad stage, particularly since yesterday evening. I'm very dissatisfied with things at the moment. Nothing to look forward to and no way out of the situation. I want to do something, go somewhere, anything. Take a holiday? That would mean leaving Jane and after a couple of days I would be even more miserable. Now Jane's mother Jean is making matters worse all the time. It's now three weeks since I went out with Jane for an evening. Now it seems that we can't even go out for a quick drink together in the evenings because Jean thinks the baby shouldn't be left with Belinda who's fifteen. Things were OK three weeks ago. Jean seemed fair enough. Jane does the housework, cooking and other chores in return for food and accommodation. Then Jean suddenly turned herself off and for about four days not a word passed between them. Then it came out, apparently, for Jane does not talk readily about such things, that Jean was angry with Jane: she must face up to the responsibility of having a child, that there were things she may have got away with at the nurses home, but not here. If Jane goes out with me she has to be back by eleven. If I come round I've to leave at eleven.

"Jane is receiving Social Security Benefits totalling £5.60 a week. Out of this, Jean takes £4. I think it fair to assume that £4 is sufficient to feed one in a group of three plus a baby including say £1 a week for the extra electricity and £1 for wear and tear. Compare this with the cost of paying for a housemaid who does every single one of the household chores, not that you could find such a person. Maids and servants went out of use long ago. Nobody would work for what Jean is effectively paying Jane. And what restrictions would this servant have? In at eleven? Possibly. But not instructions on how to look after her own child. The woman is mad. She seems to think she can play with people's lives like they are tin soldiers without even a helmet. This tin soldier doesn't have a helmet. Rather than cause mischief, hurt relationships, or make changes, Jane willingly puts up with anything that is imposed on her. She puts up with it well but it bothers her when my bitterness shows through.

"Jane and Jean both have characters that seem simple but are really so complicated. Jane is tolerant; she hides her emotions shallowly, but just deep enough to keep them hidden. Jean likes to dominate people, priding herself in doling out common sense. They can both be mean but also kind. They both hide their emotions and problems: they won't tell what's bothering them when something obviously is. Jean says nothing and goes off to Pup's. Jean seems to resent Jane staying in her house in some ways but likes her being there in others. There are clear benefits to it. But Jean has to have things her own way. To her, it's not right for an unmarried mother to lead a carefree life so it's her duty to make sure that Jane doesn't. Neither Jean nor Belinda have to baby sit. That's alright. Then it should also be alright if Jane didn't do the cooking and cleaning. It's so bloody mean.

"The other evening, I stayed in the garden with Jane. We couldn't leave the house, not even for a drink, even though Jean stayed in the kitchen and there were two responsible girls in the house. We'd met in the park earlier. Jean had told Jane not to be too long 'in case I decide to go to bed early'. Jane had just looked at her as if to say, "So what?"

"Last night I went around whilst Nicole was being fed. Jean was with them, the radio was uncomfortably loud and slightly out of tune; the Archers had just finished. After half an hour of just sitting in the kitchen Jane put Nicole to bed. Jane and I went to the living room. There were things I had been wanting to tell her for a long time but the time spent in the kitchen spoilt my mood. I've felt depressed since then.

"I found myself a job on Thursday at Lancaster's warehouse in Thornton Road. It involves picking orders from the warehouse for fairs and bingo halls. Whilst it's pleasing to know I can afford to stay in Bradford during the summer vacation there are snags. I will miss the fun of last week of term as well as an amount of unfinished work. A more interesting or higher paid job would be better but the £40 for a 50-hour week I'll be getting is higher than I was prepared to accept. I'll be spending half my waking hours filling in time and the other half trying to stop myself from missing Jane.

"I wish getting married was just as simple as signing my name. Why should it involve so much more? Jane's 'mother business' is a reason for us getting married now. Jane is just biding her time. For how long? For one year? Or two, when I have finished my studies? Or three, when I've made a start with my career? Why not make it ten years, just to be on the safe side? The time I want to get married is NOW. It's not like buying stocks and shares deciding the best time to go ahead. Neither is it like waiting until the pie is cooked before eating it. It's more like eating the apple that's already in your hand. The apple won't improve on keeping, nor will it go bad, but you may as well eat it now rather than later.

"The other night I had this strange dream:
A man in swimming trunk is standing on a high diving board above a pool of deep green water. He's a champion diver. He stands on the edge then springs upwards, taking to the air like a bird. Gracefully he turns in the air and glides perfectly, as if on wings, towards the other side of the pool, where he descends. But his glide has taken him beyond the edge of the pool and he smacks onto the concrete floor."

Thoughts on Monday 19.7.71:

"I had a feeling that Jane would not be able to come over to my bedsit tonight. Yesterday, she told me she'd come if she could. We were talking about the past last night. I suddenly seemed to see Jane's point of view of my relationship with Jo. Every time I've mentioned Jo in the past has been to make Jane sort of jealous. When I think about it now, I realise it was mean of me. It was an enjoyable piece of self-esteem to simultaneously have two girlfriends to go to bed with. Jane said yesterday that if she had known about Jo at the time she would have left me. Jane had sex with someone else once whilst I did more than a few times. In her opinion, the fact that she got pregnant after that one time does not make her sin any worse than mine. Although I disagreed, I can see her point of view. Physical and mental changes resulted from her actions but not from mine. The actual act of sexual intercourse in her case was more disloyal than in mine because of the result. I then thought about my recent bout of jealousy. I was even jealous of the boys she had been out with before she knew me and of anybody else she had ever kissed. Yesterday, I realised how comical and ridiculous this jealousy was. What difference does it make? I must have done just as many things as she did. Anyway, now I feel slightly more relaxed and comfortable when I think of Jane.

"The question of marriage has recently been revived. Jane said somewhat unexpectedly on Saturday that it would be awkward coming to see me with the baby when it got really cold so we should get married before it does. We sort of settled on December 11th or a few days thereafter. This is probably another reason for my contented feeling. Over the past few weeks I've been earnestly searching for a larger, two-roomed flat to live in, so that we don't have to think about moving when we do get married. Now I've gone back to my original idea of buying a small house or cottage. I was enlightened today by colleagues at work who thought there was no reason why I shouldn't be able to rental purchase of a house. I am now seriously thinking of doing this. If I had done this at Easter, by now I might already be financially better off. I would probably have been paying a similar rent to what I'm paying here but would have something to show for it. Mum put me off the idea at Easter. She was thinking in terms of me getting a mortgage, which I wouldn't have been able to, and on a house that will probably be demolished in a few years. As far as I can see, if I'd got a house at Easter and it was to be demolished tomorrow I wouldn't have lost anything. I like the idea of building up a collection of furniture. Carefully chosen old furniture often looks good when painted up. The warehouse where I am working now has items I can buy much cheaper than in the shops. I have visions of sandpapering and varnishing wooden floors, painting old furniture white and such things that cost little but look good. For a few weeks I'd be virtually camping in the house, but by the time we get married in December we could have a proper little house. I'm getting enthusiastic! I wish my parents weren't against my two most important decisions, that is, marriage and house. They might not be of course, but I expect they are. If I just went ahead and got a house and then got married I doubt if they'd begrudge me too much. It's nice to think that this time next week I could be in a little house of my own. I bet I won't be able to find a suitable one now!"

Thoughts on Sunday 1.8.71:
"Now I have a larger flat in St Pauls Road, a five-minute walk away from Jane's house. It's on the first floor, has two rooms and a kitchen and costs £4 a week. This is where I'll probably settle for a while but Jane seems to have taken a slight dislike to the place.

"Every so often, Jane seems to get these moods of hers. I reckon about every six weeks, though it could be more often. It's as though she's annoyed with me for something although she says she's not. This time it seemed worse than others. At the moment she's really mean. Friday wasn't particularly good. Jane came round in the morning and we went to town. That was a bit boring. She came back for dinner and that seemed very dull and we didn't talk much. In the evening Jane told me that she met Steve in the park yesterday and this afternoon and might do so again on the following day (Saturday). She meant will, not might because that is what she later claimed she said. She knew I didn't want her to go on Saturday. It's natural that I should object. I don't mind that she saw him on Thursday and Friday but Saturday is our day together. So she goes out with her old boyfriend instead of being with me. It's not jealousy this time. It's just not right for her to see him in place of me. When I told her this she said that it was not just her that Steve wanted to see but his child as well. Anyway, she went. Fortunately, I had plenty to keep me occupied that afternoon and evening, as well as this morning.

"I thought Jane might come to visit me this afternoon so I waited until three and then called at her house. Jane wasn't in. Belinda thought she was walking round the park. I found Jane in the park pushing the pram on the opposite side of the lake. I walked around and sat with her on a bench. I asked why she hadn't come to see me and she replied that she just didn't feel like it. After a while, Jane got up and left but I stayed. She didn't seem to care. I didn't expect her to. I decided that if I let her go I'd be very miserable so I caught her up after a few minutes. Fortunately, it didn't seem as if I was 'giving in'. She was a bit more amiable. She said she'd be alright in a few days. I should go and find another girl for a while. I told her she was being selfish and she replied

- 153 -

that she'd do what she wants. Normally, Jane is very unselfish but now she seems the opposite. When I told her that she doesn't care about my feelings she replied, "Why should I bother about other people?" I can't argue with Jane when she's like this. She won't listen to what I say. She just sticks to her side of the main point of the argument and nothing else. It isn't that she's taken a sudden dislike of me and it's not to do with Steve's visit. It's something to do with her and she brings it out on me. I bet she doesn't get angry with other people. It's just the way Jane is.

"On Friday night the thought of me making Jane pregnant was strongly abhorrent. I wished I hadn't had sex with her last week. At the time, the low risk didn't concern me at all. But by Friday night I was worried. The expense of keeping Jane and two children concerned me. I have been calculating the cost of keeping the three of us to determine if drastic cuts would be needed. The addition of a fourth person would be problematic. Jane would have to go out to work, leaving the children in a nursery. At the moment I'm less keen than before on marriage. Jane has another week or two before her period is due. By then, I'll probably be dead keen on the idea again!"

Thoughts on Tuesday 3.8.71
"It was not a good day at work today. At lunch time my work mates pointed out that it took me longer than them to assemble an order from the warehouse. They said that because I go to university I ought to be able to do it better than them. I realised later that they were just poking fun but I got angry and it made me unpopular. Work finished at 5.30. It was a very wet evening. The bus ride home took ages and the windows were all steamed up. I cooked a meal from what I had in stock and rounded it off with ginger biscuits dipped in tea. After clearing up I washed my hair, had a shave and cleaned my teeth. I put on a clean shirt and shoes then left the house at 7.30. It was still drizzling so I hurried to Jane's house in five minutes. I was disappointed to see that Jean's car was outside the house. Through the window I could see that Jean, Jane and Belinda were playing Monopoly. I knocked on the door and after what seemed much longer than necessary Jane opened it. She was wearing a brown tee-shirt, purple jeans and the Scholl sandals that I bought for her. Jane left me dripping on newspaper whilst being sniffed by Sambo. Jane brought in a folding chair which she opened half way for me, and placed at the corner of the table. Monopoly was resumed. Jean had bought Park Lane and Mayfair and most of the property had been sold but there were no houses on the board yet. Fleet Street was auctioned and Jane bought it for £250 to stop Belinda completing her set of reds. The boring game dragged on and I decided I would sit patiently for precisely one hour and then leave. It seemed they were being inhospitable,

especially as I hadn't seen Jean for six weeks. Jane acted as if I wasn't even there, let alone welcome. I might just as well have not been there. I thought this was very unusual behaviour: any visitor deserves at least to be noticed. The game continued. Jean threw a double and landed on Go to Jail. Belinda said that doesn't count with a double and there was a discussion about that. Nobody glanced my way so I said nothing. Bow Street goes up for auction. Jane, who already has the other two orange properties gets it for ten pounds. The game now begins to go away from Belinda towards Jane who soon has some hotels. At about 8 o'clock Belinda is out of the game and they decide to finish it, Jane being a clear winner. The game is packed away.

"Belinda says she'll make up the baby's feeds.
    'Nineteen scoops of Trufood and a pint of water. NINETEEN', Belinda emphasises as if she is mixing some magic formula.
    'One pint. How many ounces is that?
    'Oh Belinda!'
They talk about how many milligrams make a grain.
    'There's a lot of nurses who don't know whether to put 30 or 60 milligrams in for a grain and sometimes doctors give a prescription in grains and sometimes in milligrams,'
Jane explains.
    'BELINDA: not that full!'
Three high pitched female voices get tedious after a while.
    'Put some milk in Sambo's dish.'
    'What a dog! He won't drink water, only milk.'
Sambo sits on a chair or someone's knee and grunts and whines.
    'What's the matter with you poor lovely thing. What do you want eh? Ah, isn't he cute!'
Sambo drinks his milk.
    'Go on, it's not too hot for you now.'

"Belinda leaves to have a bath and Jane sits with '19' magazine in front of her. It's price is displayed both as 17½p and 3s 6d. The two talk about Jean's work and something about night work.
    'She gets paid £3 a night, works three nights so that makes £9 she gets.'
    'I think I'm going to do that.'
    'Sometimes it's easy and sometimes it's hard. It's hard when they're getting up every 10 minutes to use the commode chair. How much an hour is £3 a night?'
    'You work eight hours per night don't you?'
I automatically start dividing 300 by 8.

'37 pence,' says Jean.

'How much is that?'

'it's 7/6 which is the same as the SRNs get.'

I can't be bothered to check the arithmetic any longer. They begin to talk about Jean's patients and about dentists. Jane says that she has to go to the dentist a week tomorrow and persists that she hates dentists. She'd rather have an operation than go to the dentist but adds that it's alright when you get there though.

'Belinda HATES going to the dentist. I think it's because of old Fogarty. He took out EIGHT of her teeth together once, she bled all night. That must have put her off the dentist for life. She once told me she was going to sit in the park and say she'd been to see the dentist.'

Belinda enters wearing a dressing gown.

'What's that about me?

'We were talking about dentists.'

'Remember what Anne did? She used to eat all those sweets but never had any trouble with her teeth.'

'Oh! I haven't done Topsy the rabbit', remembers Belinda.

'It's raining as well. I'll have to put a coat on. You do her Jane?'

'I won't.'

Jean says, 'I shall have to go the phone in a minute. Does diddums want to come to the phone with me in the CAR?'

The last word makes Sambo prick up his ears.

'I just feel like having a fudge,' says Belinda.

'Can you get me a fudge?' she says, producing a 10p coin.

'Oh, and a packet of Seabrooks cheese and onion crisps.'

If Jane asks me I must tell her that I don't like the T-shirt with the butterfly thing on the front that she's wearing. It's a horrible colour. Jean has a cup of coffee.

'Would you like a cup of coffee, Mark?

'No thanks - it's not long since I had some tea.'

My spirits rise half a notch as having been recognised as being present. Jane turns the pages of her magazine displaying adverts for makeup, tampons and deodorant. There's pictures of girls and a few pages with a lot of black people on. She seems to linger on that page studying a black man and tilting her eyes slightly to get a better view. Her eyes seem to say aren't black men better looking than white, perhaps thinking of Steve. There's more talk of Jean going to the phone.

'The one at the top of Victor Road doesn't work. You should ring the operator.'

'You can't even dial.'

'Is Sambo coming? In the CAR.'

He pricks up his ears again, peering over the table at Jean from his perch on the chair.

'He wants to go for a walk in the park. Take him for a walk in the park mammy.'

'It's too wet. I'm not going there in the dark.'

'There's a fair on.'

'I haven't heard the fair, have you? You always used to be able to hear from it at night. Clearly. Just as though it was next door.'

Belinda enters the room wearing a coat over her dressing gown and goes outside.

'Oh! it's not even raining.'

She leaves doors open and a cold draught blows in. She soon returns. That didn't take long for all the fuss over the rabbit.

'Well, are you coming Sambo. In the CAR.'

Jean and the dog leave. The car starts and reverses away. Belinda is behind me.

'Have you used up all the hot water? asks Jane.

'Naw. I haven't used ANY.'

'Good.'

Jane turns the magazine over and goes through the first few pages slower than before this time. I peer over her arm.

'You're not to look at the girls,' she says.

'No. I'm going now,' I say, getting up and making for the door.

It's on the latch and I open it.

'Where to?

'Home.'

'Oh. what are you going to do?'

I step outside.

'Nothing, 'bye.'

As I step out I notice Jane making an expression that I can't interpret. It looks like she's smiling but it could be a grimace. Does she expect me to come back? Is she pleased that I'm leaving because she's in one of her funny moods? Am I doing the right thing to leave? The next few minutes are very sad but then it wears off. At least the hot, angry feeling inside me has gone. It is raining slightly and starting to get dark. I want Jane to come running after me but know she won't. It's my dramatic sense of imagination. Even so, I look back a couple of times. At the end of the street I start towards the off-licence.

No,' I say to myself, 'Save your money until pay day.'

I'm not wanting to drown any sorrows. Anyway, a cup of coffee is just as cheering as a glass of beer or wine. I decide to go back to my flat and write about the evening. Ideas form rapidly in my head. Straight away I go for paper and pen and sit at the table. That's too uncomfortable. I take paper and pen to an armchair and write rapidly for half an hour. Then I read through it, feed the gas meter, make a cup of coffee and write again. And what is the result? I've occupied myself up until 11 o'clock so far. I shall have another cup of coffee, read through what I've written and then go to bed.

Thoughts in October 1971:
"Today, the weather is beautiful, especially so for October. But I'm feeling blue, like the colour of the sky. If the sky was grey I'd be happy to be working indoors. I don't want to stay inside doing chores. But I feel lazy and don't want to go for a walk. I need to make an effort one way or another. Either go for a walk or sit down and do some hard university work. The trouble with me is that my mind wanders. I do one thing and my mind wanders into the alternative option. I should make up my mind what to do and go for it 100%. Do it enthusiastically!"

Autumn term began on 4th October. Monday nights were good: canoeing at the baths, a drink at the Westgate Hill hotel, curry at the Kash, then coffee at Val's bedsit in Merton Road. Val was a very attractive girl and wore a black bikini in the baths. We got to talking as we were having curry. She did most of the talking. I was getting on well with her. I thought it might be possible to sleep with her. I wanted to, but a little voice in my head begged faithfulness to Jane. If her room-mate Carol wasn't there with her boyfriend that night I might have stayed. Perhaps it was best that way: I didn't have to face the test.

On the second Monday I bought Val a drink and we continued chatting during the curry. I felt relaxed with her. Carol was away so I stayed in their room and slept in Carol's bed. Val had recently had an abortion and the doctor's instruction was no sex for three weeks.

On the following week, Carol was sharing their room with her boyfriend. Val came and slept with me in my flat. I told Val all about Jane and myself and she told me all about herself and her ex-boyfriend Mike. It was easy to talk about sex with Val. She needed someone and I happened to be there at the right time. I enjoyed being with Val and got to know more people through being with her. Sexually, my performance with Val was at first abysmal. I must have been feeling guilty about cheating on Jane.

My love-making with Jane had been getting riskier. I started worrying a day or two before her November period was due and she hadn't started the day after the due date. I felt sure I was going to be a daddy. I suppose you could say it was bound to happen one day. It turned out that Jane and I were wrong. I'm not going to be a father just yet. Her period started four days late. When she told me, my feelings were neutral: I was neither relieved, joyful nor disappointed. Thinking about it, the chances of her being pregnant were very low really. Perhaps it was the jolt we needed to take more care. Or perhaps the jolt was too strong because I began to feel that I didn't want to get married just yet. It was probably because I had met Val. Not just because of her, but because of the thoughts that Val set running through my mind: thoughts of living more freely and taking full advantage of student life. I went through phases of being keen on getting married as soon as possible to being a free man.

I'd been thinking of buying a car for some time. I visited Bradford Car Auctions on several occasions. It was an interesting experience. The vehicles sold very cheaply and I missed several good buys. I finally found a suitable car advertised in the paper: a black Morris Minor, registration VAK 276. I bought it for £55 and paid £29.40 for Third Party Fire and Theft insurance.

I was also reconsidering my accommodation. It was easily worth what I paid but not really what I wanted. When I moved there I wanted somewhere that Jane and Nicole could live with me when we got married at Christmas. It now seemed very unlikely that we would get married at Christmas. Anyway, Jane didn't like the place. I could be paying a pound a week less elsewhere and at times I'd be happy if there were other people about. Miss Mason, my landlady at St Pauls Road, wanted me to leave because she had been made redundant and was hoping to use the flat for full board and earn more money, so I had to get a different flat anyway.

Thoughts in November 1971:
"I'm tired. Tired at having lost a night's sleep. Tired of running around looking for a flat. From seven yesterday morning until three this afternoon everything was fine and I felt great. Now I feel lousy.

"The last twenty-four hours were good. Really good. But now I want someone to talk to. A pad of paper and a pen will have to do. It's because of Val. Our relationship was bound to improve and my feelings for Jane to lessen. Poor Jane. Do I love her? Do I love Val? I have to love Jane. I mustn't love Val. It has to be that way. I can't leave Jane. No. Never. I've never felt this way about her before. Val is great! I can (and do) confide in her like with nobody else, more than with Jane. Val has perfect breasts and a lovely shaped body. She has this trick of rolling her tummy like a belly dancer. Val is fantastic with sex. She likes to try different positions. Jane is better for making love with. Perhaps I'm bored. Jane's body has lost some of its appeal. Val's is new to me. No – I shouldn't compare.

"I got up from Val's bed at nine o'clock, allowing plenty of time to reach my flat for 9.30, which is the earliest Jane ever got there for our weekly Saturday excursion around town. The car failed to start because water from a leaking radiator had dripped straight onto the distributor. After a lot of pushing we eventually got it to go. A hundred yards before I reached my flat I met Jane setting off towards town on her own. I stopped and ran after her. It was obvious to her where I had been. I hadn't slept much and it showed. I told her that I went to Martin's the previous evening to fix the roof rack on my car (which I did) and when I set off the car wouldn't start so I stayed in Martin's room for the night to wait until morning when I could see better. I thought the story sounded believable but obviously it wasn't.

"I've become wicked. I've told lies, broken promises and have been unfaithful to Jane. It doesn't upset me though. I'm thinking of Val too much. I mustn't. I must not get hung up on Val. We even agreed on that together, such is our openness. We have talked of many things. I told her the story of Jane from the beginning to the present time. This is the first time I have told the full story to anyone. It clarified my thoughts. It was good to do that. It was good to be with Val. It was good to admire her looks. Good to hold her naked body next to mine. Good to admire her character. But I'm tearing myself apart. Jane is the one I want. Val is the one I desire.

"I couldn't even go and see Jane tonight. It would have made matters very, very bad for her. She would detect immediately how I feel and I would have to explain. If I told her truthfully why I feel this way it would almost break her heart. On Sunday, Jane begged me not to go out with anyone else. Now I'm longing to be with Val and probably will do so on Thursday. Tomorrow I see Jane. I'm not looking forward to it. I will have to be very careful not to show my feelings. I must forget about Val. But I'm looking forward to Thursday! We'll have a drink, an interesting conversation, then I'm going to take 'studio' photos of her and afterwards go to bed with her. Fantastic! I can't wait! Val is keen about the photo shoot. My thoughts are reeling. Will she stay the night? It shouldn't happen!

"In the evening, Val cooked us a fabulous meal. Her two very nice friends, Trudi and Chris joined us. Afterwards, I took Val to Baildon for a drink. Val talked and talked so much that I got a bit bored. We went back to my flat, had coffee and I took a whole film of photographs of her. It was an exercise in photographic portraiture – decent pictures of Val fully dressed, not pornographic. Only after that did we go to bed.

"Last night Jane begged me to take her and make love to her wildly. I didn't want to. When we went to bed it all went wrong. I didn't want her to stay. At 11.30 I took her home. What I did next was probably the cruellest, meanest and most unfaithful act I have ever done. After Jane had shown me how much she loves me with her heart and body I went straight round to Val's flat in Merton Road and we had sex. Now I'm missing Val. Val is beginning to like me more. Jane is beginning to love me more. I'm beginning to love Jane less and Val more. I could see Val again tonight but I shouldn't. I don't want a repeat of what happened last week when I was late for Jane on Saturday morning. Everyone tells me that I ought to be faithful to Jane. The more unfaithful I am the worse the situation becomes. Last night I made love to Jane. It was unpleasant, tainted and unfulfilling. This morning I made love to Val. It was delectable, delicious, so much sweeter, fresher…

"I was writing the above notes when Jane called and we went to her house. Jean and Belinda were both out. Now it's midnight and seeing Jane seems to have had a beneficial effect on my feelings. Jane practically insisted that we made love again and it was enjoyable this time. We had to stop and get dressed quickly when we heard the characteristic sound of Jean's Volkswagen Beetle reversing into the yard. Perhaps that was as well. I didn't want to go all the way. It's pretty safe at this time of the month but I don't want to risk making her pregnant. She's not bothered about that any more. She says it doesn't matter if we love each other. I know it's evil of me, but I was thinking of this morning when I was in bed with Val. We had no regrets about it. We both wanted to go all the way, we did and it was wonderful.

"Yesterday was a very enjoyable day. The canoe club decided on a down-river trip to Apperley Bridge. Val came along, but not to paddle. We loaded the canoes onto my car and set off, firstly to Apperley Bridge. Val and I arrived long before the others so after looking at the swollen river, Val and I went into the pub. Val had a Pony and I a glass of rum. It was delightful, and warming. The others arrived, then we all travelled in my car to the boathouse above Shipley. I showed Val how to use my camera and she was happy to follow us down river on foot as far as Shipley. The canoeing was enjoyable and Val seemed to be happy. After the trip I took her to my flat and cooked us both a meal. We spent the rest of the evening printing the photos I took on Thursday, then slept in my bed.

"It's now midnight and I'm waiting to see if Val will drop in for coffee! I doubt that she will now, although all weekend I've been hoping she would. I said she could call up to 12.30 and she liked the idea. She may be only a few doors away or she could be at her house in Merton Road. I'm not going to find out. In a way, it would be as well if she doesn't come because every hour I spend with Val makes things that bit worse for Jane. The chances of spending tomorrow night with Val are high. Whether that is good or bad is debateable. I must not place too much reliance on it as it could make me disappointed. Every time I hear a sound I jump, thinking it's the door. I want Val to stay tonight. However, if she does, it means that she has thought about me perhaps a bit too much. Our relationship must not get too serious, for both our sakes.

"At the same time, Jane loves me more than ever before. She now has set her heart on living with me. I wish she had decided this before now, such as at Easter. As it is, I feel like I'm a ping-pong ball bouncing back from one idea to another. I had decided to spend most of the Christmas vacation at home and return to live in a single flat, or even with Craig or someone else. Now my decision is to stay in Bradford and live with Jane. All her 'moral' ideas seem to have gone now. Now it's alright for her to live with me without being married. Now it's alright to fuck (what a foul word). Now she'll go on the pill for me. Previously, all these things were against her conscience, having being brought up a Catholic, so she would not do them. Now it's alright because she loves me so much. I've agreed to live with her. Financially, it's a good idea. Being unmarried, she still gets her Social Security Benefit amounting to nearly £7 a week, which should be ample to feed and clothe her and Nicole. It shouldn't make any difference to my expenditure. No more sleeping with Val of course, but that is made up for, physically if not mentally, by having Jane every night. Cooking and washing taken care of too! Never mind the pros and cons! It's a good idea. I'm sick of her living at home and being governed by her mother, even her sister as well at times. Tomorrow I will make enquiries about houses to let.

"Well, it now looks like I won't be getting my oats tonight. It was a selfish thought anyway.

"Two minutes after writing that, Val arrived.

"Jane suspects there is more going on than what I have told her. She asks about 'the girl in the black bikini' who goes canoeing."

December 1971:

In the middle of the university Rag Week there was a boat race on the frozen lake in Manningham (Lister) Park. I gave Martin, Stuart and Val a lift then picked up Jane and Nicole from Victor Road and walked down to the lake to watch the race. I thought it would be good for Val to meet Jane and Nicole. It was okay but difficult to maintain conversation that was appropriate for both and in the presence of others. Having the baby to talk about made it easier. Thursday's photo shoot must have been mentioned, but Jane said nothing about it at this stage. Martin, Stuart and Val had left some gear in my car so I promised to take it round to them later. When the time came Jane came with me, perhaps to make sure I didn't go to Val's on my own. When Jane, Nicole and I got there Val offered coffee. Still thinking that it would be a good idea for Val and Jane to get to know each other better I agreed. I thought it might make Jane less jealous and less suspicious of us if they were friends. Was I being over-optimistic or simply naïve?

Competitors in Manningham Park Boat Race

I was hoping to be with Val and was expecting to spend that evening together but Jane wanted me to be at her house. To let Val know I went to the kitchen and started scribbling a note to her. I heard someone behind me entering the kitchen and thought it would be Val. It was Jane. She caught me red handed!

My mind went frantic thinking what to write and make it look innocent. At first I just doodled, then I wrote,

"Have taken paddles to boat shed."

Later, I discreetly threw the paper into a waste bin.

Although Jane had said nothing about the photo shoot when we were in the park it must have bothered her. Sometime later, perhaps on the Thursday, Jane had been to the flat and looked at the photographs I'd left on the table. She observed that they were taken in my bedroom.

"What else did you do in there?" she asked.

I can't recall my reply but when I returned to the flat all of the photographs were gone, including the negatives. I have no photos of Val. Fifty years later, this still upsets me at least as much as it did at the time, probably more so.

Thoughts:

"It's appalling when you think about it, bedding two girls alternately at twelve-hour intervals. I ought to be ashamed of myself. Jane would murder me. She was hysterical with me for bringing Val to the flat and taking photographs of her. Jane said that what made it worse was me telling lies about it. Jane ripped up all the photographs. That didn't bother me too much at the time but now I'm annoyed about it. They were good prints and represented a significant amount of material and time. To me, being alone with another girl and taking photographs of her was perfectly innocent. Not to Jane. She was furious. Imagine her reaction if she found out the whole story as only Val and I know. That's serious. She really would do something very, very silly. She won't find out. Providing I keep my activities with Val at a discrete level Jane needn't know. I encourage Val to get herself another boyfriend to act as a 'buffer'. She thinks she needs one and I agreed. It's best that she doesn't become too involved with me. Over the last few days though Val and I have become closer. It's very nice but it makes the complications even worse. I accept that Val is friendly with a lot of different people and don't resent it. At all costs I must avoid becoming 'possessive' of her.

"Here I am sitting on my own whilst there are two girls, both easily reached, who would be glad if I went to see them. I could be with one in five minutes, the other in fifteen. Yet here I am alone. I've plenty to do, but I'm not keen on working at the moment. If I went to see Val I'd miss her over the weekend. If I went to see Jane I'd still not get any work done and it wouldn't make me happier. So, here I am, alone.

"I currently have two opposing external thoughts on my problem. Firstly, there's Val's thoughts. She's in a slightly biased position but she's the only person who understands the full picture. Then there's Craig's thoughts. He doesn't know the full story. At least, I doubt it. He won't be able to understand my feelings towards either girl because I haven't explained them to him. So, I have Val who understands but will be biased, and Craig who can't appreciate the whole situation but is unbiased. They both have pretty much opposite opinions. Val thinks I shouldn't live with Jane. Craig thinks I should. I'd rather have the freedom of living on my own. In other words, I like the freedom of not being tied to one girl! But that 'freedom' will one day get me into trouble. Living with Jane will force me to 'modify' my relationship with Val (somewhat of an understatement!) and hence avoid the associated complications that arise nearly every day and get worse each time. Living with Jane is rather a roundabout and cowardly way out of the situation. So far, I haven't mentioned the feelings of Jane and Val. Jane wants to live with me. Jane loves me. Jane has the strongest feelings of the three of us. Therefore, she should count more. If I had to leave one girl for the other, it would be best to leave Val because she would be the less upset. Leaving Jane would be serious, even if I explained my feelings for them both. But I don't think I should be over swayed by the relative strength of their feelings. I should base my decision on how I feel. The trouble is, I know what is best for me to do. For a start, I should stop sleeping with or going out with Val. But I don't want to give that up. What I want is the exact opposite of what is best. Which line should I follow? Logical or emotional? The logical line is to do what is best, leaving emotional feelings out of it. But it's an emotional problem so they can't be left out. If it wasn't for my emotions there wouldn't be this problem. It's a battle between logic and emotion. Do I use my head or my heart? My normal answer to that question would be to use my head. But as I just said, it's a problem of the heart, not the head. The thing is, I don't want to make a decision at all. I want to leave the situation as it is. In other words, do nothing about it. But it can't go on indefinitely. I've already passed the danger limit. I've gone over the red line. The longer it continues, the worse it gets. I told Val last night that I need a combination of them both! With Jane, I get the right physical responses but the wrong mental ones. With Val I get the right mental responses but the wrong physical ones. By this I mean I'm not so easily aroused by Val but I concentrate on giving her pleasure. I'm quickly aroused by Jane, but her kind words or loving kisses fail to make me feel passionate."

Val went to a fancy-dress party just down the road from my flat. The theme was Romans and Ancient. At 10.30 the following morning she came around to mine for breakfast. I was going to Ray's for him to do something on the car.

After dropping some things off at her place we both went around to Ray's in Undercliff. The work took longer than expected and it was two o'clock before we got away. I felt a bit indebted to Val for hanging around so long and because of the meal she had cooked for me on Thursday so I drove her directly to Brad and Liz, who were canoeing at Bingley weir. Val and I arranged to have a meal together later and I left to meet Jane at my flat. Jane was already there when I arrived. The two chairs that Val and I had used for breakfast were still in the kitchen.

"Who have you had in here then?" Jane asked.

The minor detail of the chairs had escaped my attention. If I told Jane truthfully that Val had come around in the morning she would have thought that Val had stayed the night before. I invented an answer.

"Martin came around for coffee and I gave him a lift to Ray's."

It annoyed me when I had to tell a lie like that more than telling a big one. Earlier, Jane had spotted that the car ashtray had been used (Val smoked) so I told her it was from Craig.

'I thought Craig didn't smoke.

'He doesn't really,' I replied, and left it at that.

As usual, I walked Jane back to her home before tea time. I wanted to buy some food and cook a meal for Val and me. I bought some onions from the Paki shop in Oak Lane. I also bought some chocolates for Val as an apology for messing her about with Jane the other day. I chose Spartan chocolates because I thought they were appropriate in memory of her previous evening's party. I went back to the flat and wrapped the chocolates, enclosing a note apologising and telling Val I would come as soon as I could. Jane had said she might come and visit me. She often said that she'd come to my flat in the middle of the night so there was a slight possibility of her visiting at any time. I sketched a graph showing the probability of Jane visiting me against time. The peak was at 7 p.m. and the graph tapered to infinity. I decided that if Jane didn't arrive by 8.30 I'd go to Val's. If Jane visited then I would go to Val's afterwards at 11.30. I occupied myself writing letters until 8.30, listening for the doorbell, not really sure of whether I wanted it to ring or not. I really wanted to see Val but felt uneasy not knowing: if Jane appeared there would be no more uncertainty. 8.30 arrived quicker than I expected, so I had to rush getting changed. I put on some smart clothes and left at 8.45. Val and I had decided earlier that we would go out to a smart place for a steak or something. I was still feeling uneasy when I got to Val's. Previously, any feelings of guilt would vanish with our first kiss. This time the worry stayed with me. I chose a dress from Val's wardrobe for her to wear and she got changed. As she changed I realised I was wearing the shirt that Jane had given me for my birthday. That made me feel even more uneasy.

Whilst Val readied herself I looked at a book of hers. It was about a woman's view of man's sexual behaviour. Its chapter on breaking up depressed me. I had just finished reading that chapter and Val was putting on her white shoes. Then Jane walked into the room.

My immediate reaction to Jane was to say, "Hello!"

"Hell-oh," Jane replied, emphasising the last syllable.

The atmosphere in the room was tense. Jane sat on Carol's bed, which was nearest the door. Val was already sitting on hers, with shoes on, dressed and ready to go out. There was a chair between the two beds. Jane insisted that I now had to decide what I was going to do. She was not going to leave until I had decided what. It took me a while to say anything constructive and in the end I was no clearer than at the start. Leaving Jane would spoil her whole life and cause great sorrow. Val would be less hurt if I left her. She understood the situation and how I felt. All of the other factors I considered simply confused the situation. I assessed the effects of my decision for the long, middle and short-terms. It was impossible for me to evaluate the relative importance of each aspect. It had to be on the strength of feeling of the two girls. Jane clearly had the stronger feelings. But I couldn't bear to leave Val at that point.

The arrival of Carol in the room must have spared me of having to make the difficult choice. Following my suggestion at 10.45 the four of us agreed to go together to the Taj Mahal for a curry. It seemed to be a good idea. Val and I were dressed smartly, which was appropriate for the Taj, although Jane and Carol wore plain clothes.

At the Taj Mahal, I was the only one with any sort of appetite. The idea of entertaining three girls at the same time made me feel good: a bit expensive perhaps, but no more than I had originally planned to spend for the evening. After the meal we returned to Merton Road and Val made us coffee. It was late when Jane and I left. I really wanted to talk with Val on her own but there was no opportunity to do so. It was awkward just saying goodbye to her. I drove in silence and stopped outside my flat in St Pauls Road. After talking for a few minutes Jane decided that she would stay the night with me in my flat.

I didn't enjoy being in bed with Jane that night. However, it amused me to think that I had expected to sleep with one girl and ended up sleeping with another. We talked a lot but it didn't achieve much and I was very tired. Jane kept whining, "Ma-aark" at me even whilst I was partly asleep. She said she didn't sleep at all and got up at about seven and went home. Her mother probably didn't realise that Jane had stayed out all night. Meanwhile, I slept again and woke up at ten and a half minutes to nine (I'd just turned on the radio).

I was pleased with myself for getting to university for a nine o'clock lecture. Mr Nunn was always late so by arriving shortly after 9.05 I didn't miss anything.

During my talks with Craig and Mandy the previous week I had predicted that the 'crunch' would come on Monday so I was one day out from my guess. Earlier, Jane had decided to go with me to the canoe club session at the baths on that Monday evening. I thought she was bound to find out something I didn't want her to know. It was better that she found out the way she did. The university white water kayak weekend at Llangollen was to be held the following weekend. Jane said I was not to go if Val was going. I made it clear to Jane that I didn't see why this should stop me from going there. For one thing, for me not to go would be letting down Ray and Martin. It was an important event and one I did not want to miss. As a child I used to visit Llangollen with mum and dad in order to attend the Eisteddfod. I knew the fast-flowing river there and was thrilled with the opportunity to paddle down it. Both Val and I assured Jane that she had nothing to worry about us two. At the time, we both meant it, but as will be seen later, minds do change.

I wanted to talk with Val but didn't get the opportunity. Jane came to the pool and enjoyed a swim but got changed early, complaining that I was ignoring her. She came and sat by me at the edge of the pool and resumed lecturing me like she had in bed the previous night.

"I trusted you once," she said.

"Now you've got to get that trust back again."

It sounded like lines from a cheap comic or a Mills and Boon book. It seemed pathetic. Compared with Val, Jane seemed childish, immature, unintelligent and boring. Afterwards, we went to the Westgate Hill Hotel for a drink and watched Steptoe and Son on their colour television as usual. The three of us went to the Kash for a curry, or rather just kebabs on this occasion. The food was interesting but the conversation dull. Afterwards we went to Val's for coffee. Carol was there busy working but she didn't appear to be especially disturbed by our talking in the same room. In the end, Val and I promised Jane that we would 'be good' and end our intimacy. I took Jane home, not talking much, then went alone to my flat. It was sad having to spend a Monday evening without Val, as we would normally do after canoeing.

I didn't see Val on Tuesday or Wednesday, and only for a short while on Thursday. Craig had gone home for Christmas so I didn't have anyone to talk to. That was alright though because I was moving out of St Pauls Road and into a smaller, but warm and cosy bedsit in Spring Place. Spring Place was close to the university. Jane thought the reason I moved there was because it was also close to Merton Road where Val was living. The main reason was really that I couldn't find a bedsit in the Manningham/Heaton area. Anyway, I went to the university more frequently than to Jane's. This would be good for the following term with exams approaching. It took all of Tuesday afternoon and most of Wednesday to transfer all my things. The trips included two full car loads of junk, a considerable difference to my first moves when I moved everything on foot. The moving kept me occupied for a week when I would otherwise have been lonely.

On the Friday lunch time I met Val, Stuart and Ray in the university bar to discuss transport arrangements to Llangollen. We decided to take three cars – mine, Stuart's and Ray's. Martin was to travel with Stuart, which meant that Val had to go with me. It felt strange at first talking to Val in the bar; not like it was before, but the sad feeling gradually brightened. We arranged a departure time and left the bar shortly before two as I had a lecture and needed to pack the car. At the lift, Val paused for me to kiss her. At that moment I think we both changed our minds about 'being good' over the weekend. Prior to this, my mind was bedevilled with constant thoughts of Val and Jane. At that moment, I knew it was going to be an amazing weekend.

We had a pleasant journey to Llangollen on Friday 10th December. The roads were still quite icy for the first part so I concentrated on my driving. After half way, I began feeling more affectionate and squeezed Val's hand or touched her knee. Where we had to stop I gave her a little peck on the cheek. We pulled up on the bridge in Llangollen. The River Dee was disappointingly low. We were staying at Mrs Jarvis's guest house, 'The Willows'. The six of us – me, Val, Stuart, Martin, Ray and Irene (Ray's girlfriend) were to stay in two of her three rooms. It meant that Val, Stuart and I would have to share a room with a single and double bed. Neither Stuart nor I wanted to sleep together in the same bed so it was quickly decided that Val and I would use the double.

After finding Martin and Stuart in town, our group had some expensive fish and chips. We spent the remaining evening drinking at the Chain Bridge Hotel and I wrote a postcard to Jane. The best part of the evening was just after 10.30, when Val and I were standing in a darkened bar room overlooking the river. It felt romantic. We all returned to 'The Willows' and went to bed. Stuart and I undressed whilst Val was in the bathroom. I thought about whether it was appropriate for me to go completely naked and very quickly decided to do so. When Val came into the room Stuart and I were both under our bedcovers.

The canoe races were on Saturday. The best and most difficult rapid was the Town Falls just above the bridge, which gave observers a grandstand view. Val took photos of our descents. As I approached the falls, I panicked, took a wrong line down the rapids and ended up swimming under the bridge. I was annoyed but consoled myself that not many people can claim to have swum under Llangollen Town Bridge in December! I was wearing a wet-suit so it didn't feel really cold.

I did not record details of that Friday night. It must have been good, and later Stuart said he heard our bed squeaking, but I'm sure that was not due to any love-making. The reason I didn't record the details is because although Friday night was good, Saturday's was fantastic. We began the evening at the Chain Bridge Hotel again but it was crowded so we spent the rest of the time in the Crown. As arranged previously, I phoned Jane at nine o'clock. It was a very pleasant talk. I told her about the canoeing, that I was sharing a room with Stuart and 'being good'. After closing time, we all went for fish and chips. Val was slightly inebriated, which annoyed me slightly. She told me I should be more assertive. I realised that I should also be more assertive with Jane. Back at The Willows Jim, a friend of Martin's from Newcastle University, talked with Val for fifteen minutes. It made me feel uneasy because they were clearly close friends too. I helped Stuart, who was drunk, get to bed. When Val and I went to bed I was a bit annoyed but that soon passed. Stuart fell into a drunken sleep. At one point, Stuart rolled out of his bed and collapsed onto Val. It was very amusing. We helped Stuart return to his bed and in a very short time he was soundly asleep. In our bed, Val and I talked for a while and then we made love. My thoughts were dedicated solely to the sensations of the act, not of whom it was with. The feeling was wonderful. A lot of the time we giggled happily, "I wonder if Stuart is listening?" It was a beautiful, exquisite, perhaps even narcotic sensation. At the end I felt so happy and contented that all my cares and worries had disappeared. I was amazed at how perfect the feeling was. Val felt the same way too. I told her that I didn't have a care in the world. There was nothing at all that worried me. I truly felt that I had never before felt so good as I did at that moment.

By Sunday morning I was still feeling peaceful but a few things came to mind. Stuart's alarm went off at 8.30 and he went down to breakfast but Val and I stayed in bed. We made love whilst the others ate breakfast downstairs. We were still embraced when Stuart walked in the room and said it's time we got up for breakfast. The canoeing went well that day. We had to hurry to get to the start on time. I didn't capsize on my run and my time of 16'03" was six seconds faster than Martin's. That fulfilled my aim of beating him. Ray was 4 seconds faster than me. After my run, I watched the others and took photos. I collected my car from the start, returned to the end, loaded the canoes, drove to The Willows and got changed. Val and I visited a pub near the finish, ate pasties and stayed there for an hour playing darts with a local. I got a bit bored and felt disappointed that the weekend was nearly over.

Town Falls, Llangollen

We left Llangollen at 2.10, drove 102.7 miles and arrived at Merton Road in Bradford at 4.45. There, we had coffee and toast and later I made cheese and scrambled eggs on toast which tasted good. It was difficult deciding if and when to go and visit Jane. I'd promised Jane I'd go but I knew I would be unable to hide my feelings for Val at that time. I very much wanted to sleep with Val that night but felt that wouldn't be fair to either of the girls for me to go off and visit Jane then come back and sleep with Val. When I explained this to Val, she said she wanted to wait for me there whilst I visited Jane. So off I went, pausing at the Waterloo on the corner of Preston Road to buy Val some cigarettes. I wondered whether I should go back to Val but continued to Jane's. As I walked towards Jane's door I knew I couldn't hide the truth.

For a start, Jane was annoyed that I hadn't arrived earlier. She asked about the sleeping arrangements and I told her I'd slept in the same room as Stuart. I knew I wouldn't get away with that. We sat in the living room and Jane asked me again so I told her I'd slept in the same bed as Val. I couldn't tell her we had made love. I had to be careful to avoid showing my impatience to leave. I didn't want her to think I was going back to Val. I knew that if I stayed much longer Jane would start crying and the situation would become steadily worse. Fortunately, I managed to leave after Jane had shed only a few tears and me showing only slight impatience. As I drove back to Val's I felt pleased with what I had done. When I got back, Val seemed a little sad, but that was perhaps because it contrasted with my happiness. We read my book, 'Sex Manners for Men' together for a while and spent a quiet night together.

In the morning I got up and made toast and coffee and just made it to university for nine o'clock. I hurried to finish the practical off in the morning and met Val in the bar at lunch time. I wanted to spend the afternoon in the darkroom, processing the two films Val had taken over the weekend. At two, Val went to her lectures and I went to see Jane.

Thoughts:
"Val's gone home to Sheffield. And I'm tired. I've been walking around since 8 o'clock delivering letters in a temporary job I've got with the Royal Mail. I wish I could talk to Val. I have often thought that I could write a book on my thoughts, my ideas, and the images that have passed through my mind this term.

"Ten o'clock on a Monday evening and I'm sat on my own waiting for the beginning of 'Steptoe and Son'. This time last week I was sitting in the Westgate Hill Hotel and looking forward to a night with Val."

"I feel that I'm destroying something precious and beautiful that took me two years to create. I'm destroying it bit by bit. I'm wielding a mighty hammer and smashing it against something I built with pride and care. It's crumbling away; slowly but surely. Tonight, I shall demolish the last remaining pieces. It's painful. Half of me cries out to stop. The other half tears, gouges and wrecks. Tonight, I will visit Jane and might never see her again. All those loving words and deeds, the letters, the kisses, making love. Together we built a house, brick by brick. Alone, I pull it down, wall by wall. Tonight, I could rebuild that house, perhaps even higher than originally planned, but I'm going to raze it to the ground. It hurts. I sit alone in my room. Looking around it I see on the mantlepiece two photographs of Jane. Hanging on a peg, Jane's mug. The teapot she gave me, the cushion, the chopping board, the washing up bowl, clothes, the bed we made love on, Fox's Jammy Dodger biscuits in the tin we bought together, Leonard Cohen singing on the tape, the woollen jumper Jane bought me for Christmas. I listen to the radio and hear records with words that could have been written especially for us."

Desiderata. Desiderata. Desiderata.
Go placidly amid the noise and haste,
and remember what peace there may be in silence.
As far as possible without surrender,
Be on good terms with all persons.
Speak your truth quietly and clearly, and listen to others -
Even the dull and ignorant, they too have their story.
Avoid loud and aggressive persons - they are vexations to the spirit.
If you compare yourself with others, you may become vain and bitter,
For always there will be greater and lesser persons than yourself.
Enjoy your achievements as well as your plans.
Keep interested in your own career -
However humble, it is a real possession in the changing fortunes of time.
Exercise caution in your business affairs,
for the world is full of trickery.

Jane was at Huby visiting the Greens, with whom she had stayed during the last weeks of pregnancy last year. This was to be the scene of our final goodbye. The moment I saw her though, it was different. A sudden change swept through me. At the Green's house I recalled the love I felt last time we were here and felt a warm affection for Jane. I think Jane was surprised, having expected me to tell her that this was our final goodbye. We sat together and spoke affectionately.

Over the next few days our affection began to fade again as I still enjoyed being with Val. Every day Jane wrote letters almost begging to see me but I wasn't going to see her just because she asked. Then one day when I didn't get such a letter I felt I wanted to see her so I decided to call at her mum's house in Victor Road. As I walked towards the house I felt unsure. It was drizzling, but warm. Her mum's car was outside and after walking round to the back I could see her mum in the kitchen. Returning to the front, I rang the doorbell. Jane was out. She had gone to visit her friend Rita, who still lived at Field House and worked at BRI. That was the result I wanted. I had given myself a test to determine how I felt when I couldn't see Jane. The test showed that I wanted to see her. I tried phoning Field House but the number was engaged. I walked back into town along Manningham Lane stopping at every phone box. Each time, the line was engaged. Finally, I rang the nurses' union number, but that didn't help. I bought a bag of toffee and continued to walk back towards Spring Place.

As I reached the corner of Great Horton Road and Laisteridge Lane I met Jane coming away from my flat. My mouth was full of toffee but that didn't matter.

Jane hugged and kissed me and jumped up and down as with childish delight. I was glad that I had found her. And it couldn't have happened in a better way.

I devoted three hours on the following Sunday to university revision work. There was an enormous amount of work to do. The thought of it can be depressing but it's often satisfying to learn something, especially when that knowledge can be used in an exam. The frustrating part is not knowing what to revise. It might be a topic you don't need to learn in detail or one that you just can't grasp. Lecture notes are often unclear and books take too long to read. Mathematical work is particularly difficult. I find the easiest way is to learn the final equation, summarise the important points, then if I can't understand the summary, learn it parrot fashion. I liked to use memory joggers, such as paragraph headings and acronyms. I invented an acronym to remember the order of the planets in the solar system: Man Very Early Made Jane Stir Up Nanny's Pie. Some acronyms that I devised for my revision made obscene words or phrases that were especially easy to remember. I wisely destroyed them after the exams.

March 1972:

By this month, Jane had decided that it would be best to arrange for Nicole to be fostered. The living arrangements at her mum's house could not continue much longer. I accompanied Jane to visit the foster mum that Social Services had selected. Jane was pleased with the arrangement. The foster mum was lovely, her home was local, Jane could visit Nicole as often as she liked and she was able to restart work at BRI. Once all that was settled, our relationship was rejuvenated.

Jane often stayed in my bedsit in Spring Place. Jane wrote me the following letter from there whilst I was studying in the university.

"My Darling Mark,
I'll try to make this a neat letter for a change! How are you doing with your revision? You must tell me if you are worried about your exams and I will try and help you, even though I'm thick! I'll tell your mummy how hard you've been working and she'll forgive you if you don't pass and I'll still LOVE YOU so just do your best.

"I'm lying here by the fire all nice and cosy and happy. Have you had a good day today? I have, even if you did leave me for an hour and I missed you. You bought me a nice cup and I shall think of you every time I use it but that's silly because I don't ever need things to remind me of you or make me think of you because I do all the time.

"It's my birthday next week, did you know? I'll be twenty-one. Ancient aren't I?

"Guess who I saw today. Sambo the woofwoof and he was pleased to see me and went all wiggly and wanted to come to the park with us.

"Are we going to the pictures on Saturday with Craig and Mandy? I'm not going unless you kiss me. Will you be too shy with Craig there?

"Did you like your sausages and potatoes for tea? I cooked them especially for you with loving care.

"I don't mind not going out anywhere honestly, as long as you're with me I'm not bothered where we go or don't go. I LOVE YOU very much now and it's lovely to have you because you're my hobbit and you're so nice. I better finish now as my arm aches and the writing is getting worse. I think I'll go to bed and cuddle Timothey the bear. He's nice and cuddly usually and is a substitute for you.

All my Love,
Jane
XXXXXXXXXXXXXXX
And lots more
I LOVE YOU"

Jane and Timothey

Following the end of the Easter term I was to start my second period of industrial training and return to Bradford in September. In the final year we had to opt to specialise in either surface coatings or dyeing. I had opted for surface coatings. When asked where I wanted to do the industrial training I was given two options: Bradford or London. Bradford was my preference because

I enjoyed being there. I could continue canoeing and see Jane or Val, depending on who I ended up with. Most of the companies offering industrial training placements in the Bradford area were in the dyeing business. Before I met Val, London's advantage was that it would be a place where I could live with Jane and Nicole. Jane was willing to work there, putting Nicole in a day nursery. That no longer applied. Therefore, either location was suitable. Mr Nunn said I had created a good impression at Laporte and he wanted a similar impression to be given to Unilever at Isleworth. London was Mr Nunn's logical choice for my placement. I was assigned a place with Unilever in Isleworth.

I once told Jane that I would never go away from her for more than a few days. I was now committed to staying away for five months. By staying in Isleworth from April to August I went away from both Jane and Val.

Basically (a word that makes me think of Val because she used it often) I felt particularly lonely because Val was going home to Sheffield. All my other friends were going home too. And I was left in Bradford. When she set off, Val gave me her usual parting call,
        "Seez-yah."
But she didn't: Val and I never saw each other again.

April 1972:
The last place I wanted to be was 200 miles from Bradford, as was Isleworth.

My first digs in Isleworth were in Harvard Road. It cost £5 a week. After a couple of weeks Jane had some time off, so she came by train to visit me. I'd had no opportunity to introduce her to the landlady and when she saw Jane the following morning she was surprised to find a stranger in the house. Later, she told me that no guests were allowed after 10.30pm. It was a reasonable rule, since they had a twelve-year-old daughter. After that I moved to a house in Worton Road. It was down the road from what used to be Isleworth Studios, where the film 'The African Queen' starring Humphrey Bogart and Katharine Hepburn was made in 1951. I first watched that film on TV one Christmas Day with dad. It was shown at the time when we both enjoyed canoeing. We were amused to watch the African Queen successfully descend rapids that we considered were too dangerous even for a kayak, let alone a steam launch.

My rent for the tiny room in Worton Road was only £3 and Jane could stay there. It was the narrowest bed I'd ever shared, but we managed.

Thoughts:

"When was I last happy? Really happy, I mean. I was just trying to think. I must have been happy before Easter even though the pressure of exams was worrying. True, I've had happy hours, even days, such as during our visit to the Lake District but that wasn't the sort of happiness I mean. True happiness is when you feel elated all of the time and have no fear of it ending. That's how it is when I see Jane nowadays. When you're truly happy you are enjoying every minute of the present time and looking forward to more happy times to follow. It's a while since I felt that way. Prior to the exams there was the problem of Jane versus Val and before that I was bored. Going back further, I was leading a dull life at home. So within the past year there can't have been long when I worried about nothing and could say I was truly happy. I remember a few happy times of course but they didn't last more than a week or so. No. I'm wrong. I was happy last autumn. The problems with Jane and Val probably added to my enjoyment of life. I've been happy this year too. I have fond memories of Spring Place. I could be happy now if I wanted. Perhaps I don't want to be.

"I'm bored. The year has completed its cycle. I'm bored because I have nothing interesting to do. There's plenty of boring things to do, like watching television, going for a drink, doing some work, assembling some slides, perhaps starting a jigsaw. Few things are more frustrating than being unable to work due to lack of literature. I've two weeks to complete a piece of work but I can't start because I don't have the necessary books. It's noisy here in Isleworth. If it's not the aeroplanes it's the TV or the girl downstairs. Jane's coming here on Wednesday.

"Last night I couldn't sleep. I tried to think of something erotic but I could not conjure up anything interesting. It was a bit like when I couldn't get an erection when I was with Val. I could do with a bit of sex now. I recently took to drawing pornographic sketches. I feel like writing about sex but it always sounds crude and rarely erotic or even interesting. I used to write such stories in the loft at Blunsden from time to time. They involved comparatively long build-up stories during which I often lost interest in sex then as the story approached the climax I became impatient and finished the story in a couple of lines. Very much like my early attempts at making love I guess. I wonder if those essays still lie under the loft insulation where I left them or has someone found them, being disgusted at the filth of the author's immature mind. I also hid a copy of Lady Chatterley's Lover and Fanny Hill in the loft. I should have saved them. I guess they seem relatively tame these days. Just look what you can read and see in 'Men Only'. Does the sight of naked breasts arouse men now? Public hairs are hardly erotic sights. John, who is an engineer at work brings in pornographic books. Nothing is left to the imagination nowadays so even the most pornographic picture might not seem interesting.

"I hope Jane doesn't read this. It's for my thoughts, not for others to read. I want to be able to record anything without worry of future embarrassment or repercussions. Even if I just wrote the word Val and Jane was to read it, she'd be upset, get the wrong idea and cause trouble. To Jane, Val is a dirty word. She turns it round and calls her Lavatory. I have to be careful to avoid the words Llangollen or Sheffield because they are both associated with Val.

"Imagine someone, anyone picking this up and reading the seedy details. They might think I'm perverted or cracking up or something. Well, I probably am when I write here: my 'crack-up' book. The writing might give the impression that this is the sort of person I am all the time. In reality, I'm quite a normal sort of person. I write here when I'm lonely, fed up, bored or feeling sentimental. Yet, while I don't want anyone to read this, in the back of my mind I feel as though I'm writing to someone. To the book itself. It's not that I want someone to talk to. It is simply an urge to record the way I feel at a particular time so that at some time in the future I can look back and see how low I was at my lowest or how high at my highest. In most cases then, the book defines the extremes of my feelings. But it's not comprehensive. Parts of my character are either grossly misrepresented or omitted entirely. Parts are manifested in other ways. For example, if I feel aggressive I'm more likely to go for a walk than write here – not that I go for walks feeling aggressive very often. This looks like an introduction to my book.

"I feel nostalgic about Bradford. I left Jane there at 4 o'clock this morning, less than 16 hours ago. I gave Andy a lift back from Bradford and we got to Isleworth at 8.10. Right now, the two kids in this house are annoying me so I can't concentrate. I've to ring Jane in 50 minutes. I'm glad we arranged to phone then. I wish she was here now.

"Jane came down here on the train on Thursday evening. The train was due at 21.10 but arrived 10 minutes early so I met Jane as she was walking across the platform. I bought her some Turkish Delight and on the way back here we had chicken and chips.

"We were going to get married on December 11th and that was the day I slept with Val after deciding not to. What was supposed to be Jane's wedding night turned out to be one of her most dreaded fears."

When I phoned Jane, she was annoyed at me for going to the company clubhouse. Suddenly the pips sounded, indicating our three-minute conversation was about to end.

"Can I ring you up tomorrow?" Jane asked.

"Of course," I replied, but we were cut off before arranging what time. When I rang back a different girl answered and I didn't have enough coins to wait. I felt annoyed with Jane and let it show in the letter I wrote her that evening. I expected it to upset her but I'd be seeing her the following evening so it didn't matter so much. It made me feel less impatient to see her although I still missed her and thought a lot of her.

Towards the end of my stay in Isleworth I took Andy, Drek (yes, it was that, not Derek), John and, on a couple of occasions Joan, canoeing. Andy and I did a bit of cross-country (or rather town) running and I played chess quite frequently. It was not so boring then and I was a bit annoyed at myself for not starting to do all of these things earlier. The Thames was nice in the evening and we had some good fun there. One day, we returned to the social club house soaking wet and walked into the bar draped in towels. But this was not typical of my time there. Mostly I was bored. The weeks that dragged by from the beginning of April to the end of June were the worst.

At the end of my industrial training during the remainder of my summer vacation I painted grandma and grandad's house at Lavendon. It was a pleasing task. Next I started on mum and dad's house at Dagnall. Jane and I came down from Bradford during her days off, mainly for the purpose of me doing that job. I prepared a successful curry the night before and brought some of the sauce home for the others to sample. We arrived at Dagnall in the morning and after lunch I started painting, beginning with my bedroom window. I borrowed a ladder from the neighbours. It only required half of the two-piece extension ladder to reach the upstairs window. Jane sat on the lawn watching whilst I completed painting the first window. I remember banging my elbow on the funny bone but the sequence of events thereafter remains blank to me. No paint was spilt, neither was the brush dropped. Apparently I slipped partway down the ladder. Jane thought I was being funny descending the ladder like a fireman. I don't remember leaving the top. I landed hitting my head on the stone path. From all accounts it was a fairly hair-raising trip in an ambulance to Hemel Hempstead hospital but I failed to appreciate anything to do with that nor of the X-ray being taken of my head. But I do remember being wheeled on a trolley into the ward. I watched the ceiling. It seemed quiet in bed. There I was in bed in a strange place wearing only my underpants. I didn't shout out where am I because I guessed it was a hospital. A dream perhaps? No, I was awake then something must have happened to me. I remembered completing the painting of that window so I must be near Dagnall. Luton hospital I presumed. Then mum, dad and Mary were standing on one side of the bed and Jane on the other. They were peering down at me. There was a lot of blood on my pillow. I just accepted that without wondering about its source. Mum told me I was at Hemel Hempstead. They all seemed concerned about me. The radiance of their thoughts about me beamed down and I felt it warmly. Then there was just Jane. The heart-warming feeling was there too. I told her I felt dizzy. When I moved my head the ward and everything in it tipped dangerously in the opposite direction. It was nice to hold her hand.

The worst night of my life followed. I was still sicking up yellow sour tasting liquid from time to time and there was shit in my pants even though I had, with help, used a bedpan. I just had to get up because it was horrible lying down but every movement I made was sickening. After a couple of seconds of movement all I could do was flop back onto my back. I tried crawling down the bed to get out but I couldn't even get on all fours. There were sides to my bed and that annoyed me. It was terrible. I appreciated the treatment given to me by the nurses. I felt worried at having no appetite for several days. As I recovered I began to feel bored. I preferred to sleep most of the time. When encouraged to walk about I became really bored. Readers Digest made me even more so. The television didn't interest me. When I listened to the radio wearing headphones I noticed that the right speaker did not work: I guessed it had a loose wire. When I turned the headphones round the other speaker didn't work for my right ear either. At first I thought it must be something to do with twisting the wires around. It was only after a doctor examined me that I accepted that I had lost the sense of hearing in my right ear.

I was very glad to leave hospital after about a week. The following week I spent indoors mostly and I hated the way time was being wasted. There was a lot I wanted to do in Bradford, not least of which was being with Jane. The defect in my hearing and balance were upsetting but gradually improved. My hope for return of hearing in my right ear dwindled by the week. Now I could almost accept it is permanent. No stereophonic listening, an incapability of locating the direction of sound and difficulty in isolating a speaker's voice from background noise. It was disappointing. It was permanent. Yet I still was contemplating buying a stereo tape deck and I arranged the speakers for the best reproduction of stereo. The human body is capable of adapting itself remarkably well to adverse changes or deficiencies; however, the loss of one small part of bodily function is most noticeable.

September 1972:
Jane had rented a bedsit ready for my return to Bradford. It was in Apsley Crescent, off Manningham Lane, only about 100 yards away from the house in Mornington Villas where Jane was born. She cleaned and made the room nice, but the shared bathroom and toilet in the house left a lot to be desired. The damp weather seemed to be making more rust on my car every day and it would often fail to start in the mornings. Then I would spray the leads with WD40 and if that didn't work, remove the distributer cap, leads and spark plugs and dry everything in the room. The slope down Mornington Villas towards Manningham Lane helped when I needed to push-start the vehicle if the battery was down.

A view towards Lister Mill chimney

Darley Street

Queensgate

January 1973
Jane and I had now moved to a ground floor flat in Heath Road, Undercliffe. It was newly decorated and comprised a lounge/dining room, kitchen, bathroom and bedroom.

We took it in turns with Craig and Mandy to visit each other for evening meals. They were living in an upper floor flat in Wells Promenade, Ilkley. They came to us on his BSA Bantam. We enjoyed our evenings together. For their last visit, the bike refused to start so they came by train. I gave them a lift back to Ilkley and on the way we stopped for a drink at the Commercial Inn in Esholt.

My car failed its MOT so I was without transport apart from my pushbike which proved very useful. I had been considering buying a motorcycle but I didn't see them being much cheaper than getting a car. There were many things that I could spend money on, most of it being for the new flat.

Hearing with my left ear only took some getting used to, but I could still hear clearly through my left one. I hoped that full hearing would be restored and I would then look back to these days and remember what it was like to lose the sense of hearing from one ear. More likely I would be looking back to see how much more used to it I had become. After all, Craig managed for years and I didn't notice until he told me.

July 1973
On the day of my graduation, mum and dad argued, apparently because I had always been her favourite. Mum came to my graduation ceremony on her own. Afterwards, we had a steak house dinner. Mary said that dad had a major outburst on the occasion of my graduation, and mum ended up going on her own, leaving her alone with a raging madman. It was yet another incident that continued to haunt her.

After applying for numerous jobs, I was offered the position of Development Chemist at Marley Foam, at Lenham in Kent. It wasn't in the area I preferred, but I was anxious to secure a position in time for Jane and I to get married and the job offer was the first suitable one I received. During the interview I felt ill and although I didn't know why at the time, it might have been because I was worried about moving away from the area I loved.

My work involved preparing alternative formulations of polyurethane foams for motor vehicle applications such as seat squabs or door handles. I would collect the raw materials, which often included handling a 45-gallon drum of isocyanate from stores, weigh and mix the ingredients then pour the mixture into a mould, typically producing a square foam cushion. We didn't usually wear gloves, so by the end of the week my hands would be covered in resin which I peeled off over the weekend. My hands would be clean by Monday for the process to begin again. One of the employees I met regularly in the canteen was Jake. To me he was a quintessential cowboy, with lean features, a moustache and brazen manners, the mature version of a schoolboy bully. Jake explained some of the nasty pranks he did to men about to get married. I took care not to tell him about my forthcoming wedding.

Marley Foam Development lab

Thoughts:

"There's not long to go now before I leave Bradford. This morning I packed up my books to take to Dagnall. It depressed me. Today I received a contract from Marley Foam in Lenham, near Maidstone in Kent. Now it's signed and witnessed that's it – I can't change my mind. I have to go to Kent. I wish I hadn't felt so ill during my interview. If I had been well I probably wouldn't have been offered the job. They put my nervousness down to me feeling unwell when it was really because I was unsure about the job. Since I felt ill, when details of the job were explained to me, I didn't take it all in. For instance, I don't remember being told that I may have to work Saturday mornings, but that's what it says in the contract."

Finding suitable accommodation in the Maidstone area proved difficult so during my first week with Marley Foam I deployed a whimsical idea and purchased (with mum's financial help) for £250 a 22-foot converted lifeboat called Juanita. She was moored on the River Medway at East Farleigh.

Juanita

Living aboard a boat had seemed like an exciting prospect and cheaper than renting a flat. Juanita needed a lot of renovation work: the engine was unreliable and the interior needed converting to be more habitable for the two of us. I spent most of my spare time and money working on it. Early on, the wooden rudder was damaged and needed replacing so I had a replacement made out of metal. Once I got the engine running I motored a mile or so upriver and it stalled so I had to pay for a tow back. Also, water was drawn in through the propeller housing when the propeller was engaged. During the two months I lived aboard I worked hard on her but failed to achieve what I set out to. The limited space made work on board much slower than when on land. My main aim was to build in more storage space and live there semi-permanently. When Jane spent a weekend on the boat with me the boatyard manager's wife asked if we were married and I lied that we were. Work on Juanita was a long way from completion when the evenings started to chill and the mornings were damp from mist that lingered above the river. In September 1973 I moved into Upper Fant Road (which we jokingly referred to as 'up a fanny' road) in Maidstone. For the two unfurnished centrally heated second floor rooms with use of kitchen and bathroom I paid £7.50 a week. Not bad value, but a significant proportion of my income. I furnished the flat with second-hand items including a sideboard donated by mum and dad. It was the one they'd had since we were living in Northampton. Maidstone was six boring hour's drive from Bradford. Fortunately, I would soon be making my last journey there to see Jane.

Jane on deck of Juanita

Thoughts in September 1973, a review of the past 4 years:
"Now I'm a Bachelor of Technology (Colour Chemistry and Colour Technology). Is that all my four years at university was for? No. The degree at the end is just a part of what those four years gave me. Now I have one week left in Bradford before I become a common citizen working a regular five-day week for 48 weeks of the year. I'm moving to Kent. Six boring hours away from Bradford and from Jane. Extortionate prices for accommodation; and I have to find somewhere to live there. It wouldn't be so bad working away from Bradford if the financial reward was worthwhile, but it isn't. For the first few weeks or more I'll be spending most of my money on accommodation and travel. It's unlikely that Jane will be able to transfer to a hospital in Maidstone

to complete her training. Even if she could it would be a number of weeks before she could actually move down there. Meanwhile, she lives in this flat on her own. Lonely and expensive. One day I shall hire a van and cart all our belongings down here: that will be tedious and expensive too. Meanwhile, I shall be kind and loving to Jane, and not allow her misery to affect me. She wants me to feel lonely and miserable too. It serves no purpose – it could weaken the bond between us, not strengthen it. I let Jane know I miss her and wish she was with me, but should not isolate myself from the world just for the sake of it.

"The decision I made four years ago to go to university was probably the best I'd ever made. They've been really good years. Nevertheless, if I had them again I hope I would manage it somewhat better. Now I'm 23 and have reached the stage where I want to stop growing older.

"Last night I told Jane the purpose of my 'Thought Book'. I believe it will be very useful to know how I really felt at a particular stage of my life. When recalling thoughts of the past, the mind subconsciously sifts out events and feelings it doesn't want, giving a distorted picture of the past. I want to be able, say in 20 years, to think back and remember what it was really like when I was at university.

"If I had no written record my recollection of these days would probably be distorted because I would have forgotten some of the important aspects. I wonder how truthful mum and dad's recollections of 20 years back were. I once asked mum if she was happier now than she was after they had just married. She said she was because then life had so many worries and money was scarce. I have worries now and tomorrow I shall withdraw the last pound out of my current account. That doesn't make me unduly unhappy. At the moment I'm depressed at having to leave the dear old town of Bradford. Maybe mum has forgotten the carefree life she enjoyed in younger days and has chosen instead to remember the difficult parts. This 'thought book' will help me recall both sides of the story to give a realistic image of the past.

"Jane seems to think that an important part of the book is to write down all my nasty thoughts about her. I gave her a little lecture about it afterwards and it upset her. Jane must have read my previous entry because she was able to repeat the contents of the whole page. Yesterday she convincingly denied ever reading this book or even knowing where it was kept: I hope she hasn't looked at it. The beauty of this book is that I can write what I want without having to bother about how others may interpret it.

"It was when I was walking around town on my own last week that I started to feel that I should recall some of my recent thoughts. Bradford is a very nostalgic place. Even when I haven't been to town for some time I get nostalgic feelings when I go there again. It is a place full of character with its hills, narrow busy streets and dark sooty buildings. It is distressing that the old Kirkgate Market is soon to be destroyed. Indeed, there are few parts of old Bradford that are not in the process of not being pulled apart. I took some photographs of the market the other day with its busy little stalls, stone floor and roof of steel, glass and dust. I had a dish of pie and peas with mint sauce in front of one of the numerous little cafes there. It was a fairly warm day and I heard one of the women working there say "it's always either too hot or too cold in here". Then looking up at the poor state of the building I could see why it has to go. But the new market will never be an adequate substitute for the old. Just as I am told that the new indoor John Street market is nothing like the old outdoor one. The new market, right in the centre of town, will have a multi-storey car park. That's ridiculous where the ratio of cars to pedestrians is already too high.

Bradford Kirkgate market

"I was walking down the stairs in Brown Muffs department store when I recalled the large part that Jane has played in my university career. Right from my first term she has affected my life. In some ways I feel it would have been better if I had met more girls. I had three girls in four years but most of the time was with one. There cannot be more than half a dozen girls (other than my sisters) that have been of any importance in my life. There was Shirley, the first girl I really kissed. Teresa, the first girl I had any sexual inclinations towards. Several other girls who really only count as one between them. Jo, the first girl I had sexual intercourse with. Val, with whom I could discuss sex most freely. And of course, Jane, from whom I have learnt everything else I know about women. These are the girls of my life up to the age of 23. There really ought to be many more. Not more to come but more past. Looking at it from a scientific point of view I would never take six samples as being an adequate representation of the whole (hole?). If I had tried more of them I could have been surer of my final choice but what if I'd had a dozen more? I doubt if I would be any better off than I am now. I would still have the urge to have sex with other girls. I guess all men are the same in their sexual desires and would like, physically at least, to have a limitless supply of sexual partners.

"What about my other leisure time activities? Canoeing of course has been my major activity. But have I done well enough in it? Certainly, I could have done better if I had tried. I could have been a Division 1 slalom canoeist for instance. I might have played a bigger part in running the canoe club. Politics has never bothered me. A canoe club is for canoeing and as far as I'm concerned the organisation can be done by others. But if I HAD played a more active role then perhaps I would be more content now. From time to time it has upset me to see newcomers learn the sport, reach my standard and then overtake me. Lately I have come to accept this, seeing myself as a veteran (it's 13 years since I started this interest now) and instructor. In this capacity I have done well, having introduced and taught a number of people.

"I could equally well have become a proficient sailor, but after the cold, wet and boring day spent with the sailing club in my first year I never went again. Trampolining to some extent may have been improved but I don't think I'd ever have been a champion; my body is not as flexible as others. Finally, there was running, walking and cycling, any of which I could have followed up but available time was the limiting factor here. Photography deserves a similar comment to canoeing although I've never seen myself as an absolute authority on the subject so it doesn't bother me. Here again my role has been one of a teacher rather than an expert.

"Academically I have no great grumbles about myself either as in my hobbies I could have done better but I came up to my usual standard – middling in everything. That seems to be me all over: a jack of all trades and master of none. Mind you, the knowledge I gained of colour measurement from ICI saw me right through the course so that I always felt top in that subject. I was expecting a 2(2) a year ago and that is just what I got.

"What about the lads at the Lodge? Brian met Mandy when we were at the Lodge. I first saw Mandy after she and Brian were locked in his room one evening. We didn't know what they were doing, but they were very quiet about it. Mandy, then a very plain 'just left school' type of girl, is now Craig's wife and has become a middle class 'I know everything because I've read it' young lady. She seems to 'out-argue' her husband. She's alright though. Brian is married to Liz, who was a student nurse at BRI with Jane. Liz is now a qualified staff nurse. After leaving Tong, Brian lived in a farmhouse with Dave and Walt and later moved to a house in Girlington, next to a house full of nurses, one of whom was Liz. Apparently, Brian sold all his drugs and bought a camera – a wise move.

"Craig got back onto the Honours course in the third year and completed his industrial training at the International Wool Secretariat in Ilkley, which is where he had worked whilst I was at Unilver. After leaving Tong, Craig had stayed in digs half a mile from the university. During his industrial training he lived in Ilkley with Mandy. After getting married at a church in Gosforth and honeymooning in the Lake District they moved to the flat in Wells Promenade. "With just one week left of being a bachelor I am having lustful thoughts of having a final fling. Once married I shall endeavour at all costs to remain absolutely faithful to Jane. But there is something fascinating about 'having it off' with one more girl before getting married. One last chance! One last shag! In future I could look back and recall my thoughts and feelings. But there's more to it than 'a quick shag'. Repercussions. Jane would add it to her list of grudges for the rest of my life. She would find out. There's a girl called Linda living downstairs. Perhaps if I tried, with a little bit of concentration, I could get her to sleep with me. But if she was the one, how could I live with Jane in the same house as her? What about a prostitute then? Again, Jane would never forgive me. If I told Jane in advance she would be very upset that I even considered it. So it's out of the question.

"Have I lost more than the sense of hearing from my right ear? Could there be more damage to my brain? Am I being more careless? Often I overlook the obvious. Could working at Marley seem worse because of me changing? Two years ago, I might have liked the job. The problems I'm faced with there are no more complex that what I've faced before but I keep making silly blunders.

Images of Jane

Chapter 4: Marriage years

I had met Jane when we were teenagers and we got engaged a few months later. A week later, Jane told me she was pregnant by another man. The following year I met Val and for six months enjoyed intimate relationships with both. Jane and I might have broken the engagement because of those circumstances but after that our love for each other strengthened. I had a serious accident and Jane showed how much she cared about me. Besides, we had already made a commitment to marry each other and it was important to me to honour my promise. As a teenager, I had found it difficult to get a girlfriend. Having found one who showed she wanted me I wanted to make sure of keeping her. Maybe at this stage I might have listened to parental advice to wait a few years. But we wanted to live together and have sex, both of which were frowned upon if you weren't married. I knew for certain that mum or dad would not condone it.

My Wedding:
We got married on 6th October 1973. The wedding went well but there are numerous parts that I would prefer to forget. I spent the night before the wedding with Craig and Mandy in their flat at Ilkley. I felt indebted to Craig and Mandy for their hospitality.. I'd borrowed mum's Citroen Ami 8 van for the following week so I drove them to Bradford Registry office in the morning. Finding somewhere to park was difficult after a traffic warden was directing all traffic away from my chosen location. Since Jane had not spoken to me for a day or two (as was normal for a bride to be) I felt she was neglecting me. I wasn't sure that I wanted to get married.

I found the ceremony nerve-racking. The reception was held at The Hare and Hounds on Toller Lane. Most of the time I felt shy and nervous. I made a cock-up of my speech by saying that the combined distance the guests had travelled amounted to 1500 miles. Anne alone travelled that far from her Army posting abroad. I felt embarrassed on opening our gifts. Dad made one of 'his' speeches that made me cringe. He included a silly story about me that I chose to forget and few found amusing. Worse of all, he said he hardly knew Jane and didn't speak well of her. Rita stood up immediately and spoke kind words about her. I felt she was gorgeous, as were Josephine and Hazel. The best part of the reception was talking to those three friends of Jane. I promised Rita that I would look after Jane. Rita said she was cross with dad, and that mum was a snob. She also disliked mum's black dress. It was good to see Dorothy and her husband Dave. They made a better couple than Dorothy did with her first husband Terry. At the end, Jane cried amongst her friends for having to leave them and Bradford.

Wedding group

And what a mistake leaving Bradford was. My biggest yet. Three years earlier I could have bought a house for £25 deposit and £4 a week. If I had I would now be more content and better financially. Two mistakes. The journey to the Lake District went reasonably well. The van was good to drive. It was spoilt by being stuck behind a herd of cows being driven along a narrow lane at 2mph. Shortly after that we stopped on open land beside a lane and I took photographs, including one of Jane sitting on the fence next to a cattle grid.

Years later, I tried repeatedly to identify that location. I assumed it would be a reasonably direct route to where we were staying. Forty-five years later whilst out for a run along a lane I used regularly I recognised that the fence next to a cattle grid was where I had taken the photo. It was just three miles from where I now live. We must have detoured away from the main road between Kendal and Windermere and gone along the narrow lanes where we met the cattle, before descending a gated road to Ings.

Jane near Ings

We arrived at our tiny cottage at Watermillock, near Ullswater before dark. The honeymoon was enjoyable but for two things. Jane had forgotten to take the contraceptive pill for two successive days so it was back to condoms. What a time to forget! But what a week to remember! One disturbing memory lingers: Jane told me that she still had to pay maintenance for Nicole. I felt that since we were married all our income should be dedicated to ourselves.

Cottage at Watermillock

December 1973:

It was good to be married, different from just living together. Perhaps that was because we both give each other a little more than we used to.

I discovered that Jane read the part that I wrote in my Thought Book just before we got married. She mocks me by repeating my words, 'With a little bit of concentration...' and 'What about a prostitute then?' She said I had written nasty things about her.

On Christmas Day Mary and I visited grandma and grandad, who were both in hospital in Newport Pagnell, but in different wards. Grandma wouldn't visit him in his ward. Perhaps she didn't want to know how ill he was. Grandad tried to say a final goodbye to Mary and I, but we didn't cotton on, and told him we would see him soon. Grandad died the following year. The memory of our last visit still haunts Mary.

January 1974:

Whilst living in Bradford we saved money in a jar, with the intention of using it to pay bills. Now the money dwindled. There was once a couple of fivers and a lot of loose silver in the jar but by now there was only about £8 left. I felt that a jinx is at work. Since starting work, my income had trebled but I could no longer save.

Thoughts in February 1974:

"Craig and Mandy have got a house now. If I had got a job in Yorkshire we would probably have one too. Instead, we're stuck in Kent with no more money than I had a year ago or even five years ago. It could be worse. If, like Craig, I'd stayed in Bradford to do a PhD I would still be in Bradford but with no prospect of buying a house. I might be able to buy a house by summer; then I may even be grateful for these months at Marley. Anyway, I've cleared my bills from Bradford, got a boat, gained a lot of experience and know what I want from life. That's a lot of improvement from eight months."

My search for a new job went well. I had strong hopes for a job in Cheshire. Then I had an interview with Formica in Maidenhead. It was a good job but a very poor place to find somewhere to live. Worst of all, I was booked for speeding in the car I hired – another chunk out of this month's salary. Two interviews followed: one at Margate, the other in Staleybridge. My interview at Margate was successful: I was offered the position of Chemist at Thor Chemicals Limited and started on 1st May 1974. They had just completed a new factory at Margate and were moving there from Crayford in southeast London. I commuted from Maidstone to Margate normally with Chris, who was a sales manager at Thor. When he was unavailable, I sometimes stayed in a caravan parked at Thor with Len, the works engineer. Len was a great character, a skilled engineer, an expert on car maintenance and a bit of a rogue. He would describe the circuitous routes he drove to avoid the police. Perhaps it was simply because he didn't tax his cars; I didn't need to know. During the evenings I stayed in his caravan I earned a bit of overtime painting the chemical plant steelwork.

Jane sarcastically suggested that I should write in my 'Thought Book' whilst I was on my own. She suspected that I would write bad things about her. I wanted this book to be a fairly continuous record of my thoughts as life progresses. Progress it must. One spends the first 21 years of life wanting to be older and the rest wanting to stay the same age. One gets funny ideas as a child. Not that I wished to be younger again. 'Just thinking'. That could be the title for this book, but it might be misinterpreted as to mean thinking justly. It would be more applicable to some parts of the book if that first word began with the letter L.

I left Marley and started working in Margate on 1st May. We continued to live in Maidstone whilst I progressed the purchase of a house in Ramsgate. It took Thanet Council seven weeks to decide if we qualified for a mortgage. I was glad I left Marley. Now I had a good job that I enjoyed doing; a job with a bright future in a friendly company. I was their only Chemist and I had a large, brand new laboratory all of my own. Ten years previously, the owners were making chemicals in a parent's garage. The company was worth £2m and expanding rapidly. If I had stayed with Marley I would probably be earning more because after I left (and probably because so many of us were leaving) the laboratory staff had enormous pay rises. My income of £2000 ought to have been enough but I was still no better off than when I was at university. For once, I could think back 12 months and be glad it was still not then. Now I felt much better off. Not financially, but in other ways. The previous year was not good at all. I could write a long account of what I should have done but that would serve no useful purpose. I wasn't very accurate with my prediction of my first weeks in Kent. The first week was as predicted in that I spent the evenings flat-hunting, but without success. I found a boat instead. On the second week I was living on the boat and from then onwards all my spare time was occupied on doing it up. Largely a waste of time really. Hours and hours of it. After spending all that time and money, Juanita was not really any better than when I bought her. Better in some ways but worse in others. A bit like me. The winter didn't help.

Craig and Mandy were doing alright financially. She got a job as a teacher and he began taking a PhD. They bought a suite for £500, a carpet for £65 and he was seriously considering spending £2,000 – £3,000 on a boat! Their house cost about £5,000. Ours was to be £6,500 which by comparison didn't seem too bad with it being in the south. Mind you, our house was nothing special. I expected that it would be a very long time before we had money to spend on luxuries.

We decided to have a baby and Jane became pregnant soon after. She completed her training at Bradford and got a job as a nurse in Maidstone hospital. When we had a completion date for the house in Margate Jane finished that job and immediately took a holiday. Guess where – Bradford of course! She planned to decorate the house in Ramsgate once we moved in. After that, she would get a job in Ramsgate, although she preferred to stay at home and look after babies, dogs, rabbits, hamsters, guinea pigs and any other friendly creatures.

We had little useful furniture for the house in Ramsgate. We put quite a lot of stuff in the front room that Jane didn't like, such as a 3-piece sofa, the old sideboard that was originally bought for our house Northampton and grandfather's old hi-fi. It was also a convenient place to store my bike.

On our walks into town we would invariably pass Thanet Pet Stores. Cocker Spaniel puppies were displayed in the window and each time we passed Jane would look longingly at one in particular. He must have been there for some weeks. It was a shame to see him kept in that window for all that time. It was as if he wanted us to help him escape, so we bought the dog and called him Ben. He had the most comfortable seat in the house – a sofa in the lounge. He was a shy little puppy and especially scared of men. His ears were so long that when he walked with his muzzle sniffing the way forward, the end of his ears would trail on the ground and needed cleaning after each walk.

Jane and Ben outside pet store

Thoughts in December 1974:

"Jane's gone to Bradford. We have a dog. His name is Ben. Despite my desire to visit Bradford I have to stay here to look after Ben because he gets car sick. I have a car: a 1500 VW saloon, left-hand drive. It goes well and should be good for long journeys. I would like to drive it to Bradford, visit Craig, see Bradford.

House and car at Marden Avenue, Ramsgate

"We now have a house in Marden Avenue, Ramsgate. We don't like Thanet – it's a boring place, lacking character. The surroundings are dull and people uninteresting. We don't go out much, but decorate instead. Jane isn't working yet. We have set a deadline of 1st January. She said she would be working if we lived in Bradford. Jane does housework, shopping and walks Ben. Work is good but I ought to be earning more than my annual salary of £2000. I need 25% more because of the enormous rising cost of living. We are spending a lot of money, mainly on the house."

May 1975:
Jane went to stay in Bradford again, this time for 3½ weeks. I found that living on my own in Ramsgate was mentally tiring. I was missing Jane and that made me feel more appreciative of her. Duties such as cleaning, cooking and taking Ben for walks were tiring. I was planning to take a holiday and go camping and walk the South Downs Way with Ben. I spent half a day packing for this. However, the car proved to be not reliable enough. The fault was a sticking push rod that operated the petrol pump. I made a repair but was not confident it would last. Instead of going away I stayed in bed until ten, had a nice breakfast, then took Ben and my camera out. I had a couple of drinks in Ramsgate and walked along the coast to Broadstairs, then got the train back to Ramsgate. In the evening I went into Margate. I walked round Dreamland then went for a drink at the West Coast near the harbour. I returned to Dreamland to look at the Big Wheel, the Cyclone and the girls. Whilst looking at the girls I felt glad I married Jane. I could see things in her that I could not expect from most others. I didn't want anyone else. I'd become adapted to Jane. Maybe I always was. As I looked at girls in the fair and mentally stripped them I always found something I didn't like about them. Some girls were too fat, others too flat. I didn't like the clothes some wore or the way they styled their hair. Some looked dirty or wore too much makeup. What was most important though, was the way they moved and how they interacted with their friends. It was difficult to describe what appealed to me about the way girls moved. I liked girls to move confidently but not in a showing-off way like a model on a catwalk. Jane was what I wanted. If you ignored everything except sex, the majority of girls would be acceptable, but so was masturbation and because sex is not all there is to a girl, that was often the better option.

I continued to have problems about money. This month it was to do with the car. I had an accident in March and faced a charge of driving without due care and attention. Last year, a pedestrian bumped his head on the roof rack of my car whilst it was parked and I got charged; then I had the speeding ticket, so the latest offence was the third within three years so my licence would be suspended. When I attended the magistrate's court my lawyer suggested that I should not have been charged for the roof rack incident: it was due to the pedestrian's carelessness and not by the roof rack being unsafe. The judge reprimanded the lawyer for questioning validity of the adding up rule. I lost my driving licence for six months.

Whilst Jane was away I feared that Henry the hamster was dead, not just hibernating. Jane would be upset when she returns. He was the second Henry hamster of ours to die. Poor Henry."

Jane found a job at a nursing home. It was not a good job and she finished work some months before the baby was due. We spent time and money decorating and carpeting the second bedroom for the baby. It was the best room in the house. Jane started being fussy about housework. Every day she brushed bare floorboards and the few carpets we had and she was reluctant for me to sit on the soft Ikea chair in the dining room because it crushed the cushions that she had plumped up. She didn't bother with Ben's room (the lounge) or the third bedroom. I set that up as a darkroom. I spent my evenings in there. One session was just long enough to develop and print a single roll of 24 exposures in black and white. I never tried processing colour film: it was too complicated and required controlling temperatures to tolerances I would be struggling to achieve.

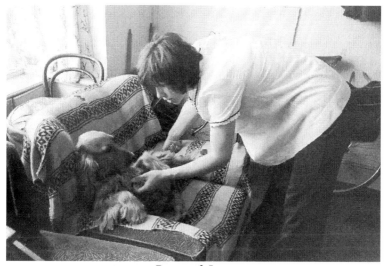

Ben and Jane

Margate maternity hospital was less than a mile from my workplace. Jane and I attended antenatal classes there and studied books about baby care. On 25th August Jane was admitted to the hospital during the night. I stayed with her for a couple of hours but there was no sign of delivery so I went back home. I went to work in the morning. The hospital phoned me in the afternoon. I hurried across and arrived in time to see the birth of my first child. It was a memorable event. I wanted to share my delight with others but there was nobody in the area that I could tell. All I could do was to go for a walk, phone my parents and write in my 'Thought Book'.

Thoughts on Tuesday 26th August 1975, 19:00 hours:
"Jane has had a baby girl! She was born today at 16.27 hours. We are both very pleased about her. Jane went into hospital at one o'clock this morning. I returned there at two o'clock this afternoon and stayed with her whilst the baby was born. It was a wonderful sight and experience.

"I realise now how tired I am, having had only three hours sleep last night, and all the excitement, and I don't think the full effect has dawned on me yet. I'm very happy about it, but with both the baby and Jane being in hospital it seems a bit lonely. I'm going back to visit them again shortly.

"We plan to call the baby Rebecca, or Bex for short. I think at first I wanted the baby to be a boy but now that it's here and it's a girl I don't mind at all. I told mum the good news on the phone and she was pleased. She says they are coming to see us in September. Mary is on holiday in France at the moment so she will have to wait until she comes back before I can tell her."

Jane and baby Bex

We brought up Bex according to what we learnt from the antenatal classes and a book we bought. Mum and dad visited us in September and in April 1976 we took her to their house. Ben had to be sedated because he suffered from car phobia. If he was made to go in the car he would poke his muzzle out of the window and the back of the car would become streaked with his saliva. Mum and dad had moved to a newly-built house in Staveley, near Kendal in Cumbria. Ostensibly, the house was a stepping stone to a future retirement cottage in a more beautiful part of the Lake District. Dad had been in the Lake District without mum and his return journey passed through Staveley – there was no bypass in those days. He saw the new estate and stopped to look at the showhouse. He decided there and then to buy the house, paid a £25 deposit and when he got home said to mum,

"I've just bought a house!"

In August that year, Jane received the following letter from the mother of Steve, who had fathered Nicole.

"I am writing this letter on behalf of Steve because he is in hospital and cannot write it himself. He want you to know that he will write to you about Nicole as soon as he comes out of hospital. The doctors don't know what wrong with him so they have him there for observation. He is in a lot of pain most of the time and they are not allowing him to sit up.

He would like to know how Nicole is getting on. He keeps saying how he wish he could see her. He asked me to say hello to the child for him.

I am Stephen's mum.

Eugene Francis

P.S. He asks me to enclose a picture of little Steve."

We later learned that Steve died.

It was good to be the Chemist at Thor. I had my own laboratory and great freedom in what I did. The company's main product was an organic mercury biocide used as a paint preservative. My main task was to analyse the mercury content of every batch by titration. There was no instrumental method available. I became skilled with the titration technique. To do the calculations I bought a programmable calculator: much quicker than using log tables. Thor also made mercuric chloride by burning the metal with chlorine inside a 2-foot diameter glass tube. A good rate of overtime work could be earned by raking out the product and packing it into sealed drums. Despite wearing full personal protective equipment, I still got mercury burns on my face. Every month, I sent off samples of urine for mercury analysis for all employees, including those in South Africa, where Thor had another factory. The results were satisfactorily low for UK employees but high for the South Africans. My job also included safety and environment. The Health and Safety at Work Act 1974 had just come into effect. I got on well with my boss, Basil, and we regularly had a meeting after 5.30 to discuss my work. One project was to investigate the production of red mercuric oxide suitable for batteries. My research involved visiting the National Library and Patents Office in London: there was no internet in those days! It was very difficult to find useful information. I carried out my own experiments using scaled up laboratory equipment. One of the challenges was to set up a 40-gallon chiller in the lab. Another was to link the equipment to the lab fume cupboards and this was far from satisfactory. The chemistry is simple enough: metallic mercury is oxidised with concentrated nitric acid. The two nasty chemicals produce a nasty biproduct of nitrogen dioxide, whose brown fumes were not always fully contained by the fume cupboards. Anyway, I made some of the required product and the customer's feedback was encouraging.

Thor Chemicals chemistry laboratory

Jars of chemicals were kept on shelves in the laboratory. On one of the shelves I had a 250ml bottle of mercury. I liked to tease visitors by asking them to pass it to me. They thought it was stuck to the shelf! Mercury is more than thirteen times heavier than water so the small bottle weighed over 3kg. I also made up my own photographic developers.

Jerry was employed there as microbiologist and he had two assistants, Mike and Judy. Jerry, Judy, Mike and I took our morning break together in the canteen, and sometimes completed the Daily Mail crossword. The canteen overlooked Ramsgate Road and another game was to guess the colour of the next passing car. It was usually red, and most likely to be a Ford Escort

Judy in microbiology laboratory

I danced with Judy at the office Christmas party and she really turned me on. Unlimited drinks were supplied by the company and at the end of the party somebody took me home but I don't remember much afterwards.

Financially, I was just about managing to make ends meet. The rate of inflation rocketed from a norm of about 5% to 24% in 1975. Accordingly, Thor increased my pay each month by an amount equal to that month's inflation. It was a good company to be with and I liked my job. However, Jane and I both disliked living in Thanet. It felt so remote. Every long journey began with an hour's journey to London and a further hour to get through or around the city, wherever we were heading. The people were nowhere near as friendly as northerners. For instance, each Friday lunchtime, a group of us went for a drink at the Windmill Inn on Newington Road. We saw the same regulars every time but they never greeted us. We decided to move back to the north.

1976 Bex

1976 Bex and Mark on motorbike

Jane became pregnant again. Shortly after her pregnancy was confirmed, our doctor in Newington Road gave Jane a routine Rubella injection. He didn't first ask or check that she was pregnant. We were advised later that as a result of the injection there was a high probability that the baby would be deformed on birth. The options were to risk giving birth to a deformed child or to have an abortion. It was a difficult decision that made us feel very angry with the doctor who gave her the Rubella injection.

Between the end of October 1975 and July 1976 I wrote eighty letters applying for jobs in the north of England. I kept a list of them all. I suppose you could call the handwritten list a spreadsheet, but such things hadn't been invented then. One of my first applications was to Listers Mill in Bradford. It would have been an ideal location, being at the top of the road where Jane used to live. I attended an interview there in December but was unsuccessful. I was interviewed and offered positions by Bradford Management Centre, BTP Cocker (Oswaldtwistle), Lancaster University, Bury & Masco and Rockware Glass (Knottingley). I accepted the offer of employment from Rockware and started working there as Environment Officer on 20th September 1976, with an annual salary of £9,351.

We moved to a rented house in Oakdale Crescent, Wibsey, Bradford. Jane had an abortion: the unborn child was a boy. He would have completed our happy family. To make matters worse, at the hospital Jane was treated with contempt because nearly all abortions were due to unwanted pregnancies.

I had already paid a deposit on a new Barratt house in Kirkthorpe, near Wakefield. This was a suitable location, being between my workplace at Knottingley and Bradford. Before we moved in, I enjoyed many evenings after work painting walls inside the new house. I would take cheese sandwiches and make Camp coffee (which was cheaper than instant) for my evening break. We liked the new house, had friendly neighbours and enjoyed the semi-rural location. The house was between 10 and 12 miles to work (depending on the route) so it was possible for me to cycle there. My target was to complete the journey by bike in thirty minutes, but it usually took me forty.

However, the house wasn't suitable for Ben. In Ramsgate, he had his own room and he didn't need to travel by car very often. Here, there was no suitable space for him and we visited Bradford every Saturday. I placed an ad in the Yorkshire Post and identified a suitable new owner in a village near Harrogate. It was heart-breaking to leave him. A few weeks later I called at the house to see how he was getting on. Ben barked at me as he did with strangers but rather than feel happy that he was clearly content with his new home it disappointed me that he did not miss me like I did him.

About 1,000 people worked at the factory in Knottingley, including many true Yorkshire tykes: down to earth, plain-talking people. I would sum it up by the saying, "They don't call a spade a spade, they call it a fucking shovel." If they had an opinion that you might not like, they told you directly. I liked that. My best friend and colleague at Knottingley was Eric, the works Fire Officer. We both enjoyed chatting together and with the joiners in particular; when I visited their workshop their typical greeting would be, "Eh up lad, are you laikin today or workin'?" A more friendly opening might be "Nah then! What yer bin up t'?" I gradually amended part of my southern dialect, such as replacing the long A with the shorter one: grass rhymes with lass, not with arse.

My main responsibilities as Environment Officer were to develop techniques and evaluate environmental hazards pertaining to factories within the Rockware Group. The main hazards within the factories were noise and dust. The monitoring techniques were at a pioneering stage and the ones I developed were later shown to match recognised standards. I also produced Material Safety Data Sheets for all the substances used in the group, similarly to my own design. In order to produce an index for the sheets I was pleased to learn and write a computer programme that arranged the list in alphanumeric order. The programme was stored on a cassette tape and took a few minutes to load onto the computer.

There were some pleasant walks around Kirkthorpe and the neighbouring village of Heath and beside the river Calder, although many of the views were marred by coal mining spoil hills or other industrial features.

On some weekends I would 'escape' (according to Jane) from home and go walking with Dave in the Lake District. Few people ventured into the more remote valleys so on a hot day it was safe to cool off by taking a 'skinny dip' in a beck.

Walk beside River Calder in Wakefield

Skinny dipping in the Lake District

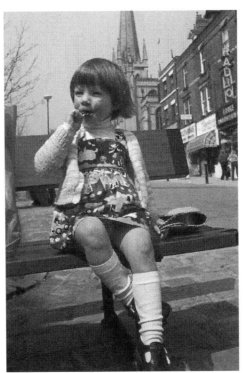
Bex in Wakefield

Jane kept the house immaculate. Her favourite piece of cleaning equipment was a dishcloth. They had to be the right sort. Ones with green borders were for wiping children's faces and hands (there was no such thing as a wet-wipes in those days) and the red ones for everything else, from window ledges to toilet seats. Jane used dishcloths so often they wore out in a couple of weeks. Ren would usually be bathed in the kitchen sink.

In April 1978 we had another baby. She was born in Wakefield and we named her Adrienne, Ren for short. Our next-door neighbour baby-sat Bex when I took Jane to the maternity hospital. By midnight there was no sight of the delivery beginning so I returned home. Consequently, I missed the birth.

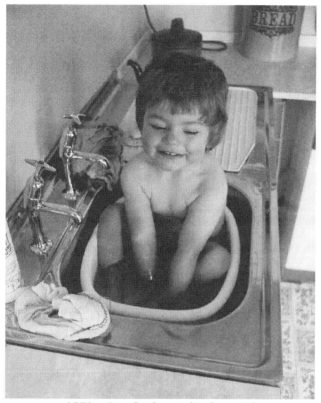
1979 – Ren bathes in kitchen sink

1980:

On Friday 30th May 1980 we went for a ride in the car, mainly to look at areas where we might choose to live next. Although we liked Kirkthorpe we wanted to move now because it was difficult to get Bex to and from school. We headed northwards and stopped first at Kippax and then Aberford. We would have liked to live there but there weren't any nice houses that we could afford, which was up to £20,000. During the trip we stopped at Coxwold and visited the Mouseman's shop. Jane wanted a cheeseboard costing £11 and sulked, calling me mean and stingy when I refused to buy it. We didn't use them anyway. We passed Rievaulx Abbey but Jane wasn't interested in looking. She preferred a visit to the seaside so we went to Staithes, arriving at four o'clock. We continued along the coast to Runswick and Whitby, where I parked just up the road from Woolworths, where Jane bought a dishcloth.

A little after five we reached Robin Hoods Bay. It was an especially peaceful place. The tide was in so we played on the seafront and sat on the cliff top to eat cherries until the fish and chip shop opened at six. It made an idyllic scene and the food was perfect.

Robin Hoods Bay

The Greens, who looked after Jane when she was pregnant with Nicole, lived nearby so we visited them and had a short chat, met their daughter and some of their pet animals. Our final call was Scarborough, but when we stopped for a wee on the way Ren dropped her can of pop on the car floor and had her bottom spanked. There were many fishing boats in the harbour and they made a pretty site. Jane enjoyed eating two waffles and the rest of us doughnuts. We left Scarborough at nine and arrived home at 10.30. Ren gave the impression that we were trying to murder her rather than preparing her for bed but she soon fell asleep again. It was a good day out: a very full one covering 200 miles but not too tiring and with plenty to see.

At the end of 1980, the works Safety Officer retired and I applied and successfully achieved the position of Safety/Fire Engineer at a salary of £7,827 per annum. Our growing family meant that we needed a larger house and we found a suitable one in Bradford. At £22,000 it was a bit more than I had budgeted for but my salary increase enabled me to get a suitable mortgage. It meant that I would have a 28-mile journey to work but it was exactly the place we wanted to live in. The house was originally part of a 17th century chapel so it had immense character. It was down an unmade lane and surrounded by newer houses but only 200 yards to the junior and infants school. A condition of the mortgage was that we had to install an electro osmotic damp-proof system. To save cost, I chose to remove the plaster to a height of two feet above the floor. This involved removing a set of bookshelves attached securely to the whole of a lounge wall and chipping laboriously at plaster that was difficult to remove in parts. When the contractors came to install the equipment, they said I could have just removed the plaster where it was damp. I also removed the dark pine kitchen fittings and replaced it with units I constructed to my own rustic design. There was a utility room that originally also served the purpose of a second bathroom. We never upgraded this area so it became a playroom for me and the girls. Bex named it the 'community centre'.

Chapel Fold, Wibsey

The "Community Centre"

We entered the house from the back, took our shoes off in the porch (which I panelled in pine) and passed through what would have been a dining room but remained an empty space for most of the time we lived there. Jane swept the bare floor every day. We upgraded the central heating system. The contractor had to weld an extension onto a drill bit to get through one of the two-feet thick walls. The house was still always cold in the winter. Two hours after turning the heating on, the room temperatures had barely risen, even though the radiators were too hot to touch. It didn't seem to obey the laws of thermodynamics.

As in previous houses, the best part of the house was the children's bedroom. Once Jane had hoovered the carpet in the morning you couldn't go in there until bedtime because that would crush the carpet pile. Shoes were not allowed to be worn anywhere in the house, except in the 'community centre', but Jane's dad never heeded that rule.

Every Saturday morning, I would take the two girls into town and do the shopping, with Ren in her buggy. I would buy chops and sausages from the pork shop in Queensgate, fish from Rawson Market and Fox's Jammy Dodgers from John Street market. Sometimes I would buy what were called something that sounds like 'ponchkers' from a Polish stall there. They were like doughnuts, only tastier. Morrisons Victoria supermarket was next door. When I came here in 1970 I think this was the first and only Morrisons supermarket. They still had a stall in Kirkgate market. We would buy a beef suet roll and jam roly-poly from Marks and Spencer's and if Jane needed some more dishcloths we would get them from Brown Muffs because that was the only place that sold the right type. Brown Muff & Co had been in Bradford since the beginning of the 19th century and was the only department store in the city since Busby's on Manningham Lane closed in 1978 and burnt down the following year. Busby's used to be best at Christmas because they had a massive toy department with a Santa's grotto. One year, Father Christmas flew in by helicopter to give his reindeers a rest.

On Saturday afternoons I cleaned the house windows.

Afterwards we went to grandad's house in West Park Terrace. He always had treats waiting for the children and there would usually be a rugby match to watch on TV before teatime.

My new job was a management grade position which enabled me to use the managers' restaurant. This was waitress-served and worked out cheaper than using the works canteen. The company also offered managers a monthly supply of free cigarettes. That was because it was normal at the start of a meeting to offer your guests a cigarette. Even at the time, it did seem odd that every monthly safety committee meeting took place in a cloud of smoke! These meetings often included heated arguments between the union safety representatives and managers. My position was usually between the two sides, aiming for a balance between costs and benefits of improvements. There were two full-time union officials, Pete and Jack. Each had his own grubby smoke-stained office. I placed myself between the managers and the full-time union officials and put up with grief from both sides.

The factory was spread over two works. I was based at the Headlands works and the Bagley works was across the other side of town. Each of the works had a medical centre and a full-time nurse, Jean and Sally. Every employee who worked in a noisy area had an annual audiometry test. The hearing in my left ear was perfect every year.

Written internal communications were done by sending a memorandum, or memo. I would give my hand-written drafts to the secretary for typing with the required number of carbon copies. Any necessary amendments would have to be made on each copy. The memo would then be sent out by internal post and the recipients would reply in the same manner. A simple exchange of memos took at least two days. This was equivalent to the few minutes that an exchange of emails takes today.

Eric now reported to me and we made such a great partnership that others referred to us as 'the dynamic duo'. Matt, whose office was near mine, was also a good friend. He was a totally dedicated Christian, keen on photography and planned to open a Care Home with his wife. Matt dismissed all scientific theory and logic to such an extent that when, as an example of logic, I tried to demonstrate 2 + 2 = 4, he replied,
    "If you say so Mark."

Matt and Eric in my office

My office contained an internal and an external phone, but of course no computer. I cultured Busy Lizzies and other plants in my office. I could be alerted by pager when out of the office. I could remember most of the phone numbers I needed. External calls went through a switchboard that was operated by two women. The Personnel Office employed four lovely ladies and it took almost a week to calculate and issue the wages. Rockware was starting to introduce computers but most records were still kept on card indexes. Sinclair introduced the ZX 81, the first home computer in 1981. It was programmed by cassette player and its memory of 1KB could manage a simple game, but little else. A new one cost £50 but I bought one second hand and used it very little.

I decided to change my car for a motorbike and an ancient Land Rover. The bike was fast and ideal for travelling to work from Bradford. One of the winters was extremely cold but I kept warm with handlebar muffs and newspaper under my jacket. The main problem was that the visor would freeze so my vision was sometimes restricted to a narrow band. The journey was mainly along the M62 which was sometimes covered in snow on all but the nearside lane. The Land Rover was fun to drive, especially when other vehicles were slithering in the snow on the steep hills in Bradford. It was awfully slow and long journeys seemed to take ages. One day, I drove it to Buckden where we met my mum and dad. I wanted to show off the vehicle's amazing ability so I drove them to the steepest gradient I could find, stopped, engaged low ratio and set off in what I thought was first gear. Unfortunately, I inadvertently selected reverse and set off downhill, much to the alarm of my passengers. So much for showing off.

I parked The Land Rover outside the house. Late one evening, following an argument with Jane, I decided to sleep in the vehicle. I had got quite comfortable when Jane came out and persuaded me to return to the house. Perhaps the argument wasn't that serious after all.

On Monday 31st May 1982 we took a train to York to see Pope John Paul II. It was so crowded in York that it took over an hour to walk from the station to the race course and when we were there the Pope was too distant for us to see him properly.

I sold the bike and Land Rover and on 1st December 1982 bought, with financial assistance from mum, a new Citroen 2CV for £2,400. We were delighted with the car. It was quirky and highly versatile. All the seats could be removed and the roof rolled back so it could carry bulky loads and the seats could be used as picnic chairs. I would take the girls out for a ride and walk on most Sundays. A packet of biscuits would often suffice for lunch!

1983:

For her fifth birthday I bought Ren a bike. She quickly learnt to ride it on grass at the end of Chapel Fold so the stabilisers were not needed for long.

Ren on her 5th birthday with Bex

By now, mum and dad had moved to live in Staveley and bought a holiday cottage in Torver, near Coniston. When we stayed 1983 but Jane didn't much like it because it was cold and damp. I regularly took the girls to play by Coniston Water from the car park at Brown Howe. Jane wasn't keen on that either, so when we discussed where to go she would say, "Not bloody Brown Howe again!"

One evening after tea I walked to the top of Coniston Old Man the 'straight' way. Before leaving, I told my family to look out of the window at 7 o'clock to spot me on the fell. I left the cottage at 6 and hurried to reach the part of the fell that was visible from the cottage by 7. My heart was really pounding as I laid my red jacket onto the ground, so I hoped they looked. I reached the summit at 7.20, descended via Cove Quarries and explored a 40-foot diameter cave, which was rather wet. An even wetter tunnel was not worth visiting. I passed an intact shelter, complete with fireplace. Its size suggested that the miners must have been very short. Further down, I tripped over a stone and did a forward roll into soft, cool, black mud, which I washed off in a stream. I was back by 9.15. The family said they forgot to look out of the window for me.

Ren and Bex at Brown Howe beside Coniston Water

1984:

Jane and I had discussed whether to have another child and although the topic was not concluded we sort of decided to have no more. Jane had already been pregnant four times. When we talked about having babies, Jane described the pain of childbirth and said that men don't know what real pain is. She had been taking the contraceptive pill for a number of years but following medical advice, decided to stop taking it. Perhaps because of a miscalculated safe time of her period Jane became pregnant.

During the pregnancy I made sure we would not have any more babies. The vasectomy operation was a good experience in itself! Perhaps it was the local anaesthetic, maybe not, but during and afterwards I felt strong gratitude to everyone involved. The surgeon would have got most of the fee but I felt the nurses deserved the same amount. They all seemed to care: it gave me a warm feeling. One nurse spent most of the operation near my head, watching and checking that everything was okay. She was the best person there for me. In the afternoon I felt fine but was advised to rest so I took Ren to see a film at the ABC cinema. When I told mum that I'd had the snip, her response was,

"So, you've sold the business!"

For the Easter holidays, we rented a Hoseasons Holiday home near Launceston, Cornwall. I watched breakfast television there for the first time. We liked to feed a goat at the site but you had to be careful to keep beyond the full extent of its chain to avoid being butted. The girls enjoyed a pony ride over the moors. On the way back home, we stopped at a Laura Ashley shop and bought some curtains. Every available space in the 2CV was filled with passengers and luggage and I had to keep the throttle on the floor just to keep above 50 mph.

Wednesday 3.10.84:
In the morning, Jane's contractions had become more frequent so I phoned work to say I couldn't attend and took Jane to the maternity hospital. The nurses thought it would be a while before the birth would start so they left us in a side ward. A few minutes later the baby started to emerge. I pressed the emergency call button before realising you had to pull, not push the button. The team arrived and out popped a baby girl.

In my 'Thought Book' I wrote about my joy:
"Jane has had another baby girl. Her name is to be Beth. She just popped out whilst I was there and I've loved her ever since. Beth is daddy's baby. I love her now more than ever."

Since Beth was definitely my last child, so I decided to watch her grow more carefully than our other two daughters, not wishing her older, but savouring every day of her development. I was pleased we had another daughter.

1985:
On Saturday 11th May I'd completed the normal morning shopping trip and in the afternoon whilst cleaning the windows noticed a large cloud of smoke. I walked to the top of St Enoch's Road from where you could look over the city. The smoke appeared to be coming from Valley Parade, the home ground of Bradford City Football Club and this was confirmed when I went back home and listened to local radio. Instead of broadcasting details of the football match, the commentator was describing horrific scenes of people with their clothes on fire. Later, it was confirmed that 56 people died and about 256 were injured when a serious fire broke out in the main stand. It was described as the worst fire disaster in the history of British football. A video of the match shows play being stopped after a small fire in a stand that was packed with spectators. The clock on the recording shows that within three minutes, the whole of the stand was engulfed with flames. The heat was so intense it ignited clothing of people escaping onto the pitch. Forensic tests concluded that the fire was probably

started by a dropped match or a cigarette stubbed out in a polystyrene cup and then spread ferociously through the old wooden stands.

Bradford City Football Club fire

I would often do our supermarket shopping at GT Smiths in Knottingley. A familiar sound would be the clicking of the hand-held machines that operatives used to put price tags on every item. Sometimes, I would buy a present for the girls, including a pull-along Snoopy dog toy for Ren. It concerned me that much of the glass packaging was being replaced by plastic. Fizzy drinks were now being sold in plastic bottles instead of glass. It seemed that glass containers were going to be used just for the higher quality goods. The glass container industry seemed to be struggling: glass was being replaced by plastic and overseas competitors were producing lighter glass containers. I decided it was time to move on and resume my career in the chemical industry. This time, I wrote 25 job application letters and attended nine interviews, including two with Glaxochem in Ulverston and two with Bayer in Newbury. I would have liked the job with Thornton's chocolate factory in Belper. I attended an interview there but was not given any chocolate and my application was unsuccessful.

A small but rapidly growing company called Fine Organics had recently been bought by Laporte. They had a small factory at Peterlee in County Durham and had started building a brand new one on Seal Sands, Middlesbrough. They wanted a Safety Officer and it seemed a great opportunity for me. I applied and attended an interview at Peterlee. The offices seemed tiny and there was no site visit. The current job holder, Ken was moving on to manage quality full time. I was offered the job and accepted and started on 2nd September. Peterlee was an 85-mile drive from Wibsey so Fine Organics paid for my accommodation until we could move nearer. I stayed in various guest houses and inns mostly around Stokesley because that was nearer Bradford and suitable for commuting to Seal Sands. My favourite place was at Harker Hill Farm. I would leave Bradford on Sunday and return on Friday. Later on, I would return home for one night on Wednesday then drive to work early on Thursday. My journeys took various routes, sometimes even passing Brimham Rocks.

On some Thursday evenings, I accompanied a fellow resident to a pub quiz at the Buck Inn, Chop Gate. One of the questions that I often repeat was this:
"If you stand on the summit of Roseberry Topping on a clear sunny day, what is the furthest object you can see?"
You can substitute any viewpoint you like. Most quizzers will ponder over the geography of the area and perhaps in this case suggest Redcar Ironworks chimneys. After allowing a suitable time for them to think I announce the answer:
"The sun."

Thoughts in November 1985:
"I've been away for four days now and I miss Beth. I miss Ren and Bex too. Beth is my baby and she's growing, changing rapidly and I don't want to miss any of it. I decided that before she was born.

"Hopefully, we shall be moving soon. It's been dragging on for three months now and this is no way to live. Not that it's unpleasant. It's not nice being away from my family, especially my daughters. Beth was born in Bradford. It's a pity to leave Bradford. Most of this book is about my life there. Bradford is where it all started. By it I mean a new phase of life for me. It was also where Beth's life started 15 years later."

Our house-hunting expeditions covered a vast area. It was essentially a triangle linking Whitby, Northallerton and Durham. We found a suitable house at Brompton, near Northallerton.

One weekend I took the three girls to Staveley for a break before we got involved in the hectic hustle and bustle of moving from Bradford to Brompton. It was a good weekend. Bex and Ren enjoyed it and were a joy to have with me. They slept in the new bedroom that had just been built. Beth hardly left my side. She wouldn't sleep until she saw that I was going to sleep in the bed next to hers too and twice she slept in my arms. People often asked Bex and Ren to stay with them but nobody seemed to want to have Beth. Beth was my baby: Daddy's baby.

As before, my normal Saturday routine was to take the girls shopping at Northallerton, then spend a lot of the afternoon cleaning windows. The house had over 170 panes of glass in its Georgian windows and every pane had to be cleaned. Jane checked every pane to make sure I got them smear-free, right into the corners.

Manor Court, Brompton

Work at Fine Organics was challenging. New processes would be introduced at lightning speed – in one meeting the engineer really did sketch plant layout modifications on the back of a cigarette packet! Odour was a problem, and complaints were received regularly from the neighbouring factory of Fisher Price Toys. The source of the foul odour was mercaptans, a type of chemical contained in our waste stream. The human nose has an unusually high sensitivity to mercaptans: we can detect it down to a few parts per billion and for that reason it is added to natural gas so that leaks can be detected by smell. Following an odour complaint, operators would sometimes pour hydrogen peroxide solution into the works drainage channels. It killed the odour but a transparent blue flame sometimes formed above the channel. My improvements to the emergency procedures included relocating the self-contained breathing apparatus to outside the hazardous area: their purpose was for tackling emergencies, not for escape. Laporte, which was a major producer of hydrogen peroxide, developed a waste treatment process using that substance to destroy the odour. The process seemed to work, but on some batches there was a sudden rise in temperature and pressure. It was the main topic of our safety meetings. We were beginning to identify the cause and a possible solution. Meanwhile the process was continued unchanged.

On my return from a shopping expedition one Saturday morning Jane told me that Ken had phoned from work at Peterlee to say there had been an explosion. I returned the call and Ken said there had been an explosion and fire, with a possible fatality. From the A19, as I approached Peterlee I observed a large cloud of black smoke above the factory. After identifying myself, the police let me through the road block and I went to the offices where the rest of the staff were gathered. There was not a lot I could do. One of the operators had been killed by an explosion of the waste treatment vessel. His work mate reported hearing a loud screaming of escaping gas immediately before the explosion. The killed operator must have been close to the waste treatment vessel when it ruptured, hurling fragments through the roof and across the tightly-packed plant. Once the fire was out, I accompanied the chief fire officer to explain the contents of remaining drums, cylinders and vessels. The wrecked plant was deep in water which covered my ankle boots. The stench lingered on my clothing and footwear for months afterwards and the memory of the disaster in my mind for ever more.

I continued to 'escape' to go walking with Dave in the Lake District. One Saturday morning in March 1987 we set off from Tilberthwaite intending to walk to Torver via Wetherlam, Swirl How and Dow Crag or Goat's Water. The weather started misty with a light fall of snow. Our walk began very pleasantly up the side of Yewdale Beck. Higher up we encountered patches of deep snow. Higher still, snow lying over ice made progress up Wetherlam Edge very difficult. Eventually, we reached a cairn by a metal stake. Visibility here was down to about 50 metres and the wind chill temperature was very low. We thought there was a trig point shown on the map and that maybe we were at Black Sails. We plodded on, the going very difficult with soft, deep snow and a biting wind that was sometimes head on and at other times from the right. We had no compass and no idea which way we were walking; there were no clues anywhere to be seen. Discretion being better than valour we decided to turn back and follow our footprints in the snow down to Tilberthwaite. It seemed to take three or four times longer to get back to the cairn by the metal stake and far from a straight line. As we began descending Wetherlam Edge we met some people coming up. Five minutes later we realised that the footprints we were following were not our own: we had ascended much more to the right. We skirted around the side of the mountain for ten to fifteen minutes but could find no other footprints so we set off back to the summit, stopping on the way to eat. We then identified that we were on the right path in the first place so we slithered off down again, with me sledging where possible on the seat of my waterproof over-trousers. Once more, we found we were following someone else's footprints so essentially we were lost! The strangers' footprints eventually merged with those of our own route of ascent. We arrived at Tilberthwaite very wet, mainly from the perspiration inside our waterproof clothing. Whilst we didn't achieve what we set out to do, the experience was certainly a contrast to everyday life!

After the explosion, work at Fine Organics was unrewarding. Laporte sent in their own safety specialists (why not before the explosion?) and everyone apart from warehouse staff moved to the Seal Sands site. I was allocated an office that was neither in the administration area nor in the production area: it was in the warehouse. A training specialist, Ted was appointed to introduce a new safety culture. He was a pleasant man but was angry when I delivered his training sessions in a different way to himself. I sought out alternative employment and was pleased to be appointed Safety, Health and Environment Manager at Rohm and Haas at Jarrow in July 1987.

The 50-mile journey from Brompton to Jarrow took over an hour if I drove there directly. Usually, I drove first to Yarm, where my work predecessor lived, then continued to Stockton, where the Environment Manager lived. The three of us took turns in driving the remainder of the journey. My little Citroen 2CV had a struggle carrying three full size men!

It was time to move house again. Durham was again the preferred location but I could find nothing suitable. In the end it came to choosing between two houses in South Shields. The two properties were similarly priced and only about 100 yards apart. Jane preferred a new build on Brandling Court. I preferred the more attractive modern house on Parkshiel and that is the one I bought.

We moved to South Shields in September 1987. For Jane, it was an even longer step from Bradford and her family and meant losing touch with friends she had made in Brompton. I decorated and furnished the house as Jane wished. Everything apart from paint came from Laura Ashley. Most weekends we would shop at either Newcastle or the Gateshead Metro Centre. Jane would buy clothes and footwear for the girls. To manage the finance each month I would use nearly all of my salary to pay off what I could from credit cards. Further purchases were made by credit card or using cash advances from a different credit card. That minimised the amount of interest payable.

The following is an actual example of one month's summary of my credit cards:

Credit Card	Due	Pay
Barclaycard	£433.89	£434
Access	£1320.91	£326
M&S card	£237.70	£140
TOTAL	**£1992.50**	**£900**

My net monthly income was about £1000 so I kept £100 for cash purchases. This month I paid off all of my Barclaycard, thus gaining up to 58 days free credit and avoiding interest charges on that card. The following month, I would try and clear the balance on Access, but each month, the debt increased. There was little scope for reducing our expenditure. We didn't go out, didn't take holidays, rarely had alcohol. Jane was not going to economise on buying stuff for the girls, nor on the amount of time she spent on the phone: one phone bill came to £200.

At work, we launched a 'Wellness Campaign'. Employees were encouraged to commit to exercise in selected activities for a specified duration each week. I chose swimming and running. A group of us swam at Hebburn baths twice a week during our lunch breaks. Another work colleague introduced me to 10k road races. The first one I entered was at Team Valley Trading Estate in Gateshead. Until then, I hadn't realised what a difference it made to run with others. The camaraderie amongst fellow competitors was unique: although ostensibly we were there to beat each other it was not about winning, everyone helped each other to do better. I ran faster than when I ran alone and at the end of the race felt great. And, of course, I got a tee shirt.

1987: The 3 girls on a restored Sunday School bench

1990:

I needed to earn at least 10% more so I looked for a different job, this time restricting my search to an area within commuting distance. I attended interviews with Hydro Polymers Limited (HPL) and Fujitsu, both requiring Safety Managers and both based in Newton Aycliffe, County Durham. Fujitsu were completing construction of a brand-new factory producing microchips. HPL, the largest employer in the town, made bulk Poly Vinyl Chloride (PVC). I had already heard of HPL through their success in Fire and First Aid competitions. After one interview with HPL, two with Fujitsu and similar offers from both I accepted HPL's offer of £23,000 starting on 1st November.

My job at HPL was similar to the previous one but better than any job I had held before. For once I could apply the experience gained over the years instead of just having to deal with day-to-day operational problems.

In August I recorded my goals as follows.

Long Term Goals:
Income sufficient to eat, clothe, house, heat, etc. family to present standard plus:

- Holidays to £2,000 pa;
- More clothes to £1,000 pa
- Go out weekly, say £1,500 pa
- Save £2,000 pa

Achieve by 2005

Property: 4 beds, double garage, utility room, nice garden, good location.

Achieve by 2010

Health: Stay well and active into old age   Achieve by 2025

Family: Achieve compatible goals   Achieve by 2010

Career: Key management position in a well-respected company with demonstrable results of work   Achieve by 2005

Other: Write to an acceptable standard either a story, book, play, music, film, etc.   Achieve by 2015

Short Term Goals:

Establish role and status at HPL	Achieve by 28/02/91
Identify key areas at HPL	Achieve by 31/12/90
Implement strategy to prevent backlogs	Achieve by 31/12/19
Income to exceed outgoings by at least £50 pa	Achieve by 31/01/91
Swim 100 miles in 1990	Achieve by 31/12/90

A big advantage of the HPL position is that it included a fully-expensed company car and I had a range of vehicles to choose from. One year earlier, I had changed my Citroen 2CV for a Citroen BX, which was a vehicle I had been wanting for some time before that. Now I could have an even better model, the fast Citroen BX GT. At 8 o'clock on 1st November, my start date, Don the company driver pulled up outside the house in my new car and we drove to work. My new career had begun.

The drive from home at South Shields to work at Newton Aycliffe took 35 to 40 minutes. During the journey I listened to spoken word tapes or CDs. I greatly enjoyed listening to books borrowed from the library; so much so that I'd welcome a traffic hold-up and sometimes I sat in the car park until a chapter had finished. In addition, I listened to self-improvement recordings that I bought, including a subscription to a monthly series.

On two or three evenings a week, I would transport Ren to Monkton stadium, home of Jarrow and Hebburn Athletics Club, where Jimmy Hedley helped her become a talented sprinter. Jimmy was internationally known as the trainer of Steve Cram, David Sharpe and Vince Wilson. I got to know Vince because he used to train at the same time as Ren and would attend the same race meetings. Vince was a great athlete, running a mile in 4 minutes and 10 seconds at that time, and had a remarkable character. Following a difficult childhood, his positive thinking enabled him to achieve everything he aimed for, be it a massive collection of CDs, a stylish apartment, or of course running excellence.

The Great North Run, a half-marathon from Newcastle to South Shields, passed through The Nook, which was less than half a mile from our house. I first entered that race in September 1991 and thereafter every year. My family would wait by the roundabout and cheer me on as I passed. In anticipation, I would relax my pace for a few minutes before reaching them so that when I passed I could look 'cool'. Jimmy Savile sometimes started the race and then ran himself. Based on the time Savile claimed to have completed the course, he would have overtaken me. He never did, so he must have cheated somehow.

Jane took Ren and Beth to and from school in the mornings, lunch times and afternoons. She spent the rest of the day and a lot of the evening doing housework. In a week Jane would spend 50 hours doing nothing but housework. On the days we went out, say to Bradford or Newcastle, the earliest we could leave would be midday so that Jane could do her minimal amount of housework in four hours before we left. To maintain Jane's standards, we did not sit on the sofas (the Laura Ashley suite was never used). The cushions remained plumped up and in perfect order. We did not use the dining room. Every day Jane wax-polished the chairs and table and if we used the furniture it would show. Instead we sat on the floor and used the toy box as a table. Bex often sat on the stairs to do her homework. Occasionally, I would suggest that we sit on the furniture. Jane would reply angrily, "Sit on them if you want." Her tone made it clear that if I carried out that suggestion I would regret it for many days afterwards. It was better to put up with the odd arrangements than try to change a habit that Jane had developed over the past decade.

When we met, Jane had a fantastic kiss. We didn't kiss now. We didn't hug each other, didn't even hold hands. In bed, Jane wore a bra, knickers and nightie. I preferred to be nude.

We often talked about getting a dog. We thought that the size and temperament of a bulldog would suit us best. Jane loved our last dog Ben and although she liked the idea of having another there was no way she would allow one in the house. I said he could live in the garage but Jane thought that wouldn't work.

One evening in April 1990, I spotted an ad in the paper for a Welsh Springer. Jane agreed that Beth and I could go and look. There were two or three pups remaining in the litter at a private house in Sunderland. We thought a dog would be better than a bitch and there was only one. They called him Pudding because he was soft. We bought him and took him home. Jane loved him and changed his pet name to Toffy because he was the colour of toffee. I registered him with the Kennel Club as Barnaby Goldwine.

Toffy

I made Toffy a cosy kennel underneath a bench in the garage and cut an opening in the bottom of the side door so that he could walk in and out of the garden at will. Toffy soon got used to his new home. At seven o'clock every morning I would take him out for a walk up to Cleadon windmill and back. We would usually meet other men walking their dogs at the same time. I never got to know the men's names and we would refer to each other by the name of our dog. One of the regulars reminded me of an older version of Jimmy Nail, so when Jane asked whom I'd met I would refer to him as Jimmy Nail's dad. On returning from the walk Toffy and I would each take a dose of cod liver oil (Toffy had his own spoon!), I would feed him then go in for my own breakfast. We followed this routine every day, whatever the weather. It made a good start to the day.

Toffy's morning walk to Cleadon Windmill

Toffy was a wonderful companion, especially to me and Beth. I would spend many evenings with him in the garage. I made a cosy den for myself in the loft space where I could read, listen to music and enjoy a glass or two of whisky. Occasionally, I carried Toffy up the ladder so that he could sit with me. Toffy's den was equally cosy, insulated underneath with layers of newspaper and heated in winter with a red incandescent bulb. Anne, Belinda and possibly others were surprised when I bought Toffy, as if they didn't think I needed the emotional support that a dog provides. I was never one for displaying my emotions openly so others must have thought I didn't have any.

At the end of February 1991 Jane found herself becoming breathless from walking up the short gradual slope to our house. At first, the doctor dismissed it as being an infection. On a second visit he reluctantly sent her for tests, thinking that there was a low probability of tuberculosis. In March, Jane spent a total of 14 nights in hospital. The tests carried out were a pleural biopsy, ultrasound scans, CT scan and a mammogram. In April, she spent four nights in South Shields hospital and five nights in Newcastle. A lymph node was removed for biopsy and tested positive for cancer cells. It was as I had expected, so when Jane told me during a hospital visit I expressed no surprise. She was angry with me for not showing remorse.

HPL was an excellent employer and supported me throughout Jane's illness, in particular by giving me as much fully paid time off work as I needed: it amounted to several months absence from work. It would have been better if we lived nearer Newton Aycliffe than the 35-mile, 40-minute journey from South Shields. We had considered moving nearer to work; in fact the house sale was with an estate agent, but at this time moving would have added even more stress to the family. Apart from that, nobody wanted to buy the house.

In May and June Jane spent eight nights in Newcastle Hospital. A chest x-ray revealed a massive pleural effusion (fluid in the lung). A sample of the fluid was found to contain adenoma carcinoma cells. No tumour could be located despite extensive tests. The fluid was removed on several repeated visits to hospital by a painful process of inserting a cannular between the ribs in her back. Over the course of a year, many litres of fluid were drawn off but the lungs seemed to refill as quickly as it was drawn off. Two separate treatments failed to stop the build-up. Although the primary tumour was never located, secondaries appeared in several locations.

Jane was given a course of chemotherapy. This proved to be the most awful experience of all. Total hair loss was bad enough but by far the worst part was the sickness. Try to imagine the worst possible hangover. Then double it. Now continue feeling that way for ten days and ten nights. Enjoy a couple of weeks break then repeat the whole ghastly process twice more. Then after all of that, discover that the whole episode has had no beneficial effect at all. It is difficult to imagine exactly how Jane felt but that's the closest description of it I can make.

In 1992, Jane was given an experimental drug. That had no effect at all, neither good nor bad. The only worthwhile drug she took was Tamoxifen and its only value seemed to be that it stopped her periods. Every month, her breathing got steadily worse. Just walking upstairs was a major effort. New setbacks appeared from time to time. She suffered new pains, lumps, sores and swollen breasts. By summer, Jane's health started to deteriorate much more rapidly. The effusion had spread to the second lung. Radiotherapy was used to stop her breasts from swelling and although it achieved a result, it caused skin burns that added to her general discomfort.

We were visited regularly by Jane's mum and sisters. Their main concern was for the future welfare of the girls. They considered that there was no possibility of me staying in full-time employment. Presumably, I was expected to sell the house and live on social benefits. Perhaps they thought I had savings. In fact, my debts continued to grow every month. We once had a family meeting with Anne and we all sat on the staircase. Anne even commented on the peculiar seating arrangement so even she did not appreciate Jane's extreme housekeeping rules.

Jane's last week was especially traumatic. By the beginning of August, it was clear that she had weeks rather than months left to live. We took each week as it came.

Anne, Belinda and their mum Jean were very supportive and everyone we knew was anxious to help in any way. In practice, there was little any of us could do. Jane's main worry was not for herself but for her children, for the future wellbeing of Bex, Ren and Beth. She was bitter with me for moving us away from Bradford seven years earlier. She was angry with me for giving a higher priority to my job than to the girls. To her, the family was everything. She didn't ask much for herself. Naturally, I kept the house clean and tidy and did all the other household chores. But nobody could possibly come close to the standards that Jane had previously maintained. Jane told her sisters and friends that the house was a mess.

A letter from Jane's friend Carole:
"Dear Jane,
I received your letter yesterday and what a shock it was. I can't stop thinking about you and feeling sorry for you especially when you say the house is in a mess because there I can sympathise. Although to some it would be unimportant to people like us it is just another burden to add to our worries, the house just has to be kept up to. (But I like your attitude when you say you'll just have to not think about it.) I'm afraid it is sensible to get priorities right, and at this time your children come first. I do think you also have the right attitude in that you will have to be strong and try to think positively, although there will be times when you will break down and say it is just too hard to fight it. I have a friend in York who has gone through a lot of trouble with her family - my husband alcoholism, two children on drugs and she says it is just the 'Yorkshire grit' that has got her through and I think there is a lot in that. It must be awful having to wait for more detailed information and treatment, as your mind must be in turmoil thinking this and thinking that. I had to smile when

you say Mark has never shown any feelings, because he must be as shocked as you but just doesn't know how to cope with it, especially when you say he's never shown any feelings about anything as long as you've known him. Because I'm a bit like that.

David many a time says, 'Just say that you love me,' but I can't say it.

I usually say, 'You ought to know I love you; I make your meals and wash your shirts, that's proof enough isn't it?'

We are all different. I put it down to the way we were brought up."

Late on 5th August Jane said she wanted Belinda, who lived in Harrogate, and Anne, who lived in Huddersfield, to come and stay. They stayed for a few days so that from then onwards at least one of us was with Jane all of the time. Jane was taking a lot of drugs but she was reluctant to do this. She hardly slept. It seemed she was afraid to sleep but she wanted to do so if only for a few hours relief. She could not find comfort. Lying down caused her to feel panic through a fear of drowning.

On 11th August the doctor offered Jane something to help her sleep. She refused, perhaps because she knew it was the final step. On the 12th she changed her mind, being desperate for sleep so she slept for a few hours that Wednesday night, often waking in the night in a confused state before falling into a few more hours of sleep.

In the morning of 13th August, Jane couldn't swallow more than a few drops of water. She needed water but more importantly although I didn't know at the time she needed her tablets. She got neither. Two small acts then stood out as tender and intimate. Firstly, she seemed to find relative comfort leaning against me instead of the pillows. Secondly, she wet the bed and was distressed by it but seemed greatly pleased while I cleaned and changed her. It sounds trivial but it meant a lot to me. At 11.00 o'clock Jane demanded to see the doctor even though he was due to call at 2.00. A doctor on call arrived and prescribed something to help her relax. It was a mistake for me to leave but I dashed down to the chemist and came back with the medicine. Anne had arrived in my absence and she was with the girls next to her. I prepared the drug which had to be squirted into her mouth with a syringe. She swallowed it, Jane then looked at me straight in the eyes and stared. It was as if she was trying to tell me something. Her eyes bulged. It must have been at that point she died. It was 12.15. It was as if she had waited until me, Anne and the girls were all there, together. And even though we knew the time would come sooner or later, when it happened it was a shock.

Baby if you've got to go away
I don't think
I can take the pain
Won't you stay another day
Oh don't leave me alone like this
Don't say it's the final kiss
Won't you stay another day

Don't you know
We've come too far now
Just to go
And try to throw it all away
Thought I heard you say
You love me
That your love was gonna be here to stay
I've only just begun
To know you
All I can say is
Won't you stay just one more day

Baby if you've got to go away
I don't think
I can take the pain
Won't you stay another day
Oh don't leave me alone like this
Don't say it's the final kiss
Won't you stay another day

Stay Another Day, East 17

I listed the drugs that remained when Jane died. They were Haluperidol, Nystatin, MST, Morphine Sulphate, Dexamethasone, Co-danthramer, Amitriptynine, Temazepam, Amitriptyline, Warfarin, Ondansetron and Temgesic.

The funeral mass and cremation took place in Bradford, one week later. So in the end I took her back to Bradford after all, even to the chapel of rest at Wibsey which was close to where we used to live. The funeral mass was at her dad's church, St. William's on Ingleby Road and it was exactly right - for Jane, for her father, her family and me. In the past I have never thought much about funerals, but to me this was a special event. Strangely, it was much more important for me to get that right than our wedding 19 years earlier and it was a much grander affair.

Make me a channel of Your peace
Where there is hatred, let me bring Your love
Where there is injury, Your pardon Lord
And where there's doubt, true faith in You

Make me a channel of Your peace
Where there's despair in life, let me bring hope
Where there is darkness, only light
And where there's sadness, ever joy

Oh Master, grant that I may never seek
So much to be consoled as to console
To be understood as to understand
To be loved as to love with all my soul

Make me a channel of Your peace
It is pardoning that we are pardoned
In giving to all men that we receive
And in dying that we're born to eternal life

I'm convinced that the cancer that led to Jane's death was due to, or at least exacerbated by, the stress caused by the circumstances in her life brought about by me.

Jane and I met each other at an age when we were both enjoying our first experiences of intimate relationships. I was anxious to retain a type of relationship that I had longed for over a period of several earlier years so when Jane agreed to marry me I was delighted. We got married when I was aged 23 and Jane 22. Inevitably, as we became older, we developed in different ways. My priority was to achieve a successful career; Jane's was to produce a family to be proud of. They could have been compatible goals, but we pursued them independently. Each of us wanted the other to change direction to suit our own aims. Jane developed what today might be recognised as an Obsessive-Compulsive Disorder (OCD) for housekeeping. Neither of us considered the obsession to be a mental disorder. It began whilst Jane was pregnant with Bex; housekeeping was perhaps just something to keep her occupied. Over the years, her expectations of housekeeping standards increased to such a level that only she could see a difference. It could be a speck of dust on a ledge, a tiny smear on a window; things that others would only notice if shown: they would regard such imperfections as insignificant. Whilst I found this behaviour irritating, I was able to tolerate it, and there was no possibility of changing it. The development of my career involved us moving to different locations. Jane was able to tolerate this but there was no possibility of me changing this behaviour either. We continued to want the other to change whilst resisting changing our own behaviours. Jane wanted me to leave her and the family. I could stay in South Shields and support them living in Bradford. That was not an affordable option and there was no way I would give up my children. When we got married I promised Jane, for better or worse, to stay together. Even though it was for the worse, that was my promise and I intended to keep it. There seemed to be no way out of the problem. As it turned out, Jane's death provided the solution.

Chapter 5: Later years

Over the two weeks after Jane's death, most conversations were about Bex, Ren and Beth. For the past few months, Anne had spent a lot of time talking to Jane who was angry with me and whose concern was for the care of the girls. Anne's suggestion was for me to give up the best job that I had ever had, move all three children away from their schools, sell the home we had lived in for five years and find somewhere to live and work in Harrogate. Another alternative could be for the girls to live with Anne and/or Belinda. This seemed to be the favoured choice of Jane, who considered me incapable of bringing up the children without her. Having just lost my wife, was I now expected to give up my children as well? I made enquiries, talked to the children and made rough financial calculations. The problem seemed insurmountable. I had no savings. For the past six years or more our expenditure exceeded my income, so I had become increasingly in debt, covered mainly by credit cards. My job at HPL included a fully expensed company car and my net pay was sufficient to cover our current expenditure. The mortgage on the house was paid off because it was covered by a life assurance policy. Now was an ideal time to recover financially. If I gave up my job for a part time one I would not be able to finance the suggested alternatives. And little or no consideration had been given to my feelings. Jane insisted that I was unable to provide the care and support the children needed, which she had devoted to them all of their lives. She wanted the girls to be living close to Anne and Belinda. It was an impracticable solution. This was of course a highly traumatic time for the children. They wanted life to continue as close as possible to the way it was before. They were being asked how they felt about the alternatives and that just added to the stress. Our doctor was surprised that a plan for our future living arrangements had not been agreed while Jane was still alive. His support for me and the girls was better than anyone else's.

I expressed my feelings in a letter to Craig on Tuesday 13.10.92:
"Time marches on. Never before has the saying 'time is a great healer' been so true to me. It is quite remarkable how over the first few days each day was better than the previous. Unfortunately, our grief was soured by a near feudal disagreement between me and Jane's sisters. My plans for life without Jane had been moulded in my mind for many months. Jane had different plans for the girls. Anne and Belinda shared Jane's plan, were indeed central to it and were committed to it. Overnight my two greatest allies became enemies. I felt everything I did or said was being questioned. We had long difficult arguments

in which I was usually defeated and made to feel worthless. Anne's husband Roger and notably the doctor were supportive of me. Most other people seemed open-minded about the situation."

In retrospect, the ongoing solution seems remarkably simple but at the time it appeared to be a daunting prospect. Once organised it worked well. At 8.00 o'clock each morning I took Beth to the house of a friend who had two daughters in the same school including one in Beth's class. Beth had lunch and tea with the friend and I collected Beth after work at 5.30. Meanwhile Bex (who was then 17) and Ren (aged 14) went to college and school respectively. The girls coped well; Bex and Beth extremely so. Beth handled Jane's death better than anyone. She was been an inspiration to us all and a great support to me.

Until July Bex and I had not been getting on well at all. I put it down to her adolescence – I was horrible when I was 16 too. Then suddenly I realised what friends and relations had been telling me for months was true: Bex was a lovely girl. After Bex turned 17 we got on with each other fine, for most of the time anyway. Ren, who had more interests and friends than the rest of us put together, found life difficult. Not at home particularly but more at school where she felt isolated. There was no-one of her own age with whom she could talk about her feelings. I guessed it must have been difficult for her friends to know how to respond; it was hard enough for adults.

Additional support (mainly for me) came from Toffy. For me at least Toffy had played a big part in helping me through the past year.

January 1993
Jane had kept in touch with a friend she had known since 1970. The friend had moved to Canada, kept in touch with Jane by letter and always signed off with the words 'love and peace'. I wrote her the following letter:
"I don't know when Jane last wrote to you but I think she must have told you that she had cancer. It was first diagnosed in March 1991. When I write this down that seems ages ago and with all the trips to hospitals, the treatments, the tablets, the pain and the suffering it must have seemed an eternity to Jane. But during the terrible illness she thought more of the children than of herself. Jane died at home shortly after midday on 13th August 1992. A funeral mass was held at St Williams church, Ingleby Road, Bradford a week later and the cremation was at Scholemoor.

"I am sorry not to have told you this tragic news earlier, but I am sure you will know that it is not easy to do. Jane went through hell during the last months and weeks and finally she got out of it. The three girls, myself and her sister Anne were around at the time and all she needed to know was that the children were alright. The girls are doing marvellously well. Considering what they have been through they could not be expected to have done so well. Bex has matured from a teenage schoolgirl to a fine young woman. She works hard studying for her 'A' levels which she will take in May/June. She will get a good grade in English Literature and passes in History and French. Bex plans to go to university in October and her favourite is York. Apart from college work, boyfriends are her major interest.

"Ren is working hard on her GCSE course, which includes GCSE PE. She is a keen athlete and trains four evenings every week. She did well in a cross-country race yesterday but her main interest is 200m or 300m races.

"Beth has been an inspiration to us all, especially me. She knew all along what was happening to her mum but I was unsure if she could really understand what it meant. Beth has been the bravest of us all and adapted to the changed circumstances admirably.

"We are all settling into the changed pattern. Obviously there are hard times, sad times, sometimes anger and bitterness. But most of the time I am proud of my family, and credit for this is due almost entirely to Jane, who devoted 17 years of her life on just that.

"The last words in each of your letters to Jane now seem all the more poignant and sincere: love and peace."

Thus, our lives continued. Bex went to university, Ren continued running and I continued working. The years that followed were the most successful of my career. We introduced what was known as Dupont's Safety Training Observation Programme, or STOP for short. Through this, we achieved a great improvement in site safety performance and became the only site in Hydro to win the President's Safety Award for two successive years. We also won the Chemical Industries Association Responsible Care Award.

When she started university, I wrote Bex my "Ten Commandments" to her. The first ones went something like this:

1. Make lots of friends
2. Don't get too attached to one lad
3. Enjoy your drink but don't have too much
4. Don't do drugs
5. Spend within your budget
6. Work hard
7. Play hard
8. Be yourself

Soon after starting at Preston University, Bex met Ray and broke Commandment number 2. Their friendship was probably strengthened by the facts that Ray had recently lost his father and Bex her mother.

In April 1993 I walked the Dalesway, an 80-mile route from Ilkley to Bowness, spread over two weekends. Toffy came too! The first two days were with Ren and we spent a night at a guest house in Grassington. It was probably about this time that Ren decided to be a vegetarian. We passed some lambs and Ren said, "We shouldn't eat lamb; we should keep them as pets." But of course, if we didn't eat lamb we wouldn't breed them so they wouldn't be born in the first place. Their lives may be short, but they are well cared for and they have no knowledge of the past or the future; there is only now. Now, life is good for them. We reached Ribblehead viaduct feeling tired, where Jane's mum Jean met us and drove us back to Ilkley. Toffy slept all the next day. A month later I walked the remaining 40 miles with dad and Toffy. Mum took us to Ribblehead and collected us from Selside at the end of the first day.

1994:
In April I took the family on a week's holiday staying in a gîte in Brittany, France. The gîte was in a remote spot, it had a lounge with a smoky fire and a kitchen/dining room with dodgy electrics. Beth and I shared the twin-bedded room. At night, it was so dark that she was scared to sleep without the light on.

As part of my development as a manager, HPL sent me on a training course that was to significantly change my life. It was the Dale Carnegie Professional Development course held in Gateshead on a Thursday evening each week. What I learnt provided me with a wealth of inspirational and practical advice on self-confidence, enthusiasm, faith, friends and the joys of living. Dale Carnegie's best known book, 'How to Win Friends and Influence People' was first published in 1936 but will always continue to apply. One of the principles I adopted and continue to apply was this:

Anything you can conceive and believe you can achieve.

At first, that looks like hogwash. People say things like,
    "Then why don't you walk on water?"
to which I would reply,
    "I believe that is impossible."

My experience showed that when you apply the principle it always works. Conceive and believe.

As a result of applying the principle 1994 was a year of great significance to me. Armed with the confidence of future success I began to think more clearly about what I wanted to achieve.

In May, I updated my goals. My targets for work were clear for the next 2 – 5 years, being based on implementation of Dupont safety systems. I had strengths in promoting action at meetings. Corporate Safety was a worthwhile goal if it were not based in Norway. Inclusion of environmental matters would increase the scope of my work in this country. A past goal had been to head safety in an organisation employing more than 10,000 people. That meant Corporate Safety within Hydro. No individual site was that big so perhaps the target should be reduced to 1,000 employees. Dupont would be good to get into, but at what location and which country? I had thought about the USA and countries other in Europe outside the UK but felt I 'belonged' in my native country.

Looking beyond retirement, I created the following vision of my seventieth birthday:
"It is now May 2020 and today I am celebrating my seventieth birthday. It's a fine age to be. I feel comfortable, assured of the future, satisfied with the past and enjoying the present. My life is interesting, my family is healthy, not far away and we have a variety of close friends. I don't feel old: only the thought of actually being seventy seems strangely unreal. I feel younger because I am fit physically and my mind is alert, my memory good and, best of all, my mind is at ease, comfortable in the wisdom acquired, the ability to understand and to change the things I need to change and to accept the things I can't.

"It's morning now. I was out walking the dog at seven as usual. Three miles before breakfast over the hills. I take my time over breakfast, sitting in this sunny room overlooking a large garden. After breakfast I shall work on my boat.

"My retirement house is in the Yorkshire Dales, Wales or Durham. I've looked at Durham so many times, so that seems to be the right place for me. I have a clear picture of what the house should look like. My activities will include constructional work like boat building or renovation, walking and swimming.

"Does my vision include a partner? When I imagine a typical scene, I don't see one. But I do see Bex, Ren and Beth. The need for a partner is to complete a balanced lifestyle "package". A solo lifestyle is incomplete. My partner must be an attractive and intelligent woman. We must both enjoy one another's company but also feel not restricted by each other. We must feel free to do what each of us pleases and that should include sharing 50% of our interests. The other 50% could be things we do individually or with others, but will include part-time involvement and a continual interest with us both. It has to be a long-term relationship, relaxed, and she must get on well with the girls, their partners and their families. Finding myself a suitable partner starts now."

Finding a partner seemed a daunting task, having not tried for 21 years! Opportunities to meet people were very limited because I didn't go to places like pubs, discos, parties and so on. So, at the beginning of May I joined a dating agency called Intro North. For my subscription I got a list of ladies: twelve pages in all. From the list I made a shortlist, phoned about a dozen numbers and had three conversations. Janice was the most interesting. She lived in Rowlands Gill, liked the outdoors, had two children and worked for the Post Office. Janice said she had now found a man but was sure that he was not her ideal partner.

Number one on my list was Patricia. I decided to phone her at 9.30 after the children had gone up to bed. Beth took a long time watching TV and getting ready for bed and by 9.50 I thought it a bit too late to phone Patricia. I phoned anyway and we talked for nearly 45 minutes. I felt good. Patricia was interesting to talk with. The more we talked the more I realised that there was a lot more to say. We made a date. Until that time came I found myself missing someone I had never met!.

This is what I wrote:
"Good things are starting to happen! I feel good about Beth, Ren and Bex. Good about the way I live, my job, Ren's work and friends, Beth's insight, Bex's adulthood. New things are starting to happen. The prospect of a lady friend. The possibility of Patricia being the ideal partner. A clearer vision of

the sort of goals worth going for. Patricia's goal of travel, demonstrating that travel could be another worthwhile goal. Australia in the year 2000 could be a real one.

"Right now, I'd like to think about the potential relationship with a woman. Already, following the 45-minute talk with Patricia I feel warmth towards her. I know what I want her to look like. And if she does look like that how will I greet her? I believe that within two seconds of meeting Patricia I will know if she is what I want. It will be in her looks, her expressions, her movements, her greeting, her words, her reaction to me and my words. Two seconds. The main thing to remember is that if she is what I want I must concentrate carefully on everything I say and do with her. Not just at first but for ever more. Now I can see what I need. I must be my best. But not just with her. With everyone, including myself. I must be my best to myself. The saying that keeps coming back to me is,

"It doesn't matter how you look, so long as you always look your best."

When Patricia and I met in a pub I applied my two second rule. She looked okay, but nothing special. We talked about where she lived in Gosforth, dinghy sailing from Tynemouth and her love of travel. I guess she didn't quite pass my test but that didn't upset me – there were more ladies on the Intro North list! I met a couple more ladies but they too failed my two second test.

Another lady on the list was Susan. She lived in Consett. After two or three enjoyable chats on the phone we agreed to meet in the car park by the clock in Consett at 7.30 on Wednesday 8th June. I estimated that the journey to Consett would take about half an hour so after leaving home at 6.30 I had time to visit South Shields harbour to see if I could spot Patricia's Enterprise that she said she would be sailing that evening. I wanted to know if the opportunity to sail with Patricia felt stronger than the wish to meet Susan. The sight of a distinctive blue sail off North Tyneside had no effect on me. If I really wanted to go sailing it was not that important who I went with. I set off for Consett keen to meet Susan. At 7.30 I was negotiating the roundabout at Stanley. I had underestimated the journey time. It must have been about 7.45 when I arrived at Consett. No Susan. Fortunately, she answered her home phone and told me to wait. Later I heard that Susan had already phoned me at home and Bex assured her that I had left to go to Consett. Susan then phoned her dad and he gave her a lift for the half mile journey to the clock. I was pleased when we met. I was grateful that she had given me a second chance to meet. Susan was dressed smartly, had taken time to look her best and she was an attractive looking woman. She passed the two-second test.

We decided to go to the Derwent Walk Inn near Ebchester. We talked about Susan's marriage and divorce and her work. I wanted to know her and she wanted to know me. It was an enjoyable meeting. It was clear that we were different in many ways. We had few common interests but we both enjoyed walking. I was more academic and career minded. Susan had done the same job since leaving school and didn't expect that to change. I was more of an outdoor person. Our personalities were different but we had similar likes and dislikes. I felt that we shared important values. For Susan, reliability was important, for me it was integrity.

When I was nine, I sometimes had a lovely dream about a girl in a yellow dress. She was soft, gentle and attractive. I was there when she needed me and I felt good. That was how I felt after that first evening with Susan.

Susan and Toffy in Durham

After that, we met most weeks. Our first weekend day together was to Blanchland. The next time I took Toffy to meet Susan in Durham. Toffy was normally very cautious meeting strangers and it was important for me to know that he would be comfortable with Susan. I needn't have worried. As soon as we met Susan, Toffy wagged his tail and was delighted to be petted by her. If Toffy could speak he would have said confidently,

"She'll do nicely, good choice Mark!"

Susan

We enjoyed being together, often taking walks in Yorkshire. However, there were times when Susan and I felt unsure of each other. On two occasions we didn't meet for two or three weeks.

In January 1995, Susan typed me the following note:
"After last night's phone call, I had very confused feelings because I felt the phone call was a bit serious and muddled and we weren't on the same wavelength. What surprised me was that it wasn't anything to get particularly concerned about but even when slight irritations occur with us I start to think if we are right together – it probably stems back to the beginning when I had so much uncertainty because you were not the type of person I would normally attach to, so at times I think I am still adjusting to your personality and everything that goes with it. Usually, I can adapt to changes in plans where the girls are concerned but last night I felt you were making a joke of the fact that

I was finding it a bit difficult to cope with. Also, I felt upset when Beth referred to me as 'her' (it sounded so unfriendly) – this may seem petty of me, the fact that she is only 10, and realise that she was getting at you as it was connected with you smiling but even this upsets me as I don't like the idea of them thinking that you are happier in my company than with them – the important thing is I don't ever want to be a threat.

"Now, I want to be completely open and tell you exactly how I feel. I definitely feel more positive than at the beginning and at times have felt that I love you, but am not head-over-heels. Sometimes I wish my feelings could be stronger but at times I believe the relationship is not necessarily lacking if you just have a great depth of feeling for someone.

"The positive things are that I enjoy being with you very much, we like virtually the same things, you are dependable, treat me very special, and we have excellent chemistry."

At the end of May, we took a holiday together in Switzerland. It started badly. We stayed at Staveley the night before because that was nearer Manchester airport. When it was time to set off, I couldn't find my passport. After searching frantically, I gave up looking and set off without it. A little later, mum called on my mobile: she had found it at the end of the bed. Dad drove out and met us at Burton Services with the passport.

Our first hotel was at Interlaken. Everything was going fine until we finished unpacking. I felt ill, not because I was sick; there seemed to be nothing wrong with me physically. All I could do was lay on the bathroom floor. Susan was upset and angry with me. I decided that the cause was guilt. Here I was in a fine hotel on holiday with my girlfriend whilst my family, for whom I carried total responsibility, stayed at home. I managed to get up and go for a walk by myself. Susan and I had an awkward relationship after that, even during a trip with stunning views to Jungfraujoch. We ascended by train and walked back down to Wengen. It was a sunny day so I wore shorts, failing to consider that at 11,000 feet something warmer would have been more sensible.

For the second part of the holiday we stayed at Zermatt. I greatly enjoyed the ascent on the Gornergratbahn, the highest open-air railway in Europe. Our hotel booking included transport from the station to the hotel in an electric car so when a driver offered to take us we gladly accepted. On arrival, when the driver asked us to pay the fare, it was clear he was a regular taxi. We wouldn't pay, so he took us back to the station. We decided to walk. Susan wanted a coffee, which annoyed me because I wanted to get to the hotel and visit the town. We argued.

Our hotel room window looked out directly towards the Matterhorn, but the cloud failed to lift during the days we were there so we never saw it. Also, following earlier upsets, our spirits were not lifted very high either. One of the few days we both enjoyed was a day trip to Stresa in Italy by rail. The warmer weather there helped.

Future holidays were better. We took Beth with us the following year and to Turkey and Greece the year after that. Our accommodation at Turkey was poor and the temperature uncomfortably hot. Susan went for a swim in the hotel pool. She's not worn a swimming costume since. By now, our relationship had become strong. We were together at least every weekend.

Running and swimming continued to keep me fit. Two or three times a week I would swim 40 lengths (1000 metres) of Newton Aycliffe baths at lunch time. I could do that and be back to work well within an hour. It was a great way of clearing my head. Sometimes, a problem at work would be making little progress at noon but after the swim I could solve it immediately. The swim was mentally relaxing, an opportunity to daydream. The hardest part was remembering the number of lengths completed. If I was unsure, I'd assume it was the lowest of the numbers I thought it was. It was important not to think numbers, such as how much cash I needed to withdraw from the bank after the swim, otherwise I would lose count altogether.

Similarly, I would run by myself on two or three evenings each week. In April 1998 I ran the London Marathon. Ren accompanied me to London, but didn't compete herself. I didn't enjoy the run because I anticipated that it would be great to see the sights of the city. Only in the last couple of miles did the route pass familiar landmarks and by that time I was too tired to care.

For my 50th birthday surprise Susan booked a stay for us in the Yorkshire Dales. She didn't tell me where but told me to drive to Leyburn. From there, I was instructed to take the A684 along Wensleydale. I knew the area from earlier walks and it was fun trying to guess where we were to stay. After crossing the River Ure at Wensley the next village was West Witton. I guessed this might be our venue so as we approached the Wensleydale Heifer I slowed down, expecting to be told to stop, but Susan told me to carry on. It was only after we had driven through the village that Susan told me to turn around. My guess was correct: we had a lovely stay at the Wensleydale Heifer.

In August 2000, Susan, Beth, Toffy and I took a week's canal cruising holiday in a narrowboat. Starting from Stone in Staffordshire we completed the 'Four Counties Ring' of 109 miles and 94 locks. I steered, the girls operated the locks and Toffy moved between us, occasionally falling into the water. Operating the locks resulted in Beth getting blisters on her hands and a wasp sting on her boobs. After a few days, we needed to top up our water supply from a hose pipe. I gave up waiting for water to appear from the tank overflow and stopped filling when I guessed the tank had to be full. That evening, when Beth went to her cabin, she found herself paddling in water. Our boat, 'Captain Smollett' didn't appear to be leaking: the flood must have come from our water tank. Next day, I stopped the boat at the top of an embankment and siphoned water from below the floorboards.

Captain Smollett

My running was at its best between 1998 and 2001. I never considered myself to be a fast runner. Like in many other respects, my standards were good but not exceptional. I ran my fastest half-marathon time of 1hr 33min 30 secs in the Great North Run in 1998. Every year I entered the Coniston 14 run, which made a circuit of the lake, and achieved my best time my best time of 1h 42m 25sec in 2000. In March 2000, I set myself a challenge of running around all the other main lakes in the Lake District and completed the last one in May 2002. Age had given me more stamina and greater endurance of discomfort and pain.

I took Susan for a surprise trip on her birthday. At every approach to a road sign she covered her eyes so she had no idea where we were when we stopped for lunch. The pub notice board displayed details of a local darts match. It showed we were in Lincoln. Susan was delighted.

Lincoln

In February 2001 foot-and-mouth was discovered at an Essex abattoir and it quickly spread across the UK. The highly infectious disease, which mainly affected cattle, pigs, sheep and goats, plunged the agricultural industry into its worst crisis for decades. Over 6 million cows and sheep were killed in an eventually successful attempt to halt the disease. Cumbria was the worst affected area of the country, with 893 cases. Footpaths across fields were closed.

Footpath closure on Cleadon Hills

At work, our site continued to achieve good results in our safety and environmental performance; this was demonstrated by us winning the company's European Safety Award.

At weekends we had often visited locations and properties with a view to moving nearer to my workplace. A suitable house was identified on The Green in Aycliffe village and we moved there in March 2001.

In June 2002 I arranged a family get-together at Carsington Water. Mum, dad, Dorothy and Mary were included and we enjoyed a meal at the restaurant that Robert, my former friend from Pinxton, then owned. This was the first of several annual get-togethers involving my side of the family.

Toffy continued to enjoy his routine walk routes, particularly along a hedgerow that was frequented by rabbits. Much as he tried, he never caught one. As before, he adopted our back garden and the garage as his domain. One evening in February 2003 Toffy declined his evening walk. He just wanted to lie on his favourite spot on the back lawn. Toffy was clearly unwell. In the morning I looked out of the bedroom window and saw that he was lying in exactly the same place. My fears were confirmed. Toffy was dead. I moved his body to one side, dug a hole in the lawn at his favourite spot and replaced the turf over him. It was a sad day.

I had enjoyed boating since being a teenager. In 2003 visited Derwent Reservoir Sailing Club and bought an old Laser. Susan had no interest in sailing and this was a boat I could launch and sail single handed. It was fast: in a moderate breeze it went in a speed boat. Another benefit was that the sailing club bar sold real ale, although it was usually warm. Races were not so good. Unlike running, where everyone was convivial, sailors seemed to change once they grasped their boat's tiller. They became intent on gaining advantages over others using tactics as much as sailing skill. The following season was dry so the level of water in the reservoir became very low. This necessitated landing the boat in mud and dragging it up a slope of more than 100 yards. Furthermore, a day sailing meant a day without Susan. I sold the Laser.

HPL won the European Safety Award for the second time in 2003 and in July 2006 the Chemical Industries Association Responsible Care Award.

Hydro Polymers

I recorded the number of times Susan and I met and by March 2007 it had reached 300. A song which reminds me of Susan at that time is 'The Closest Thing To Crazy' by Katie Melua:

> How can I think I'm standing strong,
> Yet feel the air beneath my feet?
> How can happiness feel so wrong?
> How can misery feel so sweet?
> How can you let me watch you sleep,
> Then break my dreams the way you do?
> How can I have got in so deep?
> Why did I fall in love with you?

> This is the closest thing to crazy I have ever been
> Feeling twenty-two, acting seventeen,
> This is the nearest thing to crazy I have ever known,
> I was never crazy on my own:
> And now I know that there's a link between the two,
> Being close to craziness and being close to you.

Making love with Susan was more like the closest thing to ecstasy I had ever been. More controlled, more passion, less lust than ever before.

In 2007 I arranged a holiday to the Greek Islands as a surprise birthday present for Susan. She had often shown a wish to visit Santorini so I booked flights to arrive there on her birthday. We set off the day before and at the airport I kept the destination secret until the last call to the departure lounge. The first flight arrived at Athens airport late evening and soon after midnight I gave Susan her birthday cards. When we flew onwards a few hours later, it was another pleasant surprise for her to discover that the destination was Santorini. After a couple of nights there we moved on to other islands by ferry. When asked by another passenger where we were heading, Susan had to tell them that she didn't know!

Susan in Santorini

Susan took early retirement from work in December 2007: there was too little work to be done to avoid boredom and her pension arrangement was favourable. She sold her house and started living with me permanently in November 2009. By then, my count of the number of times we had met had reached 1,554.

I was due to retire in May 2012. Financial calculations showed that I could afford to retire six months earlier than expected and reduce my working week to three days from November 2009.

We often discussed future places to live where we might wish to spend the rest of our days. Practically anywhere in the world was possible but Susan immediately narrowed the scope to Europe. Many English people retired to France and during an earlier holiday there we spoke to a couple who were enjoying their retirement in that country. I supposed we could get used to the differences in culture but were content with the English way of life so we decided to stay within the UK. Scotland and Wales were ruled out because of the extra distances away from friends and family. Also, our visits there had shown that pub food and beer in those countries was nowhere near as good as England's. The decision then was between the north and south of England. The south was warmer and drier and had more facilities, but was busier. Our weekend forays to southern counties were made more interesting by considering the possibility of permanent residence there. In the end, we decided that the north of England suited us best. North Yorkshire was the focus of our search.

Susan applied for us to participate on the TV series, 'Escape to the Country' and after each of us completing a long phone interview we were accepted. In August 2009 the crew spent a day filming us in Aycliffe. In August we spent four days staying at a hotel in Ripon and viewed four properties. The whole experience was enjoyable and every member of the film crew was friendly and helpful. At first, the interviews were a bit intimidating but assurances from the crew, especially Nikki Chapman, put us at ease. When asked to sum up my impression of the first property I spoke volubly for about three minutes. The producer responded,
"That's great. Now can you do it again in about thirty seconds?"
On completion of the shooting, we had a pub meal together with the crew. It was quite sad to be parting from them.

We were very impressed with the first property shown to us, which was in Marton-le-Moor near Ripon. I later made an offer which was accepted, but I cancelled after further consideration. Over the hedge opposite was a piece of wasteland and an old metal barn that I suspected might in the future be used for development. A property with a water feature had always appealed to me and I was keen to buy a former water mill in Kirkby Malzeard that I had looked at earlier. The property included a small woodland with the beck running through.

My offer was accepted but again I cancelled after Susan expressed her concerns about the amount of work required to modernise the house.

I had sometimes walked around the village of Staveley, Cumbria and putatively considered potential properties if they were for sale. There was none: they were either too expensive, too small or too old, with nothing in between. During a visit to mum in October 2009 I picked up a paper from an estate agent in Grange. A property just a mile away from Staveley looked interesting. The agent was closed on Sunday so a viewing appointment could not be made so Susan and I took a walk to see what it looked like from the outside. The owner was working in the garden and showed us round the house. We were impressed but Susan did not like the location of the bathroom downstairs, even though there was an upstairs shower room, so we took it no further. We explained this to the owner when he phoned but agreed to take a second look a fortnight later. On this visit we made an offer which was accepted.

For the move, I hired a van from Kendal and drove it back to Aycliffe. We loaded the van that evening, leaving enough furniture to continue staying in Aycliffe. The following morning, I drove then van to Cumbria with Susan, completed unloading as soon as the family had vacated the house then returned the van to the rental company. It was precisely one week before Christmas Day. That night, heavy snow made further travelling practically impossible and we enjoyed our first days snuggling in and exploring the immediate area.

Susan outside new House

December 2009

My dad died in March 2009. It was a pity he didn't get to see our new home. He must have driven past it a number of times. He once knew someone who lived nearby and had even considered buying a neighbour's house.

Some months later, on returning to the house after a day out I discovered the cold tap was running at full pelt into the bath. The house had been locked and there was no sign of entry. I carried out numerous experiments to determine if a tap left dripping could open fully without being manually operated. The experiments showed that drips tended to get slower rather than faster. There was nothing loose. There was no logical explanation for the tap being wide open. The same incident happened the following year. On this occasion there was also some grit suggesting that somebody had stood in the bath wearing shoes. Our water bills showed that the amount of water lost cost £100 so it must have been running for many hours. I thought that dad's ghost must have been at work and this was his way of making a joke. None of the houses he owned had a water meter so his water bill was the same regardless of how much he used. He must have overlooked that our water was metered!

One night in August 2010, Susan woke me up. Someone was banging on the front door and shouting in a frightened voice. I opened the door cautiously in case this was a ploy to gain entry into the house. A panic-stricken teenage girl was standing there. She stammered,

"I've crashed my car into the wall and the passenger's not moving!" The car was on its side on the grass verge against a demolished section of our front wall. I called for an ambulance. As I approached the car, a door lifted open and another teenage girl climbed out. Neither of the girls were seriously injured. They had been celebrating the girl passing her driving test. A police officer arrived before the ambulance and pointed out that the accident could have been far worse if the car had hit the tree immediately in front of it. He breathalysed the driver and found she was over the legal limit. After the damaged vehicle had been removed I picked up an almost full bottle of Jägermeister from the verge. The following day, the girl was brought back to our house by her father. It was a friendly visit and I felt sorry for the girl. She had behaved stupidly, but probably no worse than my own behaviour when I was her age. Her lessons were much more expensive than mine. She had written off the car she had just qualified to drive, probably lost her newly acquired driving licence and when she was permitted to drive again her car insurance premium would be prohibitively expensive. She didn't want the bottle of Jägermeister back.

Susan and I spent nearly every weekend in Cumbria. The 70-mile journey from Aycliffe usually took less than 90 minutes and I became familiar with every bend and bump in the road. One winter's evening the temperature at Scotch Corner was minus 5 and the A66 was icy even on the nearside lane. The temperature dropped further as we continued, dipping to minus 15 at Brough. On several occasions the A66 closed due to bad weather and for one return journey we took a much longer route using the M62 instead.

In November 2011 I retired from work and moved out of the former house. I had previously put the house up for sale with an estate agent. As soon as their sale sign went up a neighbour called and said she been interested in this house for a long time and she agreed to buy it. Beth was still living with us, working locally and intended to stay in the area. We found a small house for her and I used some of the funds for the sale of my house to buy it for her.

Much of my free time was spent volunteering with the National Trust and Lake District National Park in tasks such as path maintenance, wall repairs and Right of Way patrols. I also registered with Sight Advice and underwent a training course for guiding visibly impaired people. In my registration I recorded that I enjoyed running. Sight Advice contacted me and asked if I would be interested in guiding a visibly impaired person on runs. I agreed and on October 2012 started running with Bill, whose eyesight was minimal. Bill lived in Staveley and over the following years we ran together two or three times a week, entered several 10k and half marathon races and also ran the Windermere Marathon together. Bill was a great training partner. In particular, he encouraged (or rather made) me run rather than walk up hills. The sight of a long hill ahead would be daunting for me and I would slow down even before starting the climb. Bill's approach was to think only one step ahead. If that step was satisfactory, do another, and so on. That had to be the way Bill ran: it required great concentration and trust in his guide. On one occasion after a long uphill run we came to a steeper hill and I refused to run further. Bill released the guide rope and continued to run up the hill unguided. He was able to see light above the hedge ahead and waited for me at the top. Despite having minimal vision, Bill was very observant. He would alert me to the sound of birds, children playing and, most importantly, of traffic behind us. He could tell by odour if there were sheep, cattle or horses in an adjacent field or when we were passing a farm. I could also detect these things, but did not normally notice them. In addition to using these senses, Bill also used his memory to piece bits of information together. If I missed a turn on a pre-arranged route Bill would question if I had decided to go a different way. One day, when we were not running I caught a bus into town.

"Kendal please," I said to the driver.
I picked up my ticket.
"Hello Mark," said a voice from a passenger seat.
It was Bill. He knew where the bus had stopped and two spoken words were sufficient for him to confirm my identity.

I also guided visually impaired (VI) people on walks and in open canoes. It was inspiring to be with those who could only picture objects through touch. How do you explain colour to someone who has been totally blind from birth? To say that blue is like a large expanse of water or red is the colour of sunburnt skin doesn't really help. It doesn't make any difference to them of course but colour is an example of many things in life we take for granted. We can all cope with the loss a particular faculty that might be regard as vital.

In a double open canoe, the VI person paddles in the front of the boat and does most of the steering. The sighted person must look ahead and pass instructions. It provided interesting challenges when paddling down rocky rapids. In this example Bill is paddling on his left side. I peer over his shoulder and spot a submerged rock a few yards directly ahead. We need to pass to the left of the rock to reach clear water beyond. Bill could attempt a draw stroke to pull the bows left but a sweep on the right side would be better. I shout,

"Change!"

Bill knows this means he must now paddle on the right. He senses the urgency of my instruction and responds immediately.

"Sweep!"

We've practiced this manoeuvre many times and Bill executes it perfectly. The canoe swings left and glides past the rock. The time between spotting the rock, assessing actions, communicating instructions and executing them was only a few seconds. It didn't always go that smoothly and sometimes (but not often with Bill) we would end up swimming, but that's all part of the fun.

Guiding visually impaired people helped me realise that we utilise only a small proportion of our full capabilities. It shows how the application of positive thought achieves results.

This takes me back to my old school motto: *omnia experire bona contine* - try everything and continue with the good. Have I yet tried everything that I want to try? One of the exercises I learnt at the Dale Carnegie course and repeat from time to time is to picture myself sitting in a rocking chair near the end of my life. In the scene I ask myself,

"What do you wish you had done in your life?"

In the past, the exercise would have made me feel regretful for failing to achieve something important. I would then bring my mind back to my actual age and this something would be added to my list of goals. If I carry out this exercise in my seventieth year, some things may come to mind but there is nothing so important that I feel regretful for not doing. Yet, hopefully I have many years remaining to do more.

As a teenager, there were many things I needed to try. A lot of them were good, many were not. In this book I have described both the good and the bad. I believe that I have learnt a lot from the less desirable parts of my life and continued with much of the good. I feel fortunate that despite uncertainty of our future world my life feels secure.

Every year, Anne organises a picnic day at Manningham Park bandstand. It was started many years earlier by her dad and is ongoing. Many of Jane's family and mine attend and it has provided a great opportunity to watch the growing families. If Jane had survived, she would have been proud of the family. By 2018, her eldest grandchild had reached the age she was when we met. Time flies.

Susan and I often joke about getting married. I don't expect we ever will. We stay together because we want to be together, not because of a vow made during a pompous wedding ceremony. I keep returning to the dream when I was nine about the girl in a yellow dress. Now, that girl is still Susan: gentle, delicate and attractive. We love each other. I am there when she needs me.

I feel good.

Susan at Tarn Hows 2017

Printed in Great Britain
by Amazon

41338782R00156